THE AGE OF TOTAL IMAGES:
DISAPPEARANCE OF A SUBJECTIVE VIEWPOINT IN POST-DIGITAL PHOTOGRAPHY
ANA PERAICA

Theory on Demand #34
The Age of Total Images: Disappearance of a Subjective Viewpoint in Post-digital Photograhy

Author: Ana Peraica

Editing: Devon Schiller
Production: Sepp Eckenhaussen
Cover design: Katja van Stiphout

Published by the Institute of Network Cultures, Amsterdam, 2019
ISBN: 978-94-92302-54-0

Contact
Institute of Network Cultures
Phone: +3120 5951865
Email: info@networkcultures.org
Web: http://www.networkcultures.org

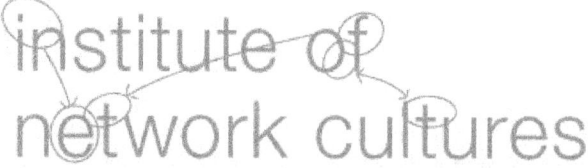

CONTENTS

PREFACE

This appropriating mirror-play of the simple onefold of earth and sky, divinities and mortals, we call the world. The world presences by worlding. That means: the world's worlding cannot be explained by anything else nor can it be fathomed through anything else. This impossibility does not lie in the inability of our human thinking to explain and fathom in this way. Rather, the inexplicable and unfathomable character of the world's worlding lies in this, that causes and grounds remain unsuitable for the world's worlding. As soon as human cognition here calls for an explanation, it fails to transcend the world's nature, and fells short of it. - Martin Heidegger, 'The Thing'.[1]

I came to realize this book unexpectedly. In 2018, during the process of analyzing the historical and technological development of post-digital photography, I studied a variety of what seemed at first to be disconnected areas of thought, including theories on the Anthropocene, artificial intelligence, cartography and geography, the perception and sociality of space, and beyond. Upon revisiting my notes, I realized that hidden within were at least two manuscripts. So, I decided to divide the single research project into two separate books: *Postdigial Arcadia* and *The Age of Total Images*. However, each has as its focus the consequences of post-digital photography for our understanding of the world. This is a major theme in all of my scholarly works. Each book is written in the domain of media epistemology and, therefore, in media ontology as well. That is, I describe the space of existence separate from a mediated space, and that theory will come back several times and twist around various topics in this book too.

During the preparation of this manuscript, I had no access to funding or research facilities because I am not a tenured scholar. Consequently, it was a great challenge for me to do this research. I would like to thank to Prof. Dr. Michael Punt, at *Leonardo Electronic Reviews*, for assigning me books to review that so perfectly suit my areas of interest, as well as for his help in gaining access to the literature that I needed to write this book. I would also like to express my gratitude to Prof. Dr. Oliver Grau and Wendy Coones, in the Department of Image Science at Danube University Krems, for connecting me to many great minds in the fields of image science and new media art, as well as for coordinating my teaching in the international graduate programs Media Art Histories and Media Arts Cultures so that I could also attend conferences and exhibitions which relate to my focus. Also, I would like to thank to dr. Oksana Sarkisova from Visual Studies Platform (VSP) and OSA Archivum for organizing and supporting my visiting fellowship at Central European University in Budapest. Their amazing offline and online library helped me a lot in formulating my thesis. Many thanks also go to Prof. Dr. Geert Lovink, a dear friend, and the editor of this book series, as well as to artist Patrick Lichty, who always gives constructive feedback and provides useful references. My former student Devon Schiller has edited the manuscript and has done a splendid job with his supreme language sense as well as his ability with questioning and theory. And let us not forget Sepp Eckenhaussen, who produced the work. Big thanks also goes to Clement Valla, an artist who permission to reproduce his artwork.

---

1   Martin Heidegger, 'The Thing' in Martin Heidegger, trans. Albert Hofstadter, *Poetry, Language, Thought*, New York: Harper and Row, 1971, 177.

Finally, I would like to thank to my mother Dragica, my Dalmatian Jere, and Marin Krpetić, each of whom helped me to remain sane and stay organized over the last few years as I was working on this book and living among the noise produced by over-tourism of Diocletian's palace in Split, Croatia.

INTRODUCTION

The crisis of physical dimensions, just as a crisis of measurement, is tied up with the crisis of determinism and affects today the whole ensemble of representations of the world. - Paul Virilio, *The Lost Dimension*.[1]

Planet Earth as a Filmic Character

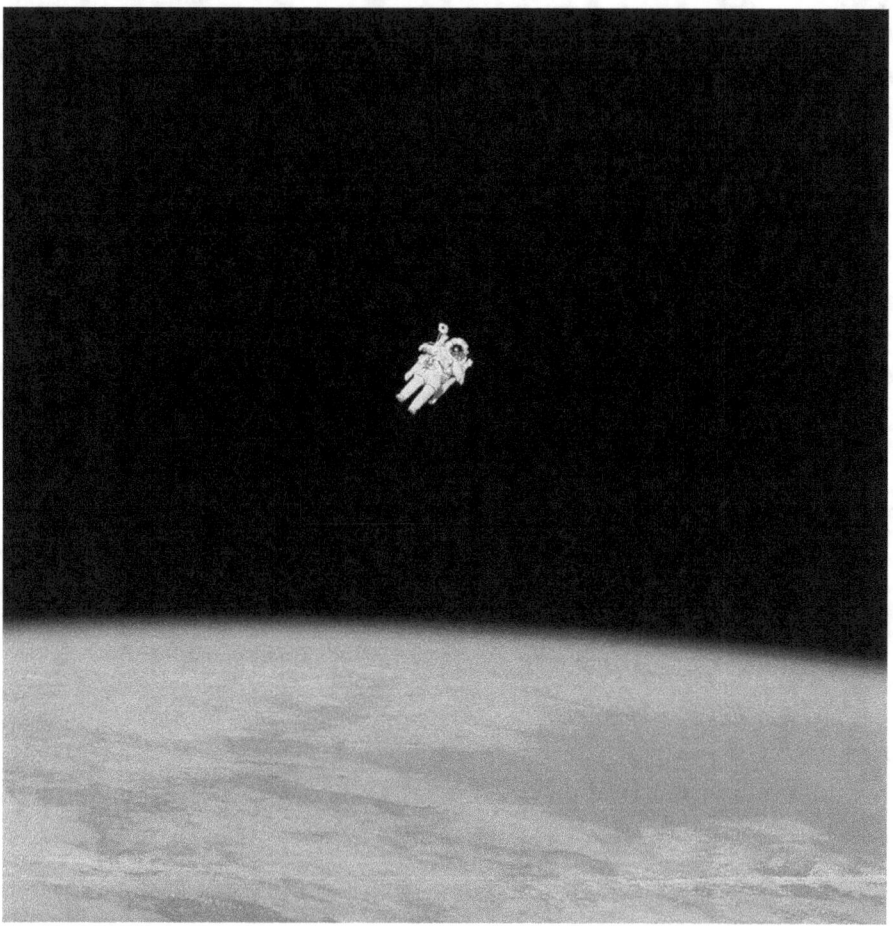

Figure 1: Astronaut in Space.

In the blockbuster film *Gravity* (2013), the actress Sandra Bullock plays an astronaut who is lost in space.[2] Constantly throughout the film, the viewer sees the planet Earth behind her

---

1   Paul Virilio, *The Lost Dimension*, trans. Daniel Moshenberg, New York: Semiotext(e), 1991.
2   *Gravity*, directed by Alfonso Cuarón, starring Sandra Bullock and George Clooney, 2013.

back. These images, we learn from the film description, were taken from NASA and Roscosmos, the American and Russian space agencies, respectively, chosen for their likeness to the views of astronauts while on missions in space. From the perspective of visual studies, these images are particularly interesting. Not only do they recall the iconic representations of the Earth, such as those from the Apollo missions, but they also serve to create a scale of the distance between the protagonist in outer space, played by Bullock, and the Earth. In addition to being a persistent reminder in the filmic narrative about Bullock's characters' motivations, these images of the Earth are also a visual backdrop for all of the events in the film. Constantly present in a film that has only few protagonists, the Earth itself becomes the movie character itself, as Bullock struggles to get back home to the planet which appears so close and yet so far away.

Our home planet has been a character in other movies as well. For example, in *The Great Dictator* (1940), Charlie Chaplin plays with the globe as if being a ball.[3] Comparing the filmmakers' approaches to the two films, the contrasts do not end at the level of filmic genre, with one film being a work of science fiction, and the other one of comedy. There are also significant differences in how the planet is represented. In *Gravity* (2013), the Earth stands for itself, appearing as a background, a two-dimensional planar image, while in the *The Great Dictator* (1940), the Earth is a model of itself, appearing as a ball, a three-dimensional globular object. Although in both movies the Earth is present via representations, we are led to believe that in *Gravity* we confront the image of the planet itself and not one in a studio. Beyond the illusion of the science fiction genre, this belief in the reality of the Earth is supported by a call upon the authority of science in general and, here, astronomy in particular. In the *Great Dictator*, on the contrary, there is no call upon such authority, but just a cynical reference to the politics while Earth appears in the form we actually know it, as an experience of the globe. Thus, between the two films we can also differentiate two epistemic relations to our knowledge about the Earth, one based on the authority of science, and the other based on everyday lived experience.

It is often taken for granted that in photography 'seeing is believing'. But there are differences in the ways in which we assign truth and trust to photographic images. For example, most of us are more likely to believe a scientific than a popular image. Therefore, we are more likely to trust an astrophotographic record than an image of an unidentified flying object (UFO). Although, in reality, we cannot verify for ourselves that the object in an astrophotographic record actually exists any more than we can that UFOs do or do not exist. None of us have ever seen either a planet or a starship with our naked eyes. Such images belong to a field of view beyond unaugmented, unprostheticized human vision. Moreover, given the 'light time delay', or the delay which is caused by the time it takes for light to travel from a celestial object in outer space to the Earth, a telescope does not provide an image of the world which currently

---

3   *The Great Dictator*, directed by Charlie Chaplin, starring Charlie Chaplin, Paulette Goddard, and Jack Oakie, 1940.

exists, but rather one which is already long-vanished.[4] Thus, even when using a telescope while in the employ of science, we can only capture an illusion of existence.

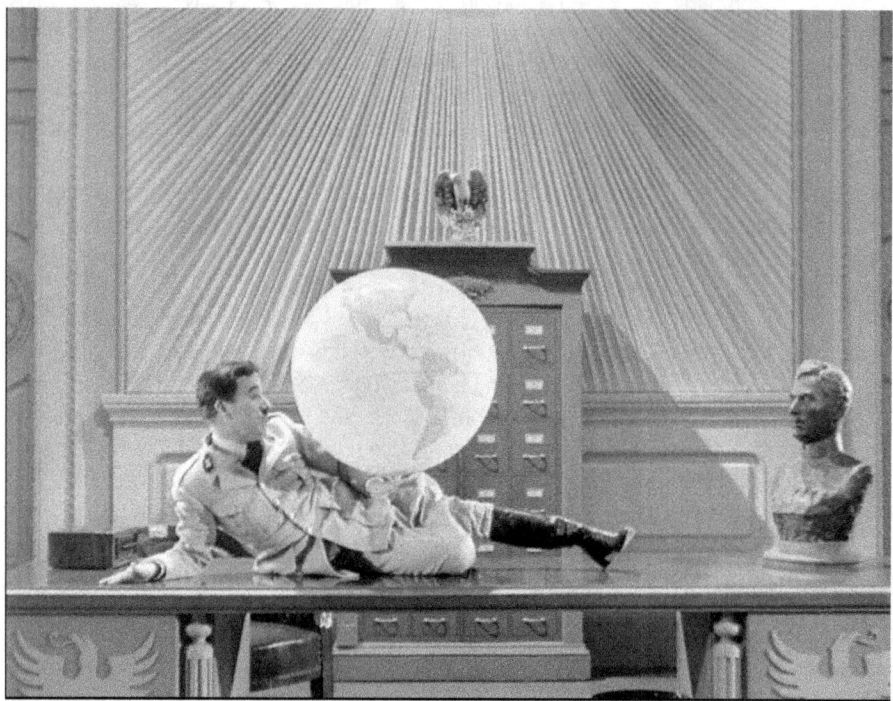

Figure 2: Still from The Great Dictator *(dir. Charlie Chaplin).*

Although it is not as problematic to try to see the Earth from space as it is to see distant celestial objects from Earth, there are still many reasons to be skeptical not only of popular imagery but also of scientific photography. For example, it is difficult to discriminate by the naked eye which picture among many pictures of the Earth that are present online are authentic. Some of these online images are in fact recorded by NASA, while others which can be found on the Internet cannot be traced back to their origin. In both cases, we are not able to access the original, which we would need to do in order to be able to validate for ourselves the truthfulness and trustworthiness of the record. For many other images of the Earth which we might come across online, whether in a Google search or on social media, there is no proof of veracity, neither photographer nor publisher given, no signature of authority. And if we go directly to NASA's online image and video library or image archive, many if not most images of the Earth and of outer space have been adjusted to at least some degree or other. Thus, our regular experience of images of the planet, whether in film or online, may be confusing. In this book, I will analyze the rise of such images in society for the general population, as well as consequences that untestable, unverifiable images of the planet are

---

4   Carl Sagan similarly writes that 'telescopes are time machines'. Carl Sagan, *Pale Blue Dot: A Vision of The Human Future in Space*, New York: Ballantine Books, 1997, 47.

having on general understanding of it. Thus, I will address two types of images: those which have a truth-claim grounded in scientific authority, and those based on either no experience or only limited experience.

Prothesis of the Eye

A large number of photographs do not show a view comparable to that of human experience. Whereas most conventional photography is used to record what may be naturally perceived, an ever-increasing segment of photographic practices focus on what may be recorded through a complex assemblage of machinic and computational processes. This development was already began in the 19th century with the merging of optical and photographic technologies. It sped up in the 20th century as the power of lenses enhanced not only distant recordings of celestial bodies from space and ground telescopes but also recording of the Earth from outer space. In parallel, innovations in lens technology have amplified our knowledge about both the microscopic and macroscopic worlds as we have become capable of recording all manner of things from the atomic to the astronomic level. The clash between these two completely different strata of universe, the micro and macro, both of which are beyond the capacity of the human gaze, were recorded in the movie *Powers of Ten and the Relative Size of Things in the Universe* (1977) by Charles Ormond Eames, Jr. and Bernice Alexandra 'Ray' Kaiser Eames.[5] Anticipating deep photography in video form, this short movie has had many reinterpretations and reiterations in the past half century. The Eames husband and wife industrial design team employed a system of exponential powers to visualize the importance of scale. Through the movie, the viewer is taken on a visual odyssey from the picture of the couple laying on the grass, far out into the distant galaxy, and then comes back again through the skin of a person and into his sub-atomic constellation. Such a view, which was based on the available scientific knowledge of the day, has further evolved in subsequent decades. Today, the power of a lens has grown to such an extent, as with the Event Horizon Telescope (EHT), that lens technology has made possible the recording of a black hole 55 million light years away.[6] And at the same time, photographic apparatuses can now be used to record the tiniest of details, down to even an atom's shadow.[7]

What such a view affords is an image which, even though it still is indexical, does not seem to be representational, but rather abstract. Despite its appearance to the naked human eye, however, such an abstract image, recorded with the aid of an extremely powerful lens, is perhaps the most real image of them all. But such images can be confusing not only because they are difficult to compare with reality, but also because the macro or micro have this strange resemblance to each other, as the Eames' *Powers of Ten* exemplifies. The abstract patterns which are shown in such images, whether a distant and outer view of the

---

5   Charles and Ray Eames, *Powers of Ten and the Relative Size of Things in the Universe*, 1977, available at: https://www.eamesoffice.com/the-work/powers-of-ten/.

6   'Event Horizon Telescope', https://eventhorizontelescope.org/.

7   Ker Than, 'First Picture of an Atom's Shadow: Smallest Ever Photographed: Technique Might Help Turn Atoms into Vehicles for Secret Messages', *National Geographic News*, 13 July 2012, https://www.nationalgeographic.com/news/2012/7/120710-first-picture-atom-shadow-photograph-science-nature-smallest/.

human environment, or the near and inner view of the human body, look like each other to a non-specialist, untrained eye.

Total Images

One reason why such aerial photographs seem so foreign to our everyday experience is that neither a human angle of view nor the subject of human vision is held in common. It is a vision fitting for machines not humans. And there is a considerable difference between machine and human vision. To briefly compare images which are produced through naked and supported vision: The human view is at once both selective and dynamic; that is, humans cannot simultaneously see details and the whole. Given the many biological, cognitive, and neurobiological factors involved in human vision, such as attention, focus, interpretation, and memory, there is great variability in what we see and how we see it.[8] Such variability would be considered errors or glitches in machine vision, would be considered unacceptable, and would be corrected during the stages of design and implementation. This difference between naked human and supported machine vision is perhaps best exemplified in the scope of the angle or field of view. Human vision lacks an overall sharpness, and the ability to provide an image that is both detailed and wide. The eye in the sky of airplane, drone, or satellite post-digital photography suffers from no such limitation.

The space of the world is continuous, but human vision, however, is constrained in various ways. For example, humans cannot see behind their own back without the help of a smart phone camera, mirror, or some other device. However, a so-called round camera system can achieve a 360-degree view by incorporating multiple lenses. Even before the invention of the round camera, the prosthetic view of photographic technologies has been extended in three principle techniques: by elevating or raising the position of the photographer and, consequently, of the viewer, thereby widening the angle or field of view; by combining a number of image together through computational or pre-computational processes and practices; and by layering other kinds of information over the original photographic record. Through these techniques, any subjective point or angle of view is dismissed, replaced by a more-than-human view.[9] The view in such a image is not described by the position of the author of the image. Rather, the view is dispersed uniformly throughout the space of the image and activated by the navigation of the user.

Discriminating between human and nonhuman images on the basis of appearance, especially in terms of the wideness of the visual field, I propose a concept of 'the total image'. The notion of such an image has already been employed by Ingrid Hoelzl and Remi Marie to describe the unique effects of Google Street View, which to date marks the furthest step taken in the totalization of cartographic or geographic imagery.[10] Expanding on their definition in this

---

8   See: Eric Kandel, *Reductionism in Art and Brain Science: Bridging the Two Cultures*, New York: Columbia University Press, 2018.

9   For more on theories of objectivity, see my book: *Fotografija kao Dokaz*, Zagreb: Multimedijalni Institut, 2018.

10   Writing: 'Google's achievement in building the 'total image' of our world has gone much further than being an interactive mapping tool.' Ingrid Hoelzl and Remi Marie, *Soft Image: Towards a New Theory of*

book, I use the term total image to mean any and all images which are liberated from the constraints of naked human vision and, particularly, the angle of view (AoV) or 'view-angle,' sometimes called the field of view (FoV), which is the extent of a given scene which can be imaged. A total image, therefore, is the result of a long process of research and development in image technologies in order to extend human vision to the point of being able to see the whole of our world all at once.[11]

Only a few theoreticians have described the various levels of such total images. For example, Christine Buci-Glucksmann defines the view from above via the narrative on Icarus, referring to an 'Icarian gaze'.[12] Icarus, son of Daedalus, fashioned a pair of wings from feathers and wax, but flew too close to the sun, until the wings melted and he fell to his death in the sea. This Icarian gaze 'opposes the vision dependent on heaviness and its constraints - horizons, orientations between the above and below - with a "being in trajectory"'.[13] The early aerial views, whether the view from the top of the hill to the view from low altitude flight, the low or the high oblique, is best described by *Ola Söderström* concept of the 'zenithal gaze'.[14] In order to describe the view of the surface of the Earth as seen from space, such as during the Apollo space missions, Denis Cosgrove referred to an 'Apollonian view'.[15] Views which simulate this view from high up above, like in a map, Claire Reddleman defines as 'the view from nowhere', 'a highly abstract viewpoint [which] is the signature viewpoint of modern cartography'.[16] Also regarding maps, Alberto Toscano and Jeff Kinkle elaborate on 'cartographies of the absolute'.[17] Irmgard Emmelhainz also writes about a groundless view, which diverges point of view and synthetic image, describing them as tautological or self-referential.

Human Photographic Condition

Aerial, drone, and satellite images afford an enhanced and extended perspective on the Earth, which is not only foreign to humans, but also surpasses the human. Indeed, this view as only been see by a chosen few, those astronauts who have journeyed beyond the boundaries of our home planet. Yet, such images have a bigger purpose, inspiring us to imagine more things than in heaven and Earth than we have dreamt in our philosophy, and transcend

the *Digital Image*, Chicago: Intellect, Chicago University Press, 2015, 24.

11   By such an expansion, I will refer also to reverberating the political idea and practice of totalitarianism, relying on Jean Luc Nancy's definition of the total human as free from alienation, emancipated from natural, economic, and ideological subjection. Jean Luc Nancy, *After Fukushima: The Equivalence of Catastrophes*, New York: Fordham University Press, 2014.

12   Christine Buci-Glucksmann, 'Icarus Today: The Ephemeral Eye', *Public* 18 (1999): 53–77.

13   Describing the Icarian as 'aeriality that re-examines and accepts a world without height or base, a world cosmically liberated from weight to become the object of artistic experimentation and conceptualization', Buci-Glucksmann asks 'have we not all become Icarian in the enchanted world of virtual map-worlds from which we cannot fall?' Buci-Glucksmann, 'Icarus Today', 58.

14   Ola Söderström, 'Paper Cities: Visual Thinking in Urban Planning', *Ecumene* 3.3 (1996): 249–281.

15   Denis Cosgrove, *Apollo's Eye: A Cartographic Genealogy of the Earth in the Western Imagination*, Baltimore, MD: John Hopkins University Press, 2001.

16   Claire Reddleman, *Cartographic Abstractions in Contemporary Art: Seeing with Maps*, London: Routledge, 2018, 11.

17   Alberto Toscano and Jeff Kinkle, *Cartographies of the Absolute*, John Hunt Publishing, 2015.

the 'human condition', as Hannah Arendt once called it in her comments about the Sputnik mission.[18] Arendt notes:

> The most radical change in the human condition we can imagine would be an emigration of men from the earth to some other planet. Such an event, no longer totally impossible, would imply that man would have to live under man-made conditions, radically different from those the earth offers him.[19]

Yet with photographic record of such a view it is not only human but also a 'human photographic condition', as a specific limited view-frame of humans, that is changed, to paraphrase Joanna Zylinska.[20] Human photographic condition is the one tied to human natural way of living, perspectival ground views, the cut-out of the view-frame, contrary to a full-round, 360-degree vision. This, ordinary, earthly, human frame, is contrasted by the nonhuman one which refers to both assisted and automated recordings made from non-natural positions. A new, nonhuman condition lifts the position of the viewer, deliberates the image of the perceptual shortening, and merges multiple viewpoints into a single image. By doing so, it undoes the human, earthly, limited, and singular act of vision, producing an unearthly, unlimited, multiplied act of visualizing in its place.

With the nonhuman photographic condition, the view is extended beyond the limitations of the human body and eyes. But, perhaps even more significantly, this set of circumstances or factors also affects the role and importance of subjectivity, especially regarding interpretation during the imaging process, through the introduction of a polyfocal perspective which distorts the order of planes and distances, even with the photographic camera which is a perspectival tool. Images are computed to lay the non-perspectival and thus non-relativist scene, the one human race never had. They are corrected to fit the frame of the non-perspectival and non-placeable intelligence. Automated and precise, the new view is also dropping the living limits of the human. Besides a viewing- subject dropout, the total image is pointing to a nonhuman creator, or at least above the human one, as its goal is to simulate the neutrality and objectivity of the image, as demanded by epistemological theories of photography, which are derived from non-locality and omnipresence. This nonhuman aspect is consisting of the simulation of the above the human being, being it physical power or the metaphysical instance, rather than a machine. Thus, all enhancements of the powers of vision from above and from outside of the Earth are necessarily non-human too, since the very beginning of conquering this position. By means of this conquering, total view is also in-human by its politics.

---

18   Hannah Arendt, *The Human Condition*, Chicago, University of Chicago Press, 1998 (1958); Zylinska. *Nonhuman Photography*.

19   Arendt, *Human Condition*, 10. Notably this discussion was so intriguing and influential that an asteroid was named after Arendt in 1990.

20   Arendt, *Human Condition*.

Post-digital Divide

The novelty of the total view comes from both its usefulness for control as well as its seeming perfection. On the one hand, the limitations of natural human sight were one of the reasons for the invention and development of such assisting, prosthetic technology in the first place. On the other hand, the application and integration of this technology has also deepened the divide between human and machine vision.

With the photographic gaze in traditional analogue photography, the two eyes work together in simultaneous action, with one eye looking through the viewfinder of the camera, while the other looks out into the landscape to control the indexical relationship between the view in the photograph and the reality of the world. With post-digital photography, however, the photographer no longer plays the part of the epistemic guarantor. And they do not themselves witness to the veracity of the image. Consequently, the parameters of the photographic medium itself have been disturbed: most importantly, the photographic claim to knowledge and truth. In essence, the truth-claim of post-digital photography is framed by the fact that humans cannot produce objective knowledge, even when using camera. Only machines can be objective, with their non-subjective, non-human artificial intelligence.

Images by Machine and for the Machine

The post-digital age is characterized by the clear and present divide (and collaboration), rather than integration, between naked human and supported machine vision.[21] New imaging techniques and technologies only serve to strengthen this divide as well as the dualistic opposition between the subjective and objective. And, I suggest, this age is also characterized by a hierarchical dynamic between these natural and unnatural ways of seeing, with the human subordinated below the machine, if not enhancing the machine working independently.

Photography in the post-digital age with both its deep combining and division between the human and machine, is characterized by two essential effects. The first effect centers around the integration of human and machine vision, and the second around an emancipated machine vision made by and for machines. As defined by David Berry and Michael Dieter, the integration of human and machine vision is 'a cultural condition which enhancements algorithmic logic, and mediated perception', emancipated machine vision in and of itself is characterized by a space without time following from the introduction of digital technologies.[22] Joanna Zylinska, one of the premier theorists on post-digital photography, describes the first effect as one in which human and nonhuman photography, in order to act together, enable different 'modes of visuality and self-identification'.[23] The second effect, however, is marked by the complete absence of humans and, consequentially, of humanity. Yet the first effect,

---

21   See: Peter McLaren and Petar Jandri , *Postdigital Dialogues on Critical Pedagogy, Liberation Theology and Information Technology*, London: Bloomsbury, 2020.

22   David Berry and Michael Dieter, *Postdigital Aesthetics: Art, Computation and Design*, London: Palgrave Macmillan, 2015.

23   Joanna Zylinska, *Nonhuman Photography*, Cambridge, MA: MIT Press, 2017, 5.

which collapses the flow between natural and unnatural perception, is a prerequisite for the second, in which control over the medium of photography is handed over in its entirety to machines. Unmanned photography, or photography which is not conducted by humans, has thus slowly become fully nonhuman, a technology that works independently from its creators.[24]

Photography done by machine no longer needs a photographer. Now, machine vision leads human vision, as even digital cameras guide a photographer where to point and shoot, offering a set of targeting tools, and have automatic settings. It is the machine that controls each step in the process of making an image, a process where photographers once exercised their free and creative will. Today, the machine is the one responsible for major decisions and actions of focusing, calculating, and measuring, thus literary commissioning, but also editing as suggesting the points of the image junction to produce a complex photographic visualization. Machines today do not even need the photographer to press the button. But photography does not only not need a photographer. Today, it does not need a viewer either. Images are not made for humans but also for another machine that will process them. We have arrived in an era of automated photography in which images are being made by machines and for them too. Such images Paul Virilio refers to as 'images without spectators' or 'images created by machine for machine'.[25] Such a photograph challenges contemporary visual culture because it is not meant neither for ordinary human affairs and sciences.

Against the emergence of new visual technologies and visualization techniques, good old human photography simply cannot compete. Without authors and audience, photographic image is no longer merely an aesthetic product, having a long-lasting purpose of musealization, but also a functional, and use- or purpose-oriented one. Images travel between one and other machine to produce a deep learning conclusion, or to select images. [26] In order to explain the intentionality of the machine image, Friedrich Kittler used concept of the 'operational images,' while Vilém Flusser referred to 'technical images,' which are themselves the end of linearity of history, existing on the basis of the text.[27] Operational images or 'image acts' as Horst Bredekamp has named them, are used in data collecting, analyzing, reconstructing and visualization.[28] And it is not only photography, but also the other means of visual representations that are failing to become fixed products but are rather becoming that what Marta Jecu names catalytic, or trajectory entities.[29] Photography and photography-based technologies have become expanded the function of the medium for storing visual memories, an immediate

24   Zylinska, *Nonhuman Photography*.
25   Paul Virilio, *The Vision Machine,* Bloomington and Indianapolis: Indiana University Press, 1994.
26   Such as GANs, Generative Adversarial Network-programs.
27   Friedrich Kittler, *Optical Media: Berlin Lectures 2009,* Cambridge: Polity Press, 2012; Vilém Flusser, *Into the Universe of Technical Images.* University of Minnesota Press, 2011.
28   Horst Bredekamp, *Image Acts: A Systematic Approach to Visual Agency*, trans. Elizabeth Cregg, Berlin: De Gruyter, 2017.
29   Marta Jecu defines postdigital architecture through a concept of catalytic space, having a mere purpose-function, staying unconsumed in the process, contrary to lived space that is altered by social processes, revoking thus again the difference of space and place and establishing the place/space mediation. 'The interplay between digital, biological, cultural, and technological elements, between conceptual and real space, between embodied and virtual media are manifestedly post-digital'. Marta Jecu, *Architecture and the Virtual*, Bristol and Chicago: University of Chicago Press, 2016, 13.

memorizing tool itself, or even a tool of a complex information storage. In addition, they have become an active agent which creates several types of visualities by rendering new from old visual information.

Nonhuman Photography

For not being objects of ordinary human affairs and sciences, but trajectory objects, non-human photography is often not taken seriously enough in analysis of contemporary visual culture. Yet, new images are fully integrated in our daily experience, also changing our understanding of the world. The reason for negligence of the role the post-digital photography has to our lives may also lie in the fact that it is not produced by humans and is thus disregarded as relevant in terms of its emancipated intentions, means and purposes. Thus, Zylinska asked for:

> Embracing nonhuman vision as both a concept and a mode of being in the world will allow humans to see beyond the humanist limitations of their current philosophies and worldviews, to unsee themselves in their godlike positioning of both everywhere and nowhere.'[30]

Finally each of these technologies influences our understanding of the world.

The use of nonhuman photography changes significantly all of the visual relationships in traditional photography, such as the plane, depth, and scale of the land, by introducing a multifocal perspective which distorts the distance and the order of planes in the image. In order to achieve a more total image, one which encompasses still more space, these images not only record from nature, but are also computed. And during these computational processes, more of the visual relationships from traditional photography are dismissed. Artificial intelligence can now be used to correct non-perspectival and non-placeable images and align them within a 'view from nowhere'. Images are adjusted, layered, and corrected *ab ovo* or from the very beginning. Therefore, these images fall outside the limits of the human. And once these photos begin to be computed by machines, there can no longer be the same truth claim about the object or objects being represented in the image.

Due to biological constraints, humanity does not have the ability to compare between technical and natural vision. These changing conditions do not support a consistent and reliable system of guaranties for the validity of an image, such as scientific authority, political institution, the credibility of the publisher, or as authors of the second order that justify the image in a certain discourse, on which I was writing elsewhere.[31] Scholars in disciplines such astronomy, criminology, ethnology, history, and medicine consider the truthfulness of the photograph to be foundational in their research. But with nonhuman photograph, the causal relationship between the image and its reference has been interrupted, and what is seen cannot be believed. We may then ask ourselves several questions: Firstly, is the existence of an object

---

30   Zylinska, *Nonhuman Photography*, 15, original Italics.
31   Peraica, *Fotografija kao dokaz.*

beyond its visual representation necessary or merely contingent? Secondly, are qualities of such an object based on a trustworthy and truthful vision, or are they being interpreted through visualization, and so only causally related to the object's existence? To simplify these questions: How do we see the world we live in? And how does our vision influence the way we know the world?

Limits of Scientific Authority

Each prospective change of technology brings a subsequent change in the culture, writes Edward Shanken.[32] With the miniaturization of the camera and automation of its functions, the prosthetic which is photographic technology records beyond the capacity of human vision, while continuing to revolutionize our relationship to reality. Aerial, drone, and satellite images, when combined into complex post-digital photographs, such as hypermaps, can serve as assistants which help us to locate ourselves, navigate our surroundings, and predict the weather, constantly intervening in our daily lives. All of the newly innovated functionalities of photographic technology, such as memory externalization, nonhuman automatization, and prosthetic extension, which characterize photography in this post-digital era, also change our actual reality. Still, they are no longer photographic visions referring to the physical reality in the indexical sense once recognized by semiotics of photography.[33] Rather, they become visualizations of some weak reality, reduced on a mere effect of realism of the photographic image.

Accordingly, photography does not necessarily record a reality, though its relationship to it remains epistemic (as it continues to bring 'some' knowledge, at least on the metaphorical level). Today it also actively produces reality as such. Thus, photographic reality can be taken as yet another one in the object-orientated-ontologies defined by Graham Harman, or as Manuel deLanda named it 'flat ontology', producing hyperobjects.[34] According them the new reality of objects would be real, independently our implementation of them, and they can actively produce it. Thus, any change in photographic medium or technology, will act on its production. But what happens when humans' sense of reality is dependent solely on images that are not made by or for humans at all? How do these images influence our knowledge about the world, in these post-digital times?

For example, there are a wide range of images of the Earth used today, including globes, landscapes, maps, and photographs, the various hybrids of these, and their digital or virtual iterations. Some of these image forms, genres, or types are integrated into satellite monitoring systems, others into smart phone applications, and some into both. But during the processes for many if not most such complex systems, the shape of the Earth is corrected, its sphericity dismissed, and flatness embraced, if only for the practical reason of efficient computability.

---

32   Edward Shanken, 'Virtual Perspective and the Artistic Vision: A Genealogy of Technology, Perception and Power', in M. Roetto (ed) *Seventh International Symposium on Electronic Art (ISEA) Proceedings*, Rotterdam: ISEA96 Foundation, 1996.

33   See, for example: Clive Scott, *The Spoken Image: Photography and Language*, London: Reaktion Book, 1999.

34   Graham Harman, *The Quadruple Object*, Winchester and Washington: Zero Books, 2011; Manuel deLanda, *Intensive Science and Virtual Philosophy,* London: Bloomsbury Academic, 2013.

Yet, all such representations continue to inform and influence our understanding of the world, especially where they are implemented with tools for our physical navigation, impacting our attitudes, beliefs, and desires toward the planet. Thus, it comes as no surprise that the aerial or bird's eye view from up above in the sky or in space has challenged our thinking about who we are and how our planet looks alike. Since the idea of the known world as a spherical shape was first introduced in Antiquity, our ideas as well as our representations for the planet have changed.

New Medievalism

The idea that the planet we live on is flat is only one among many various beliefs from the Medieval Period which some individuals and communities have started to believe in again in the late 20th and early 21st centuries. James Bridle calls this era the 'New Dark Age'.[35] The such a Dark Age indeed becomes visible in the surveillance logic of big brother and the eye in the sky. But can also be seen in economic segregation as well as the large migration and movement of entire populations. To this list can also be added the growing distrust in science and religious fundamentalism in the last decades, as is evident in the belief that chemtrails of condensed water vapor created by airplanes traveling at high altitudes are damaging to our health, or that vaccines cause autism, and on and on.

All such tendencies lead to the rise of a 'New Medieval Age', as I termed this phenomenon in my previous book, *Culture of the Selfie*.[36] As my book was published a year earlier than Bridle's, now I will further distinguish my earlier concept of 'New Medievalism" from Bridle's latter concept 'New Dark Age'.[37] There are several avenues of inquiry from which to approach how a conception of the world from the Medieval Period has returned, including educational, medial, philosophic, religious, and technological, to name but a few. It is possible, for example, to analyze the level of the education of disbelievers, in particular their mandatory education syllabus. Besides, an independency of the education can be taken into the account, as well as the impact from the religion, or families and societies in shaping belief systems. It is also possible to analyze general policy and investment in public education, and more general socio-political atmosphere surrounding the education process. The status of the public science in a certain culture can also be taken into comparison, forwarding questions if the science is meeting the criteria of the publicity and accessibility. Besides, the percentage of sceptics in a certain population can be screened as well. From there yet other questions may be raised – what the impact of the Internet on the disbelief in science is, that besides the shape of the Earth also challenges medical recommendations for vaccinating children and chemotherapy use in cancer cure etc. Finally, it is possible to approach the problem by analyzing dominant visual culture and the hegemonic elements embedded in it, which is the approach taken in this book.

---

35   James Bridle, *New Dark Age: Technology and the End of the Future*, London and Brooklyn: Verso, 2018.

36   See my: *Culture of the Selfie*, Institute of Network Cultures, Amsterdam, 2017.

37   New Medievalism is defined on the basis the theme of *acheiropoieton*, a God-made image in selfies, as well as the dismissal of perspectival knowledge as a visual and demonstrative way of measuring the space around us in technologies of selfies.

A Note on the Organization of this Book and the Definition of Terms

Through the fields of art history, media theory, photographic theory, and visual studies, I will begin my analysis in Chapter 1 by addressing some of the reasons how and why flat Earth theories have reemerged in the 20th and 21st centuries. In Chapter 2, I will elaborate on the historical development of aerial photography, and in Chapter 3, imaging of the planet from space. For this discussion, I will draw upon a diverse range of images and media, encompassing aerial photography from the civilian, geological, and military sectors, sculpted globes and digital globes, as well as drone and satellite imaging. Then, in Chapter 4, going beyond the photographic medium and all its varieties over the past hundred-and-fifty years, I will analyze maps which simulate this aerial or bird's eye view from above. In Chapter 5, I will further distinguish between two types of representations of space, the landscape and the map, as well as their contemporary hybridization. In Chapter 6, expanding upon these foundational genres, I will catalogue and categorize the diverse image forms where aerial photography and map making are in some way combined, such as the orthophoto, photomap, and hypermap, as well as computational photography and deep photographs. And lastly, in Chapters 7 and 8, I will discuss the problems of perspective and of perspectival systems in the aerial view from the Medieval Period to the post-digital age, along the theme of control by viewing from above.

Since its invention in the early 19th century, the photographic medium has for the most part been characterized by its indexical or factual relationship to reality. And today, photographs may be constructed out of many different kinds of materials. Overall, my analysis will encompass two types of representations: photographs and image constructs that might look alike photographs. Such constructs can be made on photographic and non-photographic base. Photography-based constructs, on one hand, are visual artefacts which are made out of the photographic medium, either as an element or as a layer, while constructs made on non-photographic base ones made from various materials.

To briefly introduce the terminology and typology for such photography-based constructs, as I will explore over the course of this book: I will deal here with image constructs, made out of photographic and non-photographic base. When an image is made on the photographic base, it can range from panoramic image and 360 images, connected by sides, photogrammetric image resulting from tiled constructions, to overlapping constructions of deep photo and GAN photography. When a photograph would be made out of photographs from various sources, assembling them, I will name it *pseudo-photographs*, while when made out of the photographic material of the same record - *deep photographs*. To briefly define, pseudo-photographs are visual artefacts in which a photographic realistic appearance was attributed to an artefact made out of photographic material which is not necessarily related to the same reality, or if it relates – the representation significantly oscillates from it because of interventions on the image. The most common example of pseudo-photography is today a product of neural software, creating images from other images.[38] Each section of the process of recording can

---

38   Neural network creates photorealistic images people are not real; DIY Photography https://www.
       diyphotography.net/neural-network-creates-photo-realistic-images-people-arent-real/.

be modified by computer calculus by specifically programmed computers as Halide.[39] Such software can change the appearance of the photo, as for example coloring the black and white pixels, enhancing the mobile phone image into a quality of a professional shooting. Still, the empowering is commonly not done in production, but rather post-productive choice made upon a number of deeply recorded images or by computing them (as in case of wrong exposure, motion blur, changing illumination).

To be able to clearly distinguish combinations with non-photographic materials, I will refer to genres - *orthophotographs* or *orthophotos*, that would be corrected, map-like photographs, *photographic maps* (or *photomap*) that would be maps looking like photographs, or photographs corrected to match the map that would present itself as rather more truths-worthy than the optical record itself, *photomaps* that are maps made on photographic basis and *hypermaps* which are the maps including a photo as one among layers. Also, in contrast to geographic analysis of photomaps, I will use the definition of orthophoto maps differently from that of photomap, although some authors warn orthophoto was yet another stage of developing of photomaps (the other two stages being planimetric, preceding photomaps, and satellite view, succeeding it).[40] These objects, named MLO (*map-like objects*) Dahlberg defines as 'mosaicked image tied to a coordinate base', and I will be investigating rather as photo-alike objects, as they actually employ and engage photographic realism as a bare effect in suggesting a certain conceptualization of reality.[41] In order to maintain clearance I will use, at many places, charts and tables.

Photographic constructs			
	-	On photographic base	
	a.	Sidelapped (tiled constructions, planimetric, peripheral or rollout photography)	Photomontages
			Panorama and 360 Photogrammetry
	b.	Overlapped	Deep photos GAN photographs (pseudo-photograph)
	-	On nonphotographic base	
			Orthophoto Photomaps Photographic maps Hypermaps

Table 1: Nomenclature and branching of total images.

39   Computational photography already has made an impact on commercial photography, as for example in services as Meero, that function as platform photographing. In Meero, photographers are serving as input to machines, providing an amount of RAW images of a certain kind which are latter processed by AI. See: https://www.meero.com/en/technology.
40   R.E. Dahlberg, 'The Design of Photo and Image Maps', *The Cartographic Journal* 30 (1993): 112-118.
41   Dahlberg, 'The Design of Photo and Image Maps'.

In order to compare and contrast the many differences between various images of the Earth and ways of perceiving it, for my analysis, I will bring together many different theoretical frameworks, including: space and place, art historical space studies of pre-photographic landscape, autonomous photographic theory of space (predominantly epistemology), measured space in metric and military photography. I will also approach different histories of the medium of photography, and the genre of aerial recording in social urbanism, military studies, sociology, and geography. I will lay down visual, and more specifically landscape, theories of space from above in historical perspective, so as to be able to analyses how the view from above changed our perception of our habitat, but also how it was schematized further to satisfy utilitarian ends, no longer matching the strong epistemic ties among the photograph and photographed.

Through these themes I will analyze the most radical of influences of representation onto the object: the image that attempts to bring out the definition of totality, either as being recorded from above of the object, or ones overlapping in situ, or by assembling multiple views on the horizontal axis, in order to provide a larger amount of data than the 'ordinary' photography would. I will address whether or not and to what degree this visual episteme provides sufficient grounds for different belief systems. The two already mentioned questions, ontological and epistemic, oriented the other way around and having a strong political resonance appear as assumptions in Frederic Jameson's theory of cognitive mapping.[42] According his hypothesis, the inability to map and have a total picture is a reason for the social disintegration, whereas the cognitive mapping in a total image results in identification with ideology. Although I will not deal with political theory, in the closing words of this book, I will nevertheless draw upon theory from the disciplines of philosophy and sociology in order to analyze the role and importance of total images in totalitarian systems, also referring to assembled totality of today's world. While I will not focus on political ideologies per se, I will trace the historical development of total images in our visual culture, and find the moments when these images either follow from or lead to conflict in our ideas and ideals about the world.

Although I will refer to the theme of flat Earth many times, starting with the next chapter, my purpose in this manuscript is not to question whether or not the Earth itself is actually flat; it is not. Rather, my purpose is epistemic, relating to this knowledge and the degree of its validity or invalidity. How does post-digital photography inform or inspire our perception and understanding of the planet? Further, how have views of the world been imagined and constructed at different times across history? And how have these views changed our knowledge about the Earth and how do they now?

---

42   The concept of cognitive mapping was first used by Edward Toi, back in 1948, to be redefined as cognitive by Jameson and mental by Lynch. Kevin A. Lynch: *Image of the City*, Cambridge, MA: MIT Press, 1960. Jameson also refers to writings of Lynch, see Fredric Jameson: *Cognitive mapping*, in Nelson, C Grossberg, L (eds) *Marxism and the Interpretation of Culture*, Chicago: University of Illinois Press, 1999, 347-60. See also: Fredric Jameson, *The Geopolitical Aesthetic: Cinema and Space in the World System*, Bloomington, Indiana University Press, 1995.

CHAPTER 1: FLAT EARTH

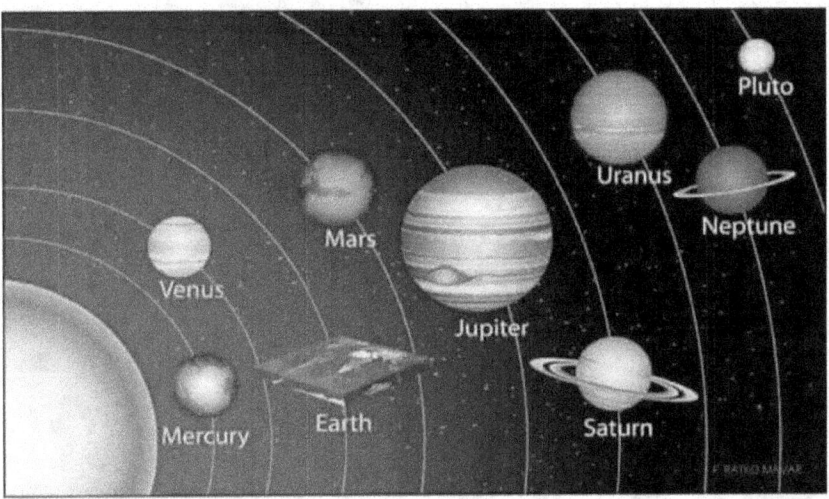

Figure 3: Flat Earth internet meme.

New Flat Earthers

At the time of this writing, people all over the world have celebrated the 50th anniversary of Apollo 11, the famous spaceflight during which humans first landed on the Moon. But there are still millions of people who are skeptical that this Moon landing ever happened. In the past half century of continuing space exploration, scientific records have failed to convince a certain segment of the population to abandon their disbelief. On the contrary, their skepticism has only increased, and not only regarding our landing on the satellite Moon, but also the shape of the planet Earth.[1] In fact, a recent article published by *The Guardian* newspaper refers to a YouGov poll which found that a third of all Americans between ages 18 and 24 were unsure about the shape of our planet.[2] This is despite the vast amount of scientific proof that has been provided over two thousand years by sources ranging from Pythagoras to NASA. Other articles in the news media suggest that about two percent of the population in the United States distrust the scientific fact that the Earth is round.[3] At first, this may not

---

1   See for example: Bill Kayasing, *We Never Went to the Moon: America's Thirty Billion Dollar Swindle*, CreateSpace Independent Publishing Platform, 2017.
2   Trevor Nace, 'Only Two-Thirds of American Millennials Believe the Earth Is Round', *Forbes,* 4 April 2018, https://www.forbes.com/sites/trevornace/2018/04/04/only-two-thirds-of-american-millennials-believe-the-earth-is-round/.
3   Richard Sprenger, James Bullock, Alex Healey, Tom Silverstone and Katie Lamborn, 'Flat Earth Rising: Meet the People Casting Aside 2,500 Years of Science', *The Guardian,* 5 February 2019, https://www.theguardian.com/science/video/2019/feb/05/flat-earth-rising-meet-the-people-casting-aside-2500-

appear to be a significant percentage. But when taking the entire United States into account, two percent of the population refers to approximately 6.5 million people who do not believe that the Earth is round. And this number does not appear to be decreasing. In the 21st century, the theory that the Earth is flat has become the source of humorous Internet memes. However, advocating this 'flat Earth' theory is far from harmless.

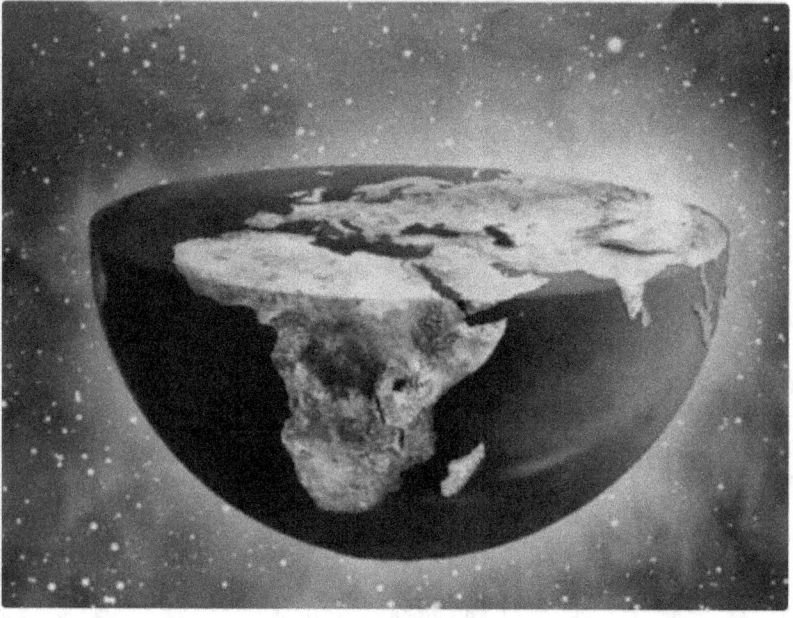

Figure 4: Flat Earth internet meme.

Flat Earth theories are no mere comedy, and the argumentation which is used in support of such theories must be taken seriously. As an educator, I am convinced that such things should not go uninterpreted. Thus, in this book I will ask the question: in the postdigital era, how this division and interaction between human and nonhuman perception, works on the rise of a belief in the flat Earth theory? As I begin to explore this question, it is important to first define what is meant by 'the flatness of the Earth'. In this book, I distinguish between three positions: ontological, epistemological, and medial. From an ontological position, to make the claim that the Earth is flat is to argue that our planet is actually, in reality, physically flat. Those

years-of-science-video.

readers who are convinced that this is indeed the case may stop reading now, as I will not try to prove, and will do everything I can to disprove, such a theory. From an epistemological position, to make the claim that the Earth is flat is to argue not that the planet is flat, but that we may experience it as flat, given a constrained view of the planet as a whole. Such a theory would enforce relativist position in the theory of knowledge, claiming that all our knowledge is partial and dependent of our view-angle. And finally, from a medial position, to make the claim that the Earth is flat is to argue that regardless of what shape the planet does or does not in fact have, the only way we can approach its shape is by the media, which determines our knowledge. In this case, according to media theory, any flatness of the Earth is a problem of mediation and the limitations of given media language. This media position is the one which I will explore in this book. I will claim that in post-digital media, the Earth is more frequently represented as a flat plane than a round sphere and, further, that this process of mediation eradicates the perspectival views of the human subject from photography.

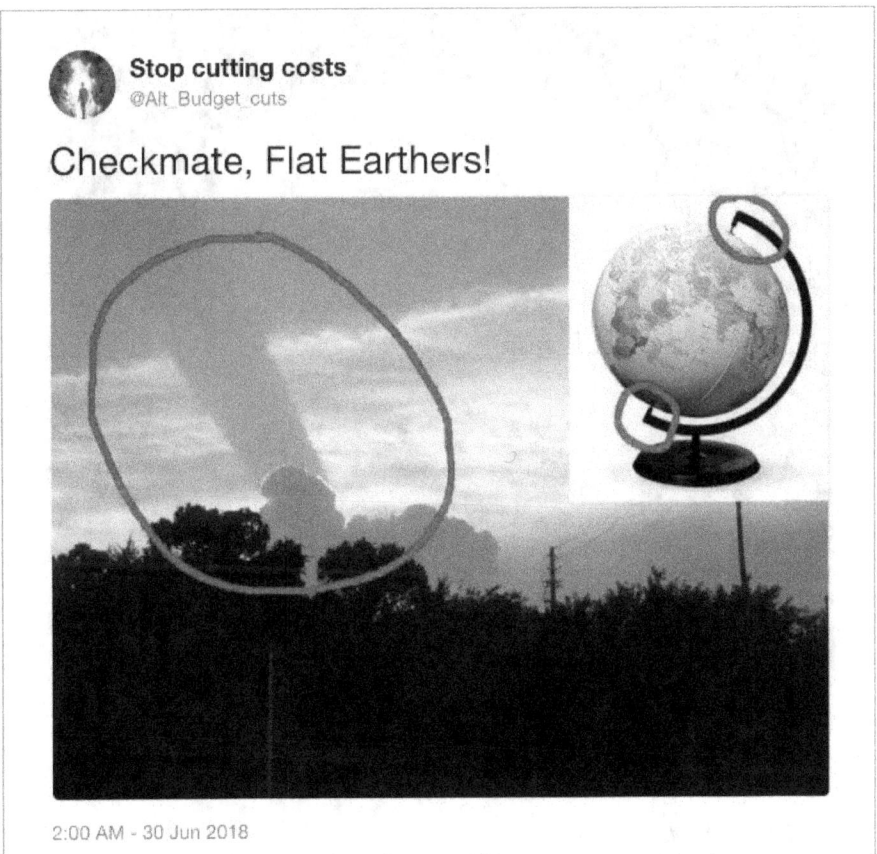

Figure 5: Flat Earth internet meme.

Throughout this book, in order to distinguish between the one and only planet Earth and its many possible representations, I will use the capitalized proper noun 'Earth' when referring to the planet and the lowercase common noun 'earth' when referring to its representations.[4] In this chapter, I will begin to address this idea of the Earth and an earth, laying down arguments for how the phenomenal world may appear to be visually flat in the contemporary era, in order to be able to analyze these representations in more detail in the upcoming chapters. My focus in the first chapter will be on the question: How does our knowledge of the Earth condition our representations for an earth and, vice versa, how do these representations for an earth influence our knowledge of the Earth?

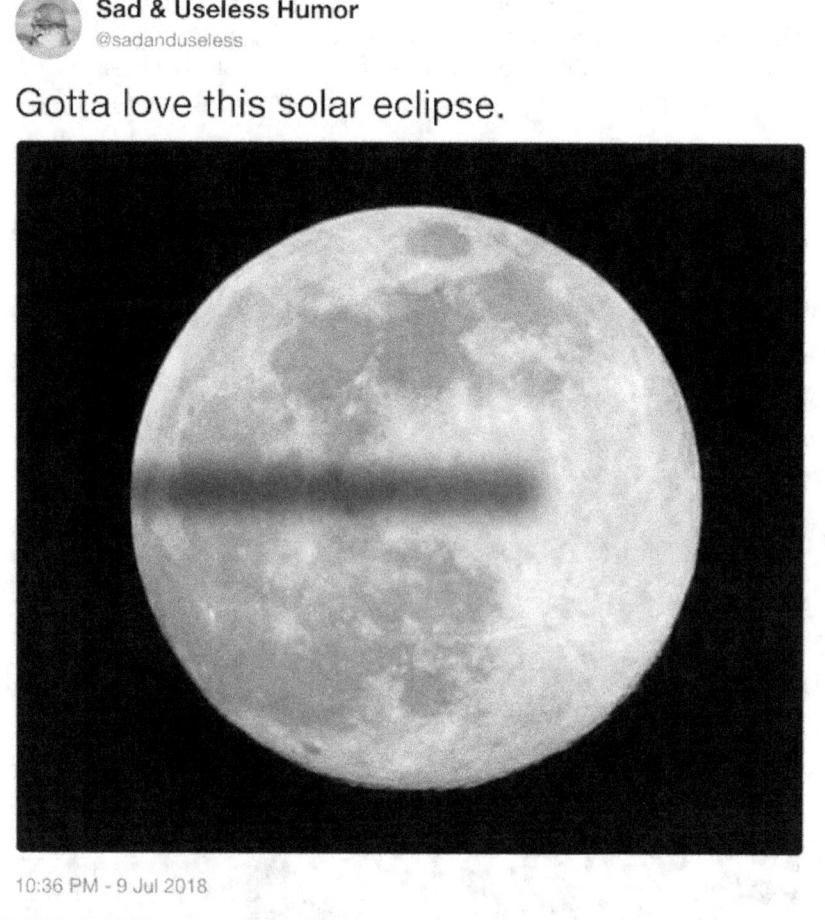

Figure 6: Flat Earth internet meme.

---

4   I refer here to the distinction Hubert Damisch made in his analysis of the visuality of clouds, using the formula /c/loud whenever he referred to its representation. See: Hubert Damisch, *Theory of the /c/loud,* Stanford, California: Stanford UP, 2008.

Down-Dimensioning

In order to understand the division between the reality of the planet Earth which we inhabit and the ways in which one may perceive and represent multiple earths, I will begin by introducing the novel *Flatland*, written in 1884 by English schoolmaster and theologian Edwin Abbott Abbott.[5] Through the voice of his narrator, 'Square', Abbot describes a hypothetical, multilayered universe. This four-dimensional system has many populations living in it. They all live in the same space and at the same time but are not necessarily able to perceive each other. or the world works as hyperworld, in which, despite its complexity, only one layer can be seen at the time. This is because each group of beings is limited in the number of dimensions which they are 'programmed' to be able to perceive. That is, each class or demographic of beings can only perceive one dimension less (-1) than it needs in order to exist. In other words, in Pointland, a single being (the universe in one) consists of a dot who has no dimension whatsoever. In Lineland, beings are lines of a certain length who perceive themselves as dots which have only a single dimension. In Flatland, which is more advanced, beings have two dimensions and perceive themselves as lines. Finally, in the last world described, the three-dimensional world of Spaceland, is being clearly visible only from a next and fourth dimension. However, Abbott does not elaborate on this last world in his book, as obviously that is the space of the Square who would need to be seen by someone in a higher dimension in order for his own world to be defined. Reading the novel *Flatland*, we learn that the inhabitants are confined to their world by their perception of that world, which therefore does not necessary correspond to reality itself. Further, most of the inhabitants stay assured and confident in the sense-data around which they build their own understanding of the world. For example, in Flatland, the inhabitants, like Square, perceive themselves as lines. To be capable of distinguishing different shapes, some of which can be dangerous, such as lines, the inhabitants introduce a strict law on the colors they should be wearing. However, such a fully ordered world would continue working according own principles in peace if there would not be a main protagonist. Square somehow manages to grasp that there exists a higher dimension beyond his direct and immediate experience, without ever having directly perceived it, after establishing contact with this dimension. And Square begins to share this knowledge with his fellow citizens in Flatland. But because this population is not able to perceive such a dimension for themselves, Square is misunderstood. And the other inhabitants of Flatland fall back on their old belief that there are hidden forces at work, controlling their world, rather than dare to imagine that there is more to their world than meets the eye. Abbott narrativizes this event through the character of the Cycle, who rules Flatland, and prophecies the arrival of a new group of invaders, giving the narrative both political and teleological significance.[6]

---

5   Edwin Abbott Abbott, *Flatland: A Romance of Many Dimensions*, new introduction by Thomas Banchoff, New York and Dover: Princeton University Press, 1993.

6   Abbott's work reminds us not only on complexity of the world but also on the cognitive distortion of individuals that might live in the downgraded dimensions, under ideologies of any kind. In addition to satirizing the stratification of the classes in Victorian society, Abbott's *Flatland* describes the ways in which religious practice and cognitive ability may be entangled.

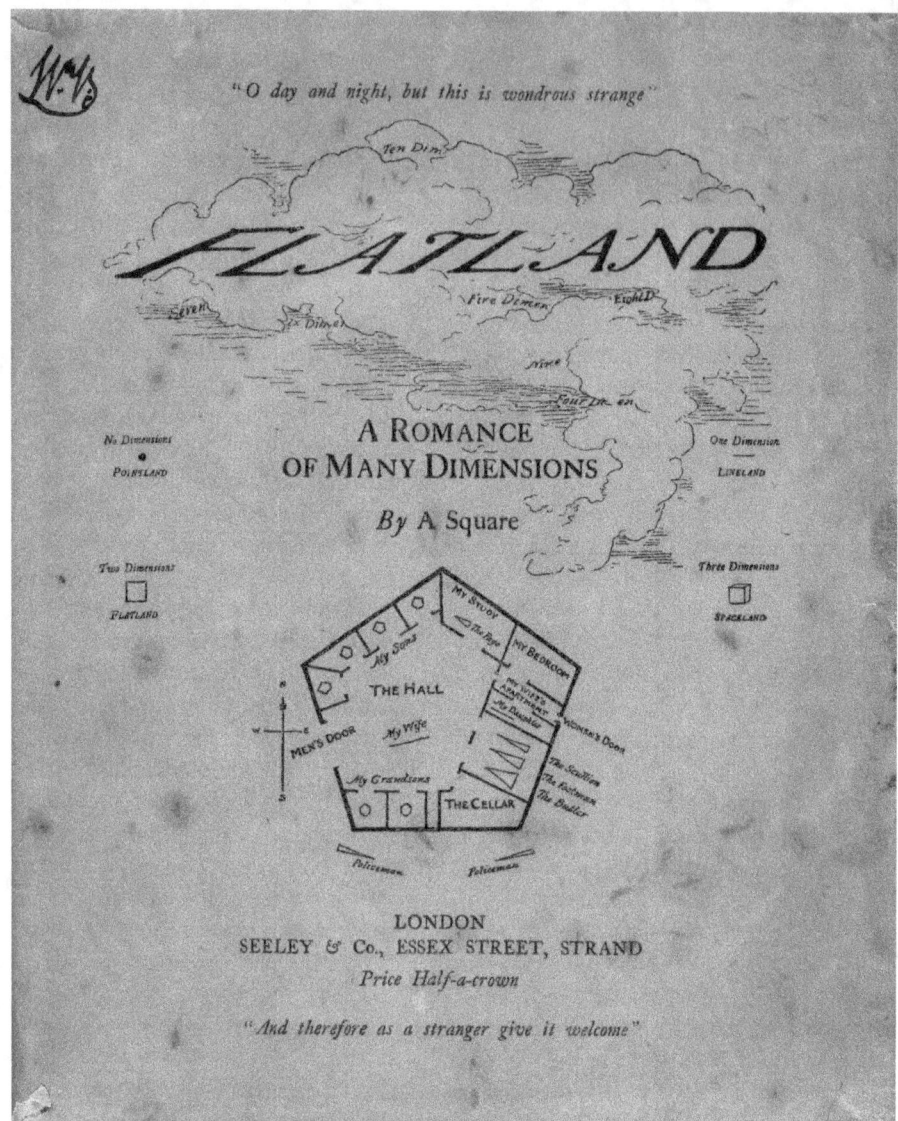

Figure 7: The Cover of Flatland *by William Abbott Abbott, 1884.*

Besides questions about how the world appears to Flat earthers, Flatland tale also raises another question: how does the same world appear to those who perceive an additional dimension? This question can be seen in the way Sphere from Spaceland sees Square from Flatland: as a two-dimensional spatial form, while Square from the Flatland sees everyone in his land as lines. Sphere is thus empowered and can control the population in the lower dimension, which, in turn is not able to directly know the upper dimension. In the real, rather than fictional world, each and every population must surpass its own image-space in order to define where they live and their place in the world. In other words, to define a space requires an additional dimension.[7]

By stratifying dimensions in a formula '+1', Abbott anticipates Austrian mathematician and analytic philosopher Kurt Gödel's incompleteness theorem. Almost fifty years after Abbott wrote Flatland, Gödel argued that in order to define a set we need at least one statement which does not belong to that set and which cannot be proven by it.[8] For Abbott, such a mathematical statement is a dimension. Furthermore, Abbott' novel *Flatland* can also be read from the perspective of Benoit Mandelbrot's notion of the degree of resolution, to which I would come back later in the book when I speak about scales of measurement.[9] Here, the perception of the size of an element, or its magnification, and therefore the determination of whether something is a dot or a ball, a line or a thread, depends upon the distance to it.[10]

Abbott's work reminds us not only on complexity of the world but also on the cognitive distortion of individuals that might live in the downgraded dimensions, under ideologies of any kind. In addition to satirizing the stratification of the classes in Victorian society, Abbott's *Flatland* describes the ways in which religious practice and cognitive ability may be entangled. To bring this discussion back to my main theme about representing the shape of the planet, in Abbott's novel *Flatland* different population groups have different perceptions of the world and experience the same world differently. An argument in favor of the parallel existence of both conceptions of the planet is especially visible in various phenomena lower dimension world ascribes to the higher dimension one, decoding them as mystic. And indeed, by reviewing the appearance in history of a thesis of the flat earth, even the contemporary one, supports the thesis of the religious background of the New Medievalism, I described in the Introduction.

Debate on the Shape

The world described by Abbott has more dimensions than can be perceived by its inhabitants. And for the most of human history, this has in fact been the case. The people who lived in ancient civilizations such as Egypt, Babylon, Mesopotamia, and early Greece thought that the world was flat largely because they did not know about other places which were far away.[11] The territories which these peoples inhabited were relatively small in size and thus appeared to be flat. It is no wonder then that an idea of the Earth as flat is also present in writings of Thales, Anaximander, Anaximenes, and other pre-Socratic philosophers. Their ideas can also be traced in the writings of other authors. And the idea of a flat Earth continued in works of Anaxagora, Leucippus, and Democritus.

---

7   Thus, Bernhard Riemann assumed the fourth dimension in defining the mathematics of the real space.
8   Also known as the Gödel's second theorem.
9   Rhonda Roland Shearer, 'From Flatland to Fractaland: New Geometries in Relationship to Artistic and Scientific Revolutions', *Fractals* 3.3 (1995): 617-625.
10   Abbott's understanding of epistemology in terms of geometry also had a direct impact on Einstein's theory of relativity, as well as theories of hyper-dimensionality. R.R. Shearer, 'From Flatland to Fractaland'.
11   For more see: Dirk L. Couprie, *When the Earth was Flat: Studies in Ancient Greek and Chinese Cosmology*, Berlin: Springer, 2018.

The idea of a spherical Earth originates in late Antiquity also with the Greeks. It appeared in works by Pythagoras and Parmenides, followed by the writings of Plato, Aristarchus, and Euclid. At 50 BCE Aristotle formulated an argument which I will call the 'argument from experience' based on the observation that the stars 'make it evident, not only that the earth is circular, but also that it is a circle of no great size. For quite a minor change of position to south or north causes a manifest alteration of the horizon', as he noted.[12] Thus, Aristotle turned to common sense, accessible and demonstrable types of evidence, and empiricism. His claim was further proved by Erastothemes, whose calculations Claudius Ptolemy later compiled in his *Almagest* or *Syntaxis*.[13] And Ptolemy's as well as Aristotle's description of the world as a sphere would be generally accepted until the fall of the Roman Empire.

But by that time, unfortunately, the idea that the world is flat came back by way of the Germanic peoples that conquered Rome.[14] This idea aligned with the doctrines of Christianity which proposed the Earth as fixed, immobile, and permanent. As such, a flat earth was soon accepted in Christian societies. Because of its consistency of Christian dogma, the idea become so popular that by the time of Saint Augustine it was accepted as the only possible truth. And from the 4th to the 12th century CE, only a few sources remain which questioned the shape of the Earth.

The idea that the Earth is spherical in its shape was revived through works by John Sacrobosco, Thomas Aquinas, Jean Buridan, and further researchers whose names are today associated with the birth of modern science, Galileo Galilei and Johannes Kepler. Yet, the processes of again proving the thesis of a spherical Earth took centuries. It took centuries for the sphericity of the Earth to be rediscovered. This was first done by sailors who had direct experience with the shape during their travels. As Richard Buckminster Fuller wrote:

> [...] the big thinking in general of a spherical Earth and celestial navigation was retained exclusively by the Great Pirates, in contradistinction to a four-cornered, flat world concept, with empire and kingdom circumscribed knowledge [...] Knowledge of the world and its resources was enjoyed exclusively by the Great Pirates, as were also the arts of navigation, shipbuilding and handling, and of grand logistical strategies and of nationally-undetectable, therefore effectively deceptive, international exchange media and trade balancing tricks by which the top pirate, as (in gambler's parlance) "the house," always won.[15]

Indeed, it took even longer to prove for a second time that the Earth is round than it did to conceive that the Earth is flat.

---

12   Aristotle, *On the Heavens*, part 13.
13   Aristotle's idea that that the Earth is a sphere not only competed with the idea that the Earth is flat, but also the idea that the Earth is a disc, presented, for example, by Thales, Anaximenes, Xenophanes, Anaxagora, Archelaus, Leucippos, and Democritus.
14   For the history of the flat earth idea see Christine Garwood, *Flat Earth: The History of an Infamous Idea*, Thomas Dune Books, Macmillan, 2008.
15   Richard Buckminster Fuller, *Operating Manual for Spaceship Earth*, Operating manual for the spaceship Earth, Lars Muller, 2008, 9.

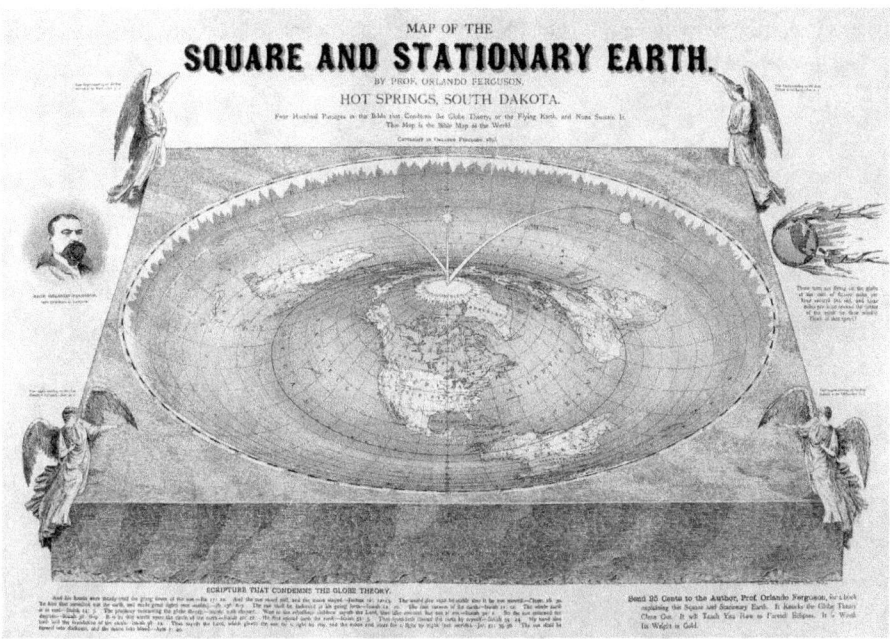

Figure 8: The Flat Earth map drawn by Orlando Ferguson in 1893.

In the centuries that followed, the roundness of the Earth became an axiom of modern science. It was an unquestionable fact. At least, that the Earth is round was a fact until some researchers began to challenge it again. Samuel Birley Rowbotham-Parallax with *Zetetic Astronomy: Earth Not a Globe* (1865), Alfred Russel Wallace with *Water Not Convex, the Earth is not a Globe* (1870), and William Carpenter *One Hundred Proofs the Earth is Not a Globe* (1885), for example, again started to cultivate the idea that the Earth has a flat surface. Today, a sect of the Flat Earthers even continues to use and expand upon arguments from Wallace, Parallax, and Carpenter. Today the idea of the flat Earth is institutionalized by the Flat Earth Society, as well as the members of other formal and informal organizations, which promote the idea that the world is flat.[16] Besides holding meetings and attending conventions, promoters of this idea also run several YouTube channels.[17] Marc Sargent, a key figure in the so-called Flat Earth Movement in California, is pictured at conventions standing in front of an image of a flat earth, as he describes the planet as being similar to this flat image, advocating for such a flatness as an ontological conception.[18] In just the last few decades, this theory has

---

16   Curiously enough, the segment of the population which believes the Earth is flat has announced their expedition to the North Pole in 2020, which reminds one of the expedition by Charles Marie La Condamine, Louis Godin, and Pierre Bouguer around the Earth in order to measure the Equator in 1735-7.

17   These YouTube channels include, for example, 'Globebusters', https://www.youtube.com/playlist?list=PLTgEApRWdweuqSBj3H7qV_GmgglJHz4ah. There are also web pages such as 'Testing Globe', www.testingtheglobe.com.

18   See: Mark Sargent, *Flat Earth Clues: The Sky's The Limit*, Booglez limited, 2016.

gained a particularly large amount of attention, reaching a peak in February 2019 according to Google trends[19].

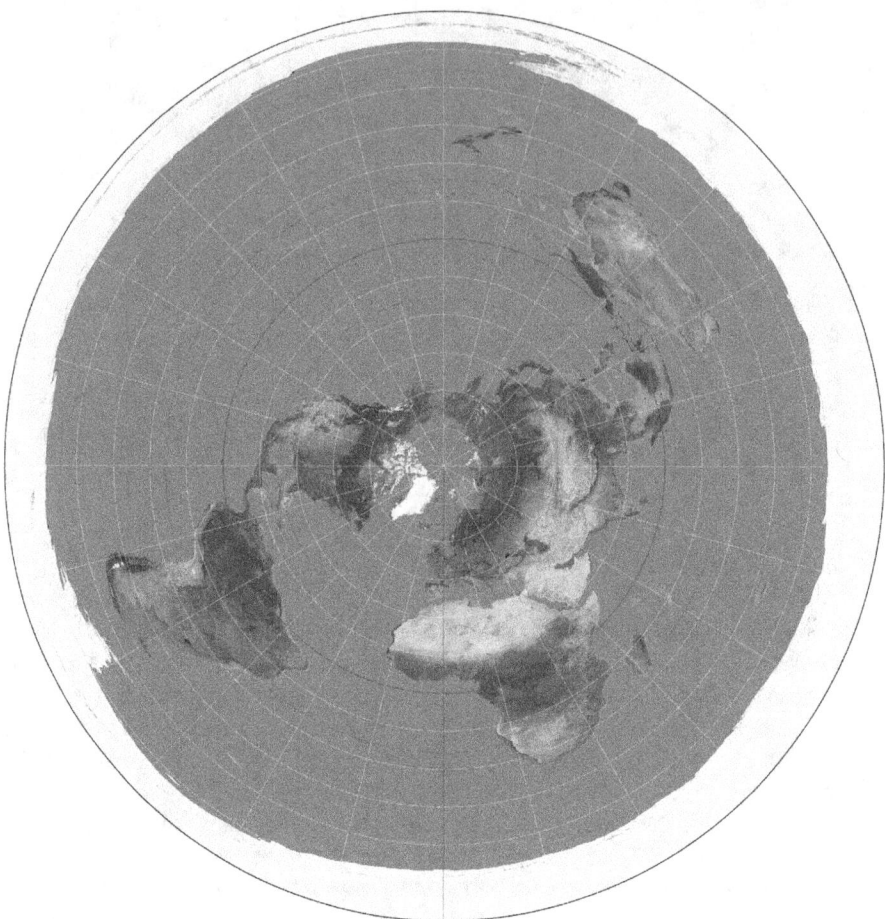

Figure 9: Azimuthal equidistant projection.

Ontological Conception

Five hundred years after the Copernican Revolution, in which our understanding of the solar system shifted from a Ptolemaic to a heliocentric model, and the likes of Marco Polo, Christopher Columbus, Bartolomeu Dias, Vasco da Gama, and Amerigo Vespucci, who sketched sections of the planet after their long sails, we once again find ourselves faced

---

19   According Google Trends, the major interest in flat Earth was by inhabitants of New Zealand, followed by Australia and United States. See: https://trends.google.com/trends/explore?q=flat%20earth.

with the growing belief that the world is flat.[20] The comeback of the flat Earth conception of the planet may be related to the rebirth of other Scholastic *doxa* or opinions, a kind of New Medievalism, if you will.[21] The relationship between such doxastic or belief-based arguments and the Flat Earth Theory is quite evident. For example, Flat Earthers rephrase the 'Intelligent Design' argument, which refers to the existence of higher intelligence on the basis of perfection of the world.[22] This theory underlines, in essence, an ontological idea that derives from a utilitarian principle which states that everything in this world happens or exists for a reason or is designed with a reason. From the ontological position of the Flat Earthers, a spherical world would be impractical to use by God, here pictured as a limited physical being, in his observation of humanity because God would not be able to see everywhere all at once on a sphere as easily as he would on a plane. Because it is implausible to think that God would create a world which he cannot use, a spherical world does not have a reason to exist. Some authors also find lines in support of the flat earth theory in the Bible.[23]

As presented in online videos, other arguments used by the Flat Earthers to support their version of Intelligent Design are based on the direct subversion of scientific authority, or by demonstrations of arguments against scientific axioms.[24] In addition to denying the shape of the planet, Flat Earthers also deny certain axiomatic scientific knowledge, such as the theory of gravity. Moreover, they propose pseudo-academic theories to explain how things do not fall off the planet. To resolve this problem, for example, they introduce a theory of continuous lifting of the Earth's crustal plates, which draws objects down to the ground by their own weight and its force. This concept is also believed to explain how water from oceans does not spill off the edge of the Earth.[25]

The Flat Earthers, while advocating for their own representation and conception of the Earth, also discredit the images from scientific authorities which do not show the planet as being flat in shape. To these sphere-sceptics, photographs of the planet do not and cannot prove

---

20   This theory is challenged by Jeffrey Burton Russell states, 'five hundred years after Christopher Columbus' who claims the idea of the backward Medieval ages was introduced by Darwinists who wanted to stigmatize critics of their theory. Columbus, according Russell did not prove the Earth was round as it was already an accepted theory. Jeffrey Burton Russell, *Inventing the Flat Earth: Columbus and Modern Historians*, New York, Connecticut and London, Praeger, 1991.

21   Among definitely medieval beliefs surely is the one by Gregory Garrett defining the new age as Era of New Luciferianism. See: Gregory Garrett, *The Flat Earth Trilogy Book of Secrets I*, Gregory Lessing Garrett, 2018.

22   The Argument of Intelligent Design is derived from Descartes' *Mediations*, in which, by the very end of the argument he resolves the total skepticism by stating that the world is conceived so intelligently that it would be impossible it was not designed by a higher being. See Daniel Dennett, 'Descartes' Argument from Design', *The Journal of Philosophy* 7 (2008): 333-346.

23   See for example arguments of Eric Tabborn, *PROOF: Does God Say the Earth is Flat?: Ending the Debate Between the Flat Earth vs. the Globe*, publisher unknown, 2018.

24   See: Elaine Chadwick Clanton: *Flat Earth for Dummies 101: Definition of Dummy: Indoctrinated in Globe from Birth*, Elaine Chadwick Clanton, 2018; Brett Salisbury, Dr. Lawrence Cohen, Dr. John Mack, Captain Obvious, *Spherical Trigonometry for Dummies*, Createspace Independent Publishing Platform, 2015.

25   For more arguments see: Kaleb Shuttleworth, *Planet or Plane?: A Debate of the 'Flat-Earth' Hypothesis*, unknown publisher, 2018.

its dimensionality. Instead, they argue, these images depict the Earth as a flat plane. And any image that shows otherwise must have been either fabricated or manipulated. To conspiracy theorists with a strong distrust in science, NASA is often the prime suspect or public enemy number one. Flat Earthers even directly accuse this independent agency of being the puppet-master behind the conspiracy of the so-called 'spherical Earth', and of secretly trying to control people through its fake images of the Earth taken from space and by satellite.

Media Argument

The skeptical attitude of the Flat Earthers is reinforced by the fact that, among the images of the Earth which are taken from outer space, there are two principle types: images which are made using powerful telescopes, and images which are visibly fused together from more than one picture in order to produce a more encompassing view.[26] Much of the variation between photographic representations of the planet can be explained by differences in the technology used to create the image, especially the lens. Moreover, as not all the parts of the Earth can be clearly seen from the point of view of a satellite or satellite system. Due to the presence of clouds, barriers, shadows, or reflective surfaces, there are always places in an image which must be completed or reconstructed. Indeed, since The Blue Marble image of the Earth was taken on December 7, 1972 from a distance of about 29,000 kilometers from the planet's surface by the crew of the Apollo 17 spacecraft, most images released by NASA have been composites made from satellites at shorter distances. In point of fact, while telephoto lenses cause less distortion than wide angle lenses, they nevertheless produce notable alterations to the measurement of reality by introducing an inherent flattening distortion. That the Earth looks like an eating plate in these images is a frequent objection made by Flat earthers, who notice variations in the sizes of the Earth as a whole, as well as its parts, but also in terms of color.[27] Yet curiously enough, it was the original photograph, and not the constructed photographic assemblages, made on the photographic base, which had this visual flattening effect. Thus, paradoxically, according the advocates for flat Earth theory, if the image of the planet is recorded using a telephoto lense, then it is shown as flat, but if it is made using a composite technique, then it is untrustworthy. In comparison, composite photography, which combines more than one photographic source into a single image, helps to create an image of higher resolution, which is also sharper, thereby avoiding the effect of making the Earth look like a flat round plate which is used for eating or serving food.

The bigger problem, however, is that some images of the Earth are not genuinely photographic but rather blended content. This can be done for many reasons. For example, clouds may have obscured the view, such that the image had to be 'restructured'. Or the recording device may have been too near to the ground. Compositing images which have been taken at different times, and from various angles, distorts the relationship between the subject position

---

26   Today, images of outer space can be realized from Earth using super-powerful telephoto lenses the shaft for which can range up to seven meters in length. See for example Pan-STARRS camera, the largest digital camera in the world, and for astronomic/space data https://panstarrs.stsci.edu/

27   This peculiar distortion of telephoto lenses and reality metering was analyzed on the Mantegna's foreshortening of the body of Christ, in the image of Christ in the temple, by Richard Latto and Bernard Harper. 'The Non-realistic Nature of Photography', *Leonardo* 40.3 (2007): 243-247.

and the object recorded, a relationship defined through focal distances, depth of field, and order of planes. Moreover, in such an image, the position of the subjective view is altered, and its original perspective is changed. What is problematic in this is that the photographic image, which historically has been taken to be indexical in relation to its reference, has been turned into a composite, which serves another purposes, as for example navigation. Although keeping the persuasive element of photographic image, these new combo-images distort the photographic description of the visual qualities of the photographic object, in a way other than by photographer decision-making or in photographic postproduction.

+1 Dimension Perspectives

Yet another change in how the photographic space is being distorted comes from the introduction of new ways in which to combine images by merging materials together that have different qualities. Today, the subjective view of the photographer and, therefore, for the viewer of the photograph as well, has been largely eliminated in order to produce a more 'neutral' view, contrary to previous use of perspectival system.

As Friedrich Kittler defines, perspective is a code for a transmission among objects and subjects.[28] Perspective system defines the space as well as the distance between objects. It not only serves representation but also metering of reality which is projected onto the flat screen or a 'veil' as Alberti names it.[29] Through a perspectival system, distance can be measured by the size of the objects relative to the vanishing point, which is usually located on horizon.

In linear perspective, a vanishing point is needed to separate image from reality, as it provided a way of measuring in terms of distance, size of objects, and the ratio between these elements. All measurements in Western, linear perspective, are both fixed and calculable. For this reason, a perspectival system can assist in the development of precise knowledge about the reality which is being represented. And because of this, perspective has long been at the center of research in science and technology.[30] Such an understanding of space continued to be present in succeeding technologies based on mirrors and mirror-reflex systems, leading to a line of historical development and media evolution from the camera obscura to photography.[31]

---

28   Kittler, *Optical Media*, 208.
29   Flat screens also function aesthetically, as in the way Alexander R. Galloway defined 'intraface':
     'The *intraface* is the word used to describe this imaginary dialogue between the workable and the unworkable: the intraface, that is, *an interface internal to the interface*. The intraface is within the aesthetic. It is not a window or doorway separating the space that spans from here to there'. Alexander R. Galloway, *The Interface Effect*, Cambridge and Maiden, Polity, 2012, 40, original italics.
30   Samuel Y. Edgerton, *The Mirror, the Window, and the Telescope: How Linear Perspective Changed our Vision of the Universe*, Cornell University Press, 2009; Martin Kemp, *The Science of Art: Optical Themes in Western Art from Brunelleschi to Seurat*, Yale University Press, 1992.
31   See Anne Friedberg, *The Virtual Window: From Alberti to Microsoft*, Cambridge, MA: MIT Press, 2009, 39 and 61.

In principle, for more than a hundred-and-fifty years, photography has served as a device of recording (and actually storing) physical reality, being an epistemic tool by which we access it, in which it simultaneously functions as a medium of transmission and a temporary screen The limits of the world are no longer the limits of the language, as Ludwig Wittgenstein noted, but ones of the physical screen. [32] Contemporary visualizations, which are tied to the screens which display an image, even when exhibited or projected within a three-dimensional environment, reinforce this idea that the Earth and its spaces are flat by constructing those spaces within the orthogonal lines of a perspective system. And even though images of the planet may represent it as a sphere, they are screened and printed on flat media such as paper or screen. Indeed, the digital world does not allow us a view which encompasses depth or distance. The flatness of the screen only supports the idea that the dimensionality of the world is just an illusion of perception, as virtual reality.

Virilio observes that in post-digital images 'depth no longer includes the visual horizon, nor the vanishing point of perspective', but rather time becomes the most essential and important dimension.[33] Our eyes move to analyze the space, not only orthogonally but also in depth, by focusing on various distances. But the interface, as a temporary image interaction, is also connected to our understanding of space as well as of time. The speed of the signal through the Internet or from a television network, as well as the speed with which this signal is carried through the device itself, has a temporal quality. This leads to the progressive disappearance of space-time, providing no illusion that the Earth is a sphere and that, hypothetically, one could travel around it endlessly, thereby introducing not only the idea of the finiteness of the planet but also the finiteness of the view. According to Virilio, this acceleration towards instantness has destroyed the fixity of both space and its visualizations.[34] Our four-dimensional world, with its three dimensions of space (height, width, depth), as well as the temporal dimension, thereby becomes fixed or flattened.

The disappearance of perspective systems and the positioning of the subject in relation to the image has lead to two phenomenon: first, the absence of a measurement of distance between the subject and the environment in the representation of space; and second, the separation between a subject and objects. This denial of perspective in post-digital photography disturbs our processes for rationalization of the world. 'Distances are no longer situated in any depth of field or "perspective"', as Paul Virilio concludes.[35] Further, the use of various technologies for transportation, such as airplanes, cars, trams, and subway systems, as well as various technologies for communication, such as cellphones, the Internet, and videotelephony, are all so pervasive that it distorts our intuitive, embodied knowledge of space.

---

32   Ludwig Wittgenstein, *Tractatus Logico Philosophicus*, London: Routledge, 2001, 68.
33   Virilio, *Lost Dimension,* 66.
34   Virilio, *Lost Dimension.*
35   Virilio, *Lost Dimension,* 103. Thus, Virilio introduces two points: a false perspective and a negative horizon. A false perspective is 'opto-electronic pseudo-perspective', 'a fantastic acceleration perspective, one ruled less by the vanishing point than b the simultaneous vanishing of all points...'. And a negative horizon, still, is based not on direct visuality of night and day, but indirect visuality. Virilio, *Lost Dimension*, 114.

COROLLARY: PHYSICAL GLOBES AND DIGITAL PROJECTIONS

Guarantor of Veracity

Because source photographs from NASA and their composite images of the Earth can at first appear similar to what can be seen by the human eye, an epistemic question may be asked: which authority guarantees the truth claims for these images, and how is it possible to determine their veracity? Moreover, the object of such qualities was not recorded as such at any point, and there is no epistemic guarantor which stands parallelly to the image recording, as for example photographer witnessing the scene while recording it. So, there is none we can blame for lying.[1]

Without the possibility of comparing an image to the reality, and with only a second-order shaky authority, the disappearance of perspectival knowledge becomes an effect of New Medievalism phenomenon. Knowledge of perspective, like the idea of the planet as a sphere, was built into the very center of our science already by Antiquity. But this knowledge was completely lost during Medieval times. It was reborn again with the Renaissance recovery of geometrical perspectival thinking.[2] But now, with the ever-increasing use of post-digital photography for representing the Earth, both our immediate surroundings and on the far side of the world, again we are suffering a loss to our ability to represent not only height, width, and depth, but our position in relation to each other. Such New Medievalism has also had an influence upon construction for the new scale model of planet Earth. This globe may actually be crucial for understanding change and abolishment of known perspective systems. In this chapter, I will analyze how our knowledge of the planet Earth has been distorted by the media used in its representation, and has become tied to the interface, or becoming the interface itself in projects as Google Earth.

Globe

A globe is a model of space presented on a three-dimensional surface. And the idea of the world as a sphere has long been closely tied to attempts to represent it three-dimensionally. As Benjamin Lazier wrote, 'Globes stand before us. We observe and act upon them from without. Globes are things that we make. They are artifacts'.[3] Globes afford a hypothetical view of the planet from space which is actually impossible, a view which is enhanced by a certain distance between the person doing the viewing of the globe itself, and a view which could never be achieved in reality or, at least, was inaccessible until the space programs of the late 20th century and remains accessible only for a select few privileged astronauts.

---

1   Which is a precondition for a lie in photography, according saying attributed to Lewis Hine: 'Photographs don't lie, but liars may photograph'.
2   Leon Battista Alberti, *On Painting*, Cambridge: Cambridge University Press, 2011.
3   Benjamin Lazier, 'Earthrise; or, The Globalization of the World Picture', *The American Historical Review* 116.3 (2011): 614.

Moreover, according to Angela Krewani, notions of the globe distance humans from subjective concepts of the Earth and world.[4] This is because, when using a globe, we imagine the planetary body on which we live as separate from us, thereby objectifying it. In order to define the shape of a thing, the observer first must be separate from that thing, and second must know their distance relative to it. Thus, to define the shape of our planet, we would need to have a certain distance from it.

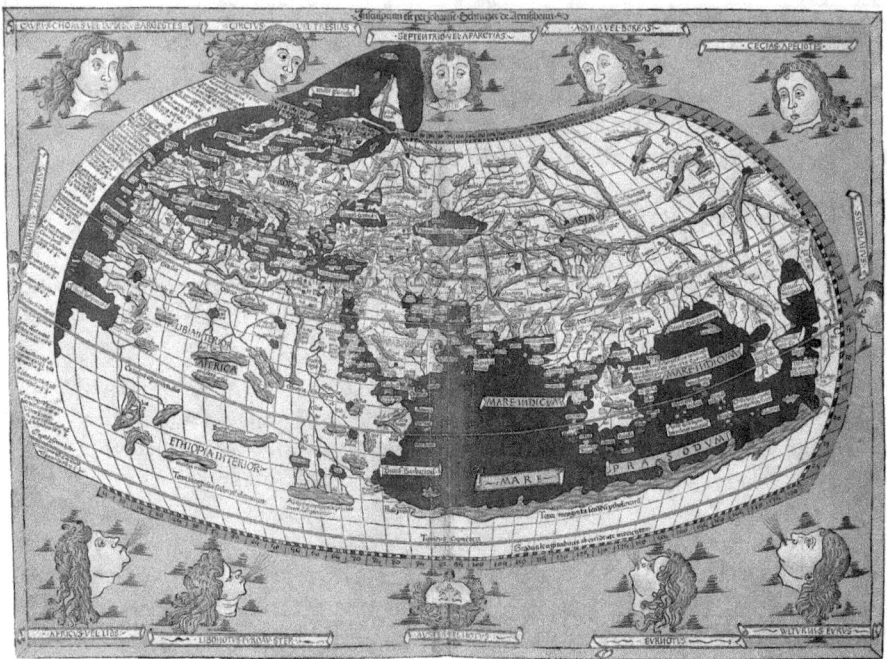

Figure 10: Donnus Nicholas Germanus, cartographer Johannes Schnitzer or Johannes de Armssheim, engraver Ptolemy Jacobus Angelus, The World.

The first representation of the planet as a globe corresponds with the time of the early imaginings of the Earth as a sphere, dating to around 380 BCE, when a first globe made by Eudoxus of Cnidus is mentioned in a poem by Aratus of Soli. Crates of Mallus is also said to made a globe by 150 BCE.[5] Ptolemy's work also refers to globes and one appears on the frontispiece of his *Geographia*.[6] One of the oldest globes, still preserved today from the time of antiquity, is called the *Farnese Atlas*, now housed in Naples, to whom Peter Sloterdijk addressed lines

---

4   Angela Krewani, 'Google Earth: Satellite Images and the Appropriation of the Divine Perspective', in Solvejg Nitzke and Nicolas Pethes (eds) *Imaging Earth: Concepts of Wholeness in Cultural Constructions of Our Home Planet,* Berlin: Transcript Verlag, 2018, 45-60.

5   Sylvia Sumira, *Globes: 400 Years of Exploitation, Navigation, and Power,* Chicago: Chicago University Press, 2014, p. 13. See also: David Woodward and RB Harley, *The History of Cartography, Volume 1: Cartography in Prehistoric, Ancient and Medieval Europe and the Mediterranean,* University of Chicago Press, 1987.

6   Ptolemy, *Geographia*. Accessible at https://archive.org/details/claudiiptolemaei02ptol.

in the middle part of his trilogy on *Spheres*, analyzing figure as an allegory of power, rather than knowledge.[7] This globe is held in hands of a sculpted marble figure from 150 CE, which represents the god Atlas.[8] Tiny metal globes named *Mainz globe* and *Kugel globe* came after.[9] Soon after these two only few centimeters large objects, the idea of the world as a sphere was terminated by growing doxas of Medieval ages.

As Western civilization fell under the influence of the Christian Church from 4th to the 15th centuries CE, the idea that the Earth is spherical in shape gradually became increasingly heretical. While the idea of the globe was absent from the West it continued to be developed in the Arabic countries.[10] Only after the mid-15th century did the production of the globe pick up again in Western culture, accelerated by new discoveries. And once the practice of globe production was reinvented, it has continued to be developed and explored, particularly in the countries of imperialist nations, such as England, Spain and the Netherlands, whose explorers were discovering new information about the planet which could be included in maps and globes, as Fuller noted.[11] A new generation of globes was made, including the *Bernkastel-Kues globe*.

One of the principle differences between types of globe is the information which they carry. Until 16th century, there were two types of globes in use, celestial and terrestrial globes. For purposes of navigation, these would be used together, supplementing each other by describing the land and the sky, respectively, with one standing for the positive and the other the negative of a total image, as if projected onto concave and convex surfaces. With increasingly varied interpretations, the information which was inscribed in globes became richer. For example, in the 16th century, terrestrial globes might encompass a mixture of narrative and symbolic elements, including Christian and pagan iconographies, such as cosmologies antique, heraldic, mythological, and zodiacal, details which were deliberate aesthetic or poetic, as well as social context. Up until the time when the Polish mathematician and astronomer Nicolaus Copernicus (1473-1543) wrote *On the Revolution of the Heavenly Spheres* (1514), sources about the sphericity of the Earth was primarily limited to antique writings of Ptolemy and calculations or notes left by of sailors. The knowledge about the shape of the Earth changes further with Gemma Frisius' *On the Principles of Astronomy and Cosmography, with Instruction for the Use of Globes, and Information on the World and on Islands and Other Places Recently Discovered by 1529*. This book summarized all of the knowledge that was used in practice by sailors, providing a compendium of most of accessible knowledge of the time.

Still, not only general knowledge about the planet but also its precise measurements were necessary in order to produce these accurate '3D maps'. Starting in the 16th century, after the projections calculated by Flemish geographer Gerardus Mercator, globes began to be

7   Peter Sloterdijk, *Spheres, Volume 2, Globes: Macrospherology*, South Pasadena: Semiotext(e), 2014.
8   In Roman mythology, Atlas was one of the Titans, cursed by Zeus to stand on the Western edge of Gaia to carry the sky, or, according to some, the celestial bodies.
9   The Mainz and Kugel globes are Roman celestial globes from 2nd century A.D. The first one is kept in Mainz, while the second is in Paris.
10   Sumira, *Globes*.
11   Buckminster Fuller, *Operating Manual for Spaceship Earth*.

used as precise tools for geographical orientation.[12] Mercator introduced a projection of the three-dimensional planet onto a flat two-dimensional surface that would serve as the base calculus for representations of the Earth over the next hundreds of years, and is even used today in the Google Earth project. From the 17th to the 19th centuries, numerous models of globe covers were designed. The azimuthal is still used today, as is Gleason's, which is important to the Flat Earthers.

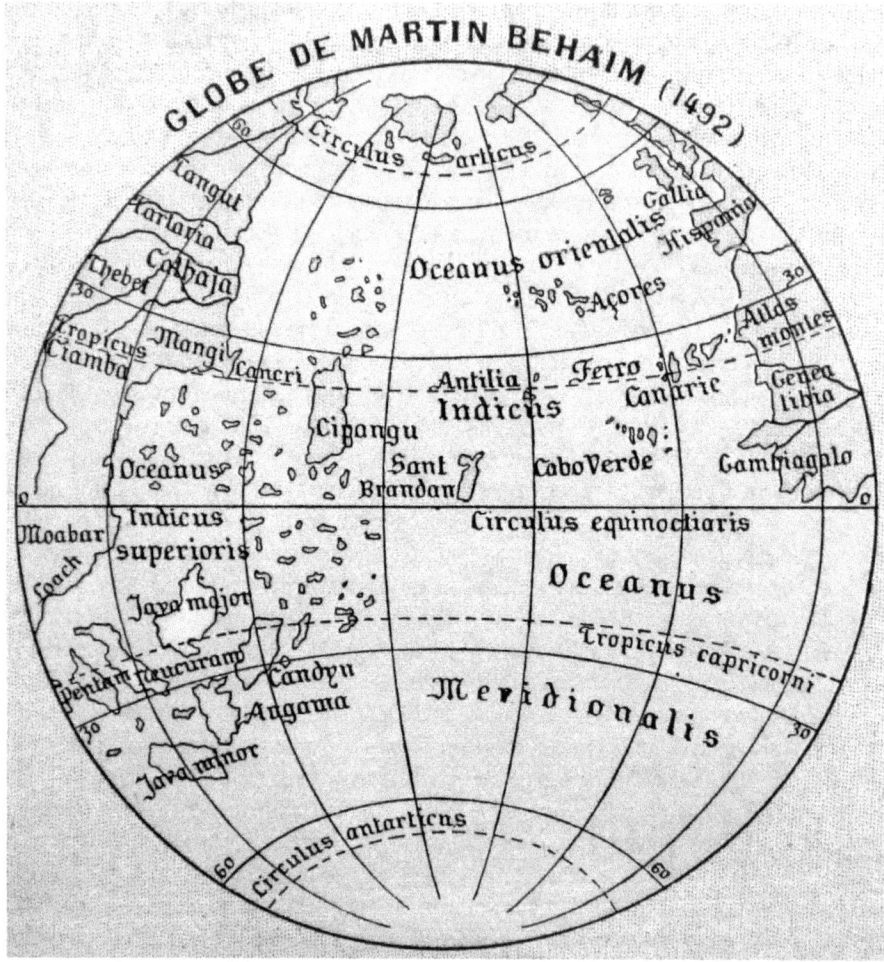

Figure 11: Martin Behaim, Globe, *Nouveau Larousse illustré.*[13]

---

12   Mercator was also the first person to name a book of maps after the Roman god Atlas.
13   The *Behaim Globe* was named after Martin Behaim from Nurnberg was the first to start a larger
     production of globes by the end of the century.

Across time, globes have been made from many kinds of materials, with some more expensive and some more luxurious than others. At the turn of the 16th century, each globe was a unique object, made manually, and decorated, painted, or sculpted by hand. Because of their uniqueness, which was similar to the uniqueness of manuscripts, Sylvia Sumira, specialist in the conservation of printed globes, named the globes produced at the time 'manuscript globes'.[14] And indeed, printed information was often attached to the wood structure from which some globes were carved. As with books, the invention of the printing press greatly diminished the labor costs for the production of globes, rendering them more affordable. In the late 15th and early 16th centuries, Martin Waldseemüller, who is credited with the first recorded usage of the word America in honor of Amerigo Vespucci, was also the first to produce a printed globe. These processes in turn would enhance the future mass production of globes. With the invention of the printing press, complex calculations could now be undertaken to produce the gore of a globe.

The gore was literally a sheet of paper. It was designed for the sphere of a globe. And it was printed with a map and geographic information which, once cut, would perfectly match the surface area of the spherical globe. This gore was a way of representing 3D space in a 2D print, and was designed as a series of thin vertical sections printed on a single piece of paper which, when cut and glued onto the surface of the globe, depicted the sphere of the Earth. Variations to the design of the gore might include its size, production materials, surface quality, and information. Some producers explored the production of miniature globes, while others, like Vinzenzo Coronelli, produced globes with a diameter of one meter or more, as with the *Marly Globe* (1688). One globe which was uniquely tailored, and described with substantial detail in the history of globes by Sumira, is Abraham Nathan Myers' globe from 1866. This globe is a 3D puzzle, in which the surface as well as subface of the sphere is dissected into eight layers, each of which consists of an additional six cuts.[15] The purpose of the globe was educational. To compile the information from the globe, its sections had to first be arranged into shape of the ball, and using the information which was represented on its printed texture or gore.[16]

Throughout the centuries, globes have also been desirable objects which decorated the libraries and living rooms of the upper class. This can be seen, for example, in the work room depicted in the *Geographer* (1668-9), a painting by the 17th century Dutch artist Johannes Vermeer. Three hundred years later, however, with the mass production of globes in the 20th century, these illustrational and informational spheres have become a common decorative element in public and personal libraries as well as also practical tool used in school. Also, many playful variants on the idea of the globe have been invented, such as the balloon globe, ball globe, and lighting globe, which can also be used in toy designs. In fact, today the majority of physical, spherical models of the Earth which exist and are still in active use are those which

14   Sumira, *Globes*, 14.
15   The idea of the gore was elaborated by many but Fuller's projection Dymaxion shape made by Buckminster Fuller might be the most challenging. His dymaxion (from; dynamic, maximum, and tension). His projection of a gore was made in order to show all the continents are connected as an island. See: Buckminster Fuller, *Operating Manual for the Spaceship Earth*.
16   Sumira, *Globes*, 35-36.

serve as toys for young children or for pet animals, who play with them like the actor Charlie Chaplin did in the satirical film *The Great Dictator* mentioned in the Introduction. And there are fewer and fewer decorative globes standing on the writing desks of academics and politicians or in the working rooms of institutions and libraries, as there has been for some five centuries.

Today, the over-exploitation of globes for non-educational purposes has produced a strong reaction among many artists, who respond by intervening in the discourse about globes and the practice of globe-making through personalizing them. As the terrestrial part of the Earth has by now been fully discovered, and a globe which represents the surface landmass has been made into a mechanically-reproducible object, artists have started to reinvent its use. Some examples include Yves Klein's *Blue Globe* (1957), Claudio Parmiggiani's *Pelle Mondo* (1969), and the many globes made by Dimitrije 'Mangelos' Bašičević. Such artistic experiments with the globes culminated during the time of James Lovelock's thesis of Gaia in which he claimed that the planet is a self-sustainable system like an organism.[17]

The materials used to model and conceptualize the Earth have gradually shifted from dimensional globes to dimensionless globes. A large number of the globes which are produced today are neither concretely physical nor as stable and fixed as sculptural objects as they once were. For example, Andreas Riedl describes virtual hyperglobe, such as Google Earth, the tactile hyperglobe, which serves as an interface, and the hologlobe, which is a holographic projection.[18] The digital or virtual globe serves both as a data cloud as well as a visual metaphor, simultaneously having a powerful influence on our lives materially and with all-to-real consequences, as it begins to be the only Earth that we know. Such virtual globes can function on a different level of complexity than can physical ones, simultaneously providing us with many layers of variously coded information, which in turn influences our experience and understanding of the Earth itself.[19]

For example, Ingo Günther makes numerous references to the shape of the world in his media art. He has made approximately two hundred globes, including tactile hyper globes, such as in his *Geospace Project*, *Omniglobe*, *Terravision*, *Magic Planet*, and others, but also hologlobes, such as *Perspecta* by Actuality systems (2002) and *Heliodisplay* (2005).[20] Günther's series *The World Processor* powered by Geo-Cosmos WP(x)GC (2013), produced in collaboration with the Miraikan National Museum of Emerging Science and Innovation in Tokyo, is built around the idea of the digital globe as a physical object in space which has been made into a projective surface in order to host various data. Still, Günther is not trying to present a realistic image of the Earth through his globes, but rather to visualize information about the Earth. When an audience interacts with *World Processor*, it displays various data and data visualizations on the surface of the globe, such as data on population, life on the planet, languages used, the laying of fiber optics, life expectancy, or geopolitical symbols.

---

17   James Lovelock, *Gaia: A New Look at Life on Earth*, Oxford/New York: Oxford University Press, 2000.
18   Riedl, 'Digital Globes', in W. Cartwright, M.P. Peterson, and G. Gartner (eds) *Multimedia Cartography*, Berlin/Heidelberg/New York: Springer, 2007, 256.
19   See Manuel deLanda, *Assemblage Theory: Speculative Realism,* Edinburgh: Edinburgh University Press, 2016.
20   See Ingo Gunther, 'Ingo Gunther', https://ingogunther.com.

Therefore, like in early days of globe production, this globe carries data which is iconograph-ically, symbolically, heraldically, or zodiacally contextualized, bringing extended information up and onto a visible surface.[21] Such globes, whether in the media arts or beyond, are the rare instances where the idea of the Earth as a sphere have survived.

The model of planet Earth slowly dematerialized in digital hyperimages which consist of photographs and maps, but also other data. As globes have vanished as functional physical objects, in the following subsections, I will give further attention to two types of data that would be applied to contemporary data globes: photographic or visual layouts which bring the visual appearance and recognition, and mapping measure that add the precision, as well as their integration into hybrids. I will analyze two forms, the landscape and a map, separately, then following their merge in hybrid forms, trying to understand what their gains and losses in description of the planet are. Although our actual place can indicate certain elements of the shape of the planet, there are various reasons that prevent us from experiencing it.

---

21 Similarly, Google Ocean consists of icons and symbols. Helmreich writes: 'Google Ocean as existential graph is a logical diagram that conjoins multiple representations, real and fictive, and multiple semiotic registers, iconic, indexical, symbolic, which can operate independently of one another (in different layers) while still forming part of a composite.' See Stefan Helmreich, 'From Spaceship Earth to Google Ocean: Planetary Icons, Indexes, and Infrastructures', *Social Research* 78.4 (2011): 1235.

CHAPTER 2: VIEW FROM ABOVE

The Control-view

A view of the Earth as seen from up above flourishes in contemporary science and technology. Yet it can be traced back to the origins of human culture. Such a view has held special importance, for example, in the Egyptian idea of 'The Eye of Horus' as well as the Catholic idea of 'The Omnipresent Eye'. Many authors from antiquity to today have written about such an 'Eye in the Sky', including Hesiod, Callimachus, Theocritus, Heliodorus, Diodorus Siculus, Plutarch, Pliny the Elder, and Aulus Gellius. Indeed, as Hubert Damisch noted the metaphor of a god as an all-seeing architect has existed since long before Plato's description in the *Timaeus*, in which god is described as a lonely being creating the universe.[1]

Further, an aerial view, or viewpoint seen at a high elevation, has existed in some form even before the invention of technologies for flight, although only at the level of predicting such a way of seeing. As shown in archaeological artefacts, this bird's eye view was already introduced to visual culture in the Neolithic Age.[2] And over six thousand years later, during the Renaissance, it developed further into a mathematically-based means of perspectical construction, which in turn influenced the development of the discipline of cartography.[3] At the time, an aerial or bird's eye view was of course impossible. Besides perching at the summit of a mountain or atop a building, humans were contained to a pedestrian or street-level point of view. Leonardo Bufalini in *Roma* (1551), Etienne Dupérac in *Nova Urbis Romae Descriptio* (1577), and Antonio Tempesta in *Recent prout hodie iacet almae urbis Romae cum omnibus viis aedificiisque prespectus accuratissime delineatus* (1593), all imagined the city of Rome from above. The images by Bufalini, Dupérac, Tempesta, and others, while not entirely abstracting their point of view as in a high angle oblique, employed a low angle oblique to depict Rome from a perspective much higher than that which was physically possible in their day. The motif was simple: to represent an entire city or large structure all at once.

In order to imagine an objective space, a culture has to have an idea of the absolute or total one. Absolute space consists of those parts of space that are experienced by the viewer as well as those part of space that are non-experienced. Such a space is said to exist a priori, a prerogative of any perception of the given (visible) space in particular. It is a space which Wilhelm Wurzer defines through concepts of a priori perception and 'transcendental apperception, by which defines a priori perception'.[4] James Elkins claimed the idea of the absolute space did not exist as a concept in Renaissance, which was to re-invent perspective, but

---

1   Hubert Damisch, *Noah's Ark: Essays on Architecture*, Cambridge, MA: MIT Press, 2016.
2   As for example in the image which is an aerial view of the city of Çatalhöyük in Turkey, 6200 BC. See: Stephanie Meece, 'A Bird's Eye View - of a Leopard's Spots: The Çatalhöyük "Map" and the Development of Cartographic Representation in Prehistory', The British Institute of Archaeology at Ankara, 2006.
3   Michael Bury, 'The Meaning of Roman Maps: Etienne Duperac and Antonio Tempesta', in *Seeing from Above: The Aerial View in Visual Culture*, London: IB Tauris, 2013, 26-46.
4   Wilhelm S. Wurzer, *Panorama*, London and New York: Continuum, 2002.

emerged latter.[5] Many authors refer to the rise of the absolute space in Baroque illusionist paintings as envisioning something like an aerial view. Certainly, the absolute space of the Baroque period was connected to ideas of absolute power, coinciding with a fully analytical perspectival model, Cartesian dualist philosophy, and the rise of the idea of panoptic control. Martin Heidegger referred to such a view as the rise of modernity itself.[6] It was by the end of the 18th century, he noted, that people began to conceive of the world as such.[7] Although Heidegger made no mention of totality, he described the subjective view of the 'world picture' (*Weltbild*) for a given era, an image of what is not only seen but also grasped as the whole. 'The world does not change from an earlier medieval into a modern one, but rather the fact that the world becomes picture of all is what distinguishes the essence of the modern age', he specified.[8] Yet this picture is not complete, because it is developed in parallel to the subjectivization of the human.

As with all general theories, the world soon again became fragmented. Relativism arose around 1620 in the Netherlands and reached its peak in German and British Romanticism. When applied to images of the Earth, as Christine Buci-Glucksmann analyzes, relativism predominantly describes the point of view and the angle of view, which later was reformulated into the epistemic perspectivism used in the wider implementation of world explanation with it.[9] An interest in maps was replaced by the one more into intimate genre of the landscape. During Romanticism, the genre of the landscape was the most popular way to represent space, highlighting the position and interpretation of space through the placement of the viewer. Some new geographic systems were introduced, enforcing geocentrism, but also homo-centrism and egocentrism.[10] They were consequences of the 'Copernican turn', commonly defined as this positioning the subject at the very center of not only epistemology, enforcing ontology based on a mere experience or phenomenology (including consequently, science).[11] With the innovation of flight, however, Baroque idea of absolute space would again be revived.

---

5   James Elkins, *The Poetics of Perspective*, Ithaca and New York, Cornell University Press, 2018 (1994).

6   Martin Heidegger, 'The Age of the World Picture', A.I. Tauber (ed) *Science and the Quest for Reality*, London: Palgrave McMillan, 1997, 70-88.

7   Heidegger, 'The Age of the World Picture'.

8   Heidegger, 'The Age of the World Picture', 84.

9   Contrasting to the space of perspective, described by Alberti, the one of Baroque ecstasy found by Andrea Pozzo, describes a total place.

10   Cosmogony defines the system of geocentric universe, cosmography, studying the planet, chorography (systematic geographic covering of the regions), defining landmaps, but also – 'geosophy' being the philosophical system of beliefs related to the earth, represented by John K. Wright. Besides Wright, Alexander Von Humboldt was writing in both cosmography, egocentricity and homocentric universe.

11   Also observation by Mitchell. See: W.J.T. Mitchell, *Landscape and Power*, Chicago: University of Chicago Press, 2002. Thus, Edmund Husserl sees difference between pre-Copernican and post-Copernican world. Edmund Husserl, *Foundational Investigations of the Phenomenological Origin of the Spatiality of Nature*, Edmund Husserl Shorter Works, Notre Dame, Ind.: University of Notre Dame Press and Brighton, Sussex: Harvester Press, 1981.

Early Flights

Taking images from the air was already a practice in the 18th century with the early tests of hot air balloon flight. In America, Benjamin Franklin was the first to witness the flight of a balloon, he wrote in his notes.[12] In France, the Montgolfier brothers invented the first practical hot air balloon and succeed in lifting themselves up off of the ground in 1783.[13] And two years later, American pioneering balloonist Thomas Scott Baldwin described balloon flight in detail in his *Aeropaidia*.[14] This book, besides describing general phenomena connected to flying, pointed out two visual phenomena that occurred along with the increased elevation of the viewpoint from the Earth's surface: confusing distortions of measurement due to the curvature of the Earth, and changes to the colors of the Earth as a result of atmospheric density. The photographic genre of aerial photography, when it fully emerged in the 19th century, had to address both of these visual phenomena and their respective image distortions.[15]

The first aerial record to be made during a flight was taken only in 1857, some twenty years after the invention of photography. Gaspard-Félix Tournachon, known by the mononymous pseudonym Nadar, took this photograph while flying over Paris in his balloon. Unfortunately, the technological constraints of the time, when photography was still at its early stages of development, resulted in several difficult conditions for taking the picture. The exposure time could last up to twenty minutes (when using the wet-plate technique).[16] Besides this slow exposure, chemical instability might also be one of the reasons that Félix Nadar's earliest photographs have not survived. As Stephen Bann explains, 'the gas [...] from the balloon reacted with the emulsion of photographic plates, and the result was a blackened image'.[17] The oldest surviving aerial photograph, therefore, in fact dates to three years later. It was recorded by James Wallace Black while flying in a hot air balloon over the city of Boston in the US.[18] Wallace's photographs were shot in a low oblique view which distorted the space depicted in the image. Further, Wallace merged aerial photographs taken from different locations during his flight, producing a kind of perspectival amalgam. A significant amount of information was lost from the corners of these aerial photographs. This was due to the

---

12   Abbott Lawrence Rotch, 'Benjamin Franklin and the First Balloons', *American Antiquarian Society*. April, 1907, 259-174,

13   Martin van Creveld, *The Age of Airpower*, New York, Public Affairs, 2011.

14   'Aeropaidia: containing the narrative of a balloon excursion from Chester, the eighth of September, 1785, taken from minutes made during the voyage: hints on the improvement of balloons to which is subjoined mensuration of heights by the barometer, made plain; with extensive tables. The whole serving as an introduction to aerial navigation.' 'Aeropaidia', https://archive.org/details/Airopaidia00Bald. It is important to distinguish the balloonist Thomas Baldwin from the inventor of the same name.

15   Today, calibrations are used when taking an aerial and satellite photograph of a large-scale settlement. For example, with *Terrestrial Test Patterns Used for Aerial Imaging* from 2013, a huge calibration target was built on the ground which an unmanned camera could detect from a large distance into order to focus in on various object and thereby sharpen the image.

16   Not interested studio photography, Nadar invested most of his energy in aerial photography. See: Félix Nadar, *When I was A Photographer*, trans. Eduardo Cadava and Liana Theodoratou, Cambridge, MA: The MIT Press, 2015. Nadar's interests in aerial technologies and archaeology merged in contemporary discussions on post-digital and post-human photography.

17   Stephen Bann, 'Aerial View', in Dorrian & Frederic Poussin, *Seeing from Above*, 86

18   James Wallace, 1860.

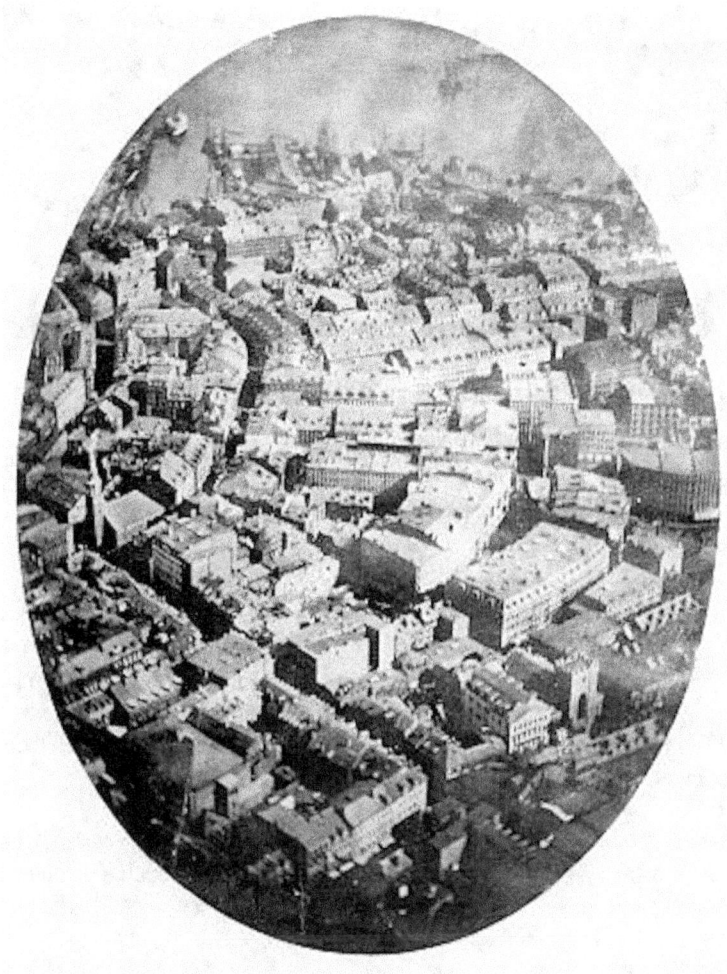

Figure 12: James Wallace Black, View of Boston, *1860.*

relative positions of the many different points of view, in relation to the curvature of the Earth's surface, the curvature of the camera's lens, as well as the distance between the camera and the subject. Given the long exposure time for these aerial photographs, these factors shortened the depth of field. Consequently, the resulting amalgamated images have faded edges, indefinite border, and vignette shape. Besides these spatial and temporal distortions, the overall sharpness of the image was also low and the exposure uneven, because some parts of the photograph were overexposed and other parts were underlit. Nevertheless, the end result was far more chemically stable than with the first aerial photograph taken by Nadar.

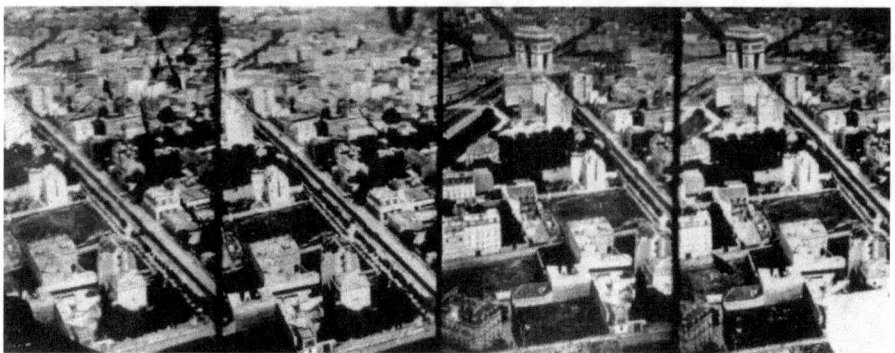

Figure 13: Gaspard-Félix Tournachon Nadar, Aerial view of Paris, *1868.*

In aerial photography, depth is fixed on the object. The horizon is that of a high oblique taken with the camera inclined about sixty degrees from the vertical. And the vanishing point is that from a linear perspective, which creates the illusion of a flat surface. To a certain extent, this is similar to how space was interpreted in the 15th century, an absolutistic rhizome seen from the perspective of a singular authority or viewpoint.[19] Since then, however, new techniques of image-making have been developed which bypass the limitations of a human-based point and angle of view, which relies today not upon the integration of multiple viewpoints but rather their computation. In the 19th and 20th centuries, innovation in aerial imaging technologies led to a new kind of totality, the totality of a computational view of the world. And because this was not possible on the basis of any one point or even angle of view to reach it, new technologies have been created in order to compute recorded sections into a whole.

Although Nadar's earliest aerial photographs have not survived, so that Wallace's aerial photographs are the are oldest which are today extant, Nadar himself found a unique solution to the problem of perspectival distortion: to employ sequential recording. Therefore, in a way, he produced the first computed total image, and did so solely using analogue photographic material. Such a way of recording, Nadar found, to some extent corrected both the curvature of the Earth as well as the problem of distributed points of view. This photomontage produced a more map-like appearance to the aerial shot. Nadar's technique was followed by that of Arthur Batut, who went even further, carrying with him into the sky a camera as well as an altimeter in order to measure the rate of exposure for the photographic plate. Batut invented a process of image correction for the raw aerial photograph by making an effective altitude map. With this proto-computational process, Batut's images would influence the birth of the orthophoto method, leading to maps which are produced from the original aerial photographic source, rather than just measurements of the land from the ground.

With the further development of technologies for flight across the late 19th and early 20th centuries, photography from the air became increasingly accurate. In Germany, Ferdinand

---

19   For more on the amputation of the vanishing point, see Denis Cosgrove and William L Fox, *Photography and Flight,* London: Reaktion Books, 2010.

von Zeppelin pioneered the first rigid-structure airship between 1874 and 1893. In the succeeding years, the Wright brothers in America continued to experiment with flight, building the world's first successful airplane, and undertaking the first flight in 1903. Their endeavors led to the accelerated development of a new aerial industry. And the first airplanes were tested by 1906.[20] Thus, historians usually consider military aviation to have already been born by 1880, but it would not really be developed until a short time period twenty-years before World War I. After WWI, photographic technology was also miniaturized, so many planes were supplied with cameras.[21] In such military context, aerial photography took over the role of the map, with each subsequent technological innovation respectively informing use .[22] For example, the stabilization of flights in turn led to a better quality of record and, eventually, to the automation of recording. In this regard, one crucial test was Oscar Messier's flight with an airborne camera. With the full integration of automated recording, the military also began to use aerial cameras to document the battlefield. And the numbers of such photographs grew rapidly. By 1915, the British army, amidst war with the Germans, shot about 1500 photographs in the field, making The Great War also the first war to encompass an 'image–coordinated action'.[23] Indeed, the innovation of this technology changed the entire course of WWI, as Peter Sloterdijk claims, because the target was no longer a person, but the landscape.[24] Since WWI and WWII, the military industrial complex has remained the largest investor in the research and development of aerial photography. This funding, in turn, has led to the complete panopticonisation of the land through photographs taken from the sky.

And, unfortunately, these techniques were soon used for the purposes of military intervention within the urban landscape. For example, Lucien Le Saint, who worked for the army, was on the team which documented the war damage. And in his film *Aerial views of Ypres* (1919), he recorded a completely destroyed or flattened city.[25] The power of such new aerial photography came into full force by WWII, when many cities were not only bombed, but this bombing was also simultaneously recorded.[26] Indeed, as Antoine Bousquet points out, ever since WWII we can speak of a 'martial gaze' which combines photographic technology with the purposes of military perception, used in order to attack or defend.[27] Apart from such visual phenomena, as Jussi Parikka also observers, when aerial photography is applied in concert with aerial bombardment, the landscape is not only literally flattened, but also represented as being flat.[28]

20   In 1885 in France and, notably, in 1900-1914 in the UK.
21   And a revolution in photographic technology came with the portable Leica camera.
22   Antoine Bousquet, *Eyes of War: Military Perception from the Telescope to the Drone*, Minneapolis: University of Minnesota Press, 2018,
23   See: Hillel Schwartz, *Culture of the Copy*, New York: Zone Books, 1996.
24   Peter Sloterdijk, *Terror from the Air*, Los Angeles: Semiotext(e), 2009.
25   Lucein le Saint, 'Aerial Views of Ypres', YouTube, 1919, https://www.youtube.com/watch?v=8IsITVwW7nY.
26   Leica's Russian copy Zorgi and Fedj123 served the same purpose. Based on a camera found when the German plane crashed on Swedish border, company Hasselblads Fotografiska AB developed a camera that was commissioned by Swedish air forces to counter fight German Leica.
27   Sloterdijk, *Terror from the Air*.
28   Jussi Parikka, *A Geology of Media*, Minneapolis: University of Minnesota Press, 2015.

	LAND PHOTOGRAPHY	AERIAL PHOTOGRAPHY
Distance	Opening the view	Closing the view with the surface
Planes	Order of planes	Single plane
Measure	Composition of elements	Single element
Angle	Various	Single or amalgamated with little oscillation

Table 2: Changes to image elements caused by shifting the point of view from land to air.

Expanding the Game?

Aerial photography would become one of the most important photographic genres of 19th century and would in turn inform the genres of other artistic mediums. Besides Nadar, more and more artists were becoming interested in making photographic records during flight.[29] At the beginning of the 20th century, at the early stage of aerial photography, some famous photographers even joined the air force in their respective countries so that they could have the opportunity to take such pictures. This included American photographer Edward Steichen, a pioneer in aerial intelligence during the WWI. The images recorded by Steichen brought a further aesthetic element to this view from above, an abstraction of territory, elevating not only the sensory perspective but also the social position of the viewer.[30] The effects of such images on the general public, who themselves did not yet have their own experiences of flight, as many if not most of us do today, was significant enough that the famed author and benefactor to the arts Gertrude Stein was herself convinced that the aerial view influenced the rise of abstraction in painting.[31] As Siegfried Kracauer later noted, 'The ornament resembles aerial photographs of landscapes and cities in that it does not emerge out of the interior of the given conditions, but rather appears above them'.[32] Aerial photographs actually look more like maps, or what Claire Reddleman terms 'cartographic abstraction.'[33]

---

29   Marc Dorrian and Frederic Poussin (eds) *Seeing from Above: The Aerial View in Visual Culture*, London: I.B. Tauris, 2013.
30   Few artists also participated in the WWII. One of the most intriguing acts of the art-world was that Joseph Beuys a pilot during the WWII and has survived a crash of the plane in Tatar country where was rescued by shamans who had rubbed him with fat, wrapped him in blankets, both he later used as parts of his art installations. Still, later found letters witness the event hasn't took the place. See: http://www.spiegel.de/international/germany/new-letter-debunks-myths-about-german-artist-joseph-beuys-a-910642.html.
31   Allan Sekula, 'The Instrumental Image: Steichen At War', *Artforum* 14.4 (December 1975): 26-35.
32   Siegfried Kracauer, *The Mass Ornament: Weimar Essays*, trans. Thomas Y. Levin, Cambridge, MA: Harvard University Press, 1995, 77.
33   Reddleman, *Cartographic Abstraction in Contemporary Art*.

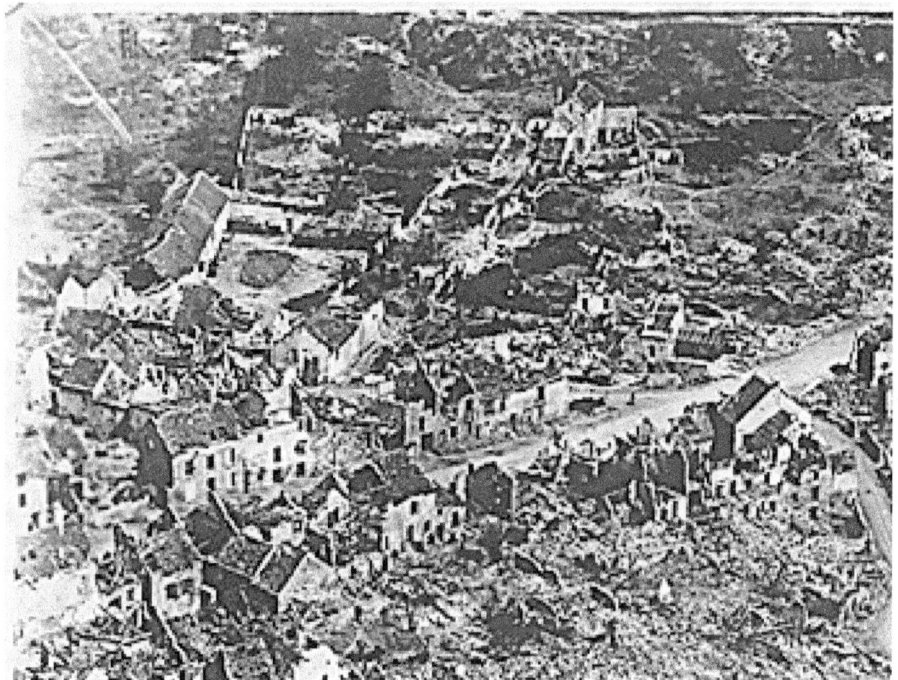

Figure 14: Edward Steichen, Aerial view of ruins of Vaux, France, *1918.*

In fact, artists were fascinated by modern technologies for flight in particular and aeronautics in general in many artistic and social movements of the early 20th century. To name but a few, Constructivism which originated in Russia and influenced the Bauhaus and De Stijl movements, and Futurism which originated in Italy, were in one way or another centered around the idea of the human surpassing his earthly conditions and limitations to finally overtake the position once reserved for the gods. Suprematists, in particular, were perhaps most fascinated by this 'new dimension,' and introduced an aerial-like imaging. In Russia Kazimir Malevich gave a speech praising aerial view aesthetics.[34] In 1916, Vassily Kandinsky painted *the Red Square from Above*, a painting said to be composed from a 'collapsing perspective,' as if the artist was standing in the middle of the square.[35]

Further exemplifying the appropriation and integration of the bird's eye view from aerial photography in other art forms and medias, in Hungary, László Moholy-Nagy, while not taking to the skies himself as did many other artists, used aerially recorded city imagery.[36] At the

---

34   Christina Lodder, 'Malevich, Suprematism and Aerial Photography, *History of Photography* 28.1 (2004): 25-40.
35   Among other reasons, Christina Lodder, finds reasons also in the relationship of the Russian spiritual relationship to the icon and aerial dematerialization as both, physically or spiritually, privileged views from above. Lodder, in Dorrian and Poussin, *View from Above*.
36   Laszlo Moholy Nagy, *The New Vision: From Material to Architecture*, New York: Brewer, Warren and Putnam, 1932.

beginning of his movie *Impressions of the Old Part of Marseille* (1929), Moholy-Nagy displayed a map of the French city of Marseille. In succeeding shots, this map is then cut with a hole in the middle in order to allow a view of the harbor. Seen through the hole, the first shot is an aerial one, followed by shots of street angles. Throughout the film, records from the sky are superimposed onto those at street level, contrasting corrected and purified aerial vision from approximate angular view and land view. Aside changing positions in heights, Moholy-Nagy also shifted details, as for example portraits and generalized views from above, strongly dividing the private vs objective story, but also realistic vs abstract field.[37] He used aerial shots, and the interchange between wide-views and close-ups, to depict different places of the harbor from the seashore to small dirty streets.[38] At certain moments, the film camera surveilled the local population in upper view close-ups from the window. The aerial view here contributed to a modernistic, abstract-geometric layout, especially in places where the camera focused on the construction of building systems, such as bridges and various console type of supports as pillars. This 'Icarian' view did not only have an influence on artworks by artists such as Malevich, Kandinsky, and Moholy-Nagy, as Christine Buci-Glucksmann recognized, but also on the work of Marcel Duchamp, who used it to destroying the paradigm of the horizon to arrive at the 'null point' or 'zero forms'.[39]

Flattening the Ground

The aerial or bird's eye view, beyond influencing the birth of abstract art, has also provoked changes in the paradigm of vision, which has become increasing schematic, symbolic and, as such, nonhuman. Although we tend to think about the development of unmanned aerial vehicles (or UAVs) in the context of contemporary warfare, the first tests of such flying devices were already done by the time modern artists recognized the importance of the view of the Earth from the sky up above.[40] Image-led weapon and surveillance machines were perfected in the 1970s during the Cold War. Although, before development of the global positioning system (GPS) it was still impossible to send an automated plane. With this invention the interest in using imaging the war led by imaging greatly accelerated.[41] And the initial use of image-lead flying devices would be during the Gulf War (1990-91).

---

37   László Moholy-Nagy, 'Impressions of the Old Part of Marseille', *YouTube*, https://www.youtube.com/watch?v=-gzEKwuh3ok.

38   See: https://www.youtube.com/watch?v=FhrMGj73-eg. Apparently, this scenario was used by Leander Kruizinga, Vincent Bonefaas, and Daniël Oliveira Prinsand to make an animation movie in 2002. See: https://www.youtube.com/watch?v=hfQiMXKfZCo.

39   See Duchamp's *Analytical Chart No. 16* (1927) in which he directly refers to Suprematism as an idea of flying. Ten out of seven images represent flight. See: Christina Lodder, 'Transfiguring reality: Suprematism and the Aerial View'. See also: Kazimir Malevich, *Non-Objective World* (1927). Art has certainly got used to this view quite early. Modernists, Kazimir Malevich and Vasili Kandinsky, among others, have been fascinated with the abstract insight of the aerial view. Malevich directly referred to the importance of the aerial view in his lecture in Warsaw, 1927. His opera *Victory over the Sun* (1913) directly refers to aerial power. Four of thirty-nine works at the *0,10 The Last Futurist Show* (1915) referred to the fourth dimension, she concluded, while *Analytical Chart No 16* is referring to Suprematism as directly connected to flight and flying, compared to both Futurism and Suprematism.

40   By 1939, the USA constructed the first control plane for remote actions, but it was not fully functional.

41   Leading to a SR-71 bomber.

This was the first war that, according to Jean Baudrillard, 'did not took a place', but rather brought together separate places within a produced space with its victims as well as its attackers at distant points on the planet.[42] Thus, Paul Virilio defined it as the war in two dimensions.[43] At the time of the Bosnian War (1992-95), the first planes that could operate on autopilot were not yet ready for implementation. The first aerial photographs done using self-flying planes were only during the Kosovo War (1998-99), which was followed immediately by a NATO bombing campaign of Yugoslavia. And the use of unmanned aerial vehicles in war came as a direct consequence of the 9/11 attack on the United States. The so-called 'targeted killing' program was ordered by U.S. President Obama's administration.[44] Targeted assassination by drones were at full force in the Afghanistan War (2001-4). Since then, the countries which are most often bombed remotely include Afghanistan, Pakistan, and Yemen.

Besides passive surveillance, drone technology was autonomously, physically engaging towards the viewed. Or, to paraphrase Virilio, the visual field has become the battlefield.[45] Literally, the targeting of weaponry was integrated with the imaging of photography, such that the eye itself, in essence, become a weapon, in a technologization of the Evil Eye concept.[46] In other words, the gaze of the drone or, as the artist and geographer Trevor Paglen calls them, 'the meat-eyes,' is not simply the a gaze which views but also a gaze which destroys.[47] And, as Grégoire Chamayou points out, these image technologies become objects of 'lethal surveillance'.[48]

Moreover, these machines analyze and compute images autonomously of human agents. As Harun Farocki stated, 'The missile search-head reads the images. Image processing presents itself'.[49] Farocki further described how '"The key to 'intelligent weapons' is image processing. Images of the terrain it is to traverse are stored in a rocket. During its flight, it photographs the terrain below and compares the two images, the goal image and the actual image.'[50] Empow-

42 Jean Baudrillard, *The Gulf War Did Not Take Place*, Sidney: Power Publications, 2012.

43 Virilio, *The Lost Dimension*.

44 It was, however, operated by the United States Air Force, as journalists such as Chris Wood note. See: Chris Wood; *Sudden Justice: America's Secret Drone Wars (Terrorism and Global Justice)*, Oxford: Oxford University Press, 2015.

45 Paul Virilio, *Pure War*, New York: Semiotext(e), 1998.

46 All of these concepts serve to demonstrate the ways in which the eye of today's drone, missile, and other intelligent weapons is not just that of a passive observer, but one which actively interferes with chain of causality in reality. Such a concept of vision is already present in the negative mythological concept of the 'Evil Eye', an autonomous and powerful all-observing eye, capable of intervening into reality affairs of what it observes. Similarly to the Evil Eye, the machine eye has a performance capacity. It changes the course of events according to the pre-programmed instructions, directions, or coding of its operator and designer as well as their political context or instigation.

47 Trevor Paglen, 'Operational Images', *E-flux* 59 (November, 2014), https://www.e-flux.com/journal/59/61130/operational-images/.

48 Gregoire Chamayou, *A Theory of the Drone,* trans. Janet Lloyd, New York: The New Press, 2015.

49 See: Martin Blumenthal-Barby, '"Cinematography of Devices": Harun Farocki's Eye/machine', *German Studies Review* 38.2 (2015): 332.

50 For more on the work of Farocki, see: Thomas Elsaesser, 'The Future of "Art" and "Work" in the Age of Vision Machines: Harun Farocki', Randall Halle (ed) *After the Avant-garde: Contemporary German and Austrian Experimental Film,* Rochester: Camden House, 2006.

ered to make complex decisions on their own, and even further equipped with such features and functions as facial recognition, these intelligent weapons have a degree of autonomy on par with robots. Yet, their analytic functions are far from perfect.

The view from a drone is limited, and while the camera may be rotated, it cannot simultaneously provide near and far vantages. Thus, a pilot cannot maintain close and distant views of a subject or subjects at the same time, or comparatively analyze both the context and the detail, while making the final decision about what action to take. If they zoom in, the wider picture is lost. And if they zoom out, the finer detail is lost. This in turn can increase the likelihood of mistaken interpretations about what is shown in an image, such as the circumstances surrounding an event, or the identity of a person of interest. And such mistakes can result in an unwanted fatality.

A pilot in the feature-length documentary film *Unmanned: America's Drone Wars* (2013), for example, states that she was not sure whether the something which she had killed was a dog or a child. Given this absence or variability of information during a combat situation, some people have been killed not because of their identity, but for their behaviors, which to a drone operator seemed suspicious. This 'uncertain or undeciding vision' is even challenged by some artists. Tomas van Houtryve, for example, addressed the ethics involved with distance in war through his photographic series *Blue Sky Days* in 2015.[51] By recording images of gatherings such as weddings, funerals, and groups of people at prayer, such as those which have become habitual targets for foreign air strikes, and would be classified and not made available to the public, only created in the public spaces of the US where foreign air strikes do not occur, Houtryve points to the role of identification in remote perception and its relativism when deprived of the context. Such an aerial, bird's eye, or eye-in-the-sky view cannot discriminate between the objects, people, or things which are being perceived.

Errors are due mostly to the necessity of representing distance in war as well as the compression and distortion from physical space to image space. For the pilot of a drone, war can seem far away even though no distance is crossed, and no place is experienced. For drone pilots, the world they view on their monitors appears immediately before them, while it is in fact thousands of miles away. Because there may often be an entire ocean between the drone pilot and drone target, there are many possible points in the chain of events in which technological may break down. Physical distance between the body of the person who operates the drone and the person who is the victim of the drone produces a gap between visual space and real space which in turn leads to psychological distance like that between the virtuality of a game and reality of the environment, polluting them, to employ Virilio's expression.[52] Indeed, drone pilots often refer to their work as gaming and compare the experience of running a drone strike to the experience of playing a computer game. And these military

---

51   See Tomas Van Houtryve's series of pictures: http://www.worldpressphoto.org/collection/photo/2015/
      contemporary-issues/tomas-van-houtryve. This series was awardded the second prize at *World Press
      Photo 2015*.
52   Virilio and Lotringer, *Pure War*.

officers are often recruited from among video gamers.[53] This collision between wargames and warfare is perhaps best illustrated by the movie *Drone* (2013), in which a pilot also plays games of war, and shifts back and forth from virtual to real war.[54] Because of the game-like experience of such warfare, questions of its ethicalness can be more easily separated, both procedurally and psychologically, to address the drone pilots and military authorities.[55] In *The Eye in the Sky* (2015), the screenwriters criticize such 'disgraceful [behavior] done from the safety of one's chair'.[56] Situated in a military campus, or a castrum, such as Fort Bragg in North Carolina, these pilots intervene in someone's life while their own combat experience is abstracted and schematized.

Comparing these different viewpoints, in the *The Eye in the Sky* the director superimposes images from above as recorded by the drone as well as from below as seen by a boy.[57] The first view is aerial, the second grounded. As Branden Hookway writes, the drone pilot's 'cockpit is at once a sphere of inhabitation, an ergonomics of use, an assemblage directed to weird control surfaces and the materiality of the air flow, and a threshold between human and machine whose mediation is expanded in trajectory of flight'.[58] The 'psychology of distance in war' is, reductively, that the further we are from the victim, the likely it is that we will act harshly.[59] And it is this distance which 'has influenced a construction of senseless jargon naming killing a "bug splat"'.[60]

---

53   A number of recent movies, such as *The Eye in the Sky* (2015) as well as the earlier *Drones* (2013), address the chain of command which, although a canonical plotline for the filmic war genre, here deals particularly with the civilian casualties which may be incurred in parallel to drone raids. 'By the time this arrives to TV there won't be twelve, there won't be babies' – a pilot of the pilot – bomb comments in Drones.

54   *Drone* (dir. Daniel Jewel, 2013).

55   See for example the analysis by George Monbiot, 'Deadly Drones: Cowards War', *The Guardian*, 30 January 2012, https://www.theguardian.com/commentisfree/2012/jan/30/deadly-drones-us-cowards-war.

56   In another dialogue in *The Eye in the Sky*, the Prime Minister of the United Kingdom says 'Legally we don't have a problem', while an advisor in war room in London asks: 'Has there ever been a British-led drone attack in a friendly country that is not at war?'.

57   But, according to other confession of some pilots from the documentary, they can read up even the car's registration label while others they can only see the silhouette. As we do not know how the drone's view look like, there can only be an imagination of that. Comparing how the 'cockpit' of the real drone and the same instrument in the movie look like, differences are visible. Both the real and imaginary drone, from documentary *Rise of Drones* (2013) and fiction movie *Eagle Eye* (2008) show the low image resolution, still – the abstract data presented is quite different. Whereas the real document provides only longitudes and latitudes, as well as the zooming distances, the cockpit in the movie buffers sound and shows different sound controls, as; volume, pitch etc... Still, as most of drones are having propellers, it is quite unimaginable how it would record sounds or other machine sounds.

58   Branden Hookway, *Interface*, Cambridge, MA: MIT Press, 2014, 6.

59   *Psychological Distance Psychology* is an important factor when addressing the effect of *distance in war*. See for example: Paul Joseph (ed) *SAGE Encyclopedia of War: Social Science Perspective*, Thousand Oaks, SAGE, 2016.

60   See the #NotABugSplat-project, which is a collaboration of Pakistani, American and French artists using large scale printed posters which can be visible clearly from satellite. See more at: https://notabugsplat.com.

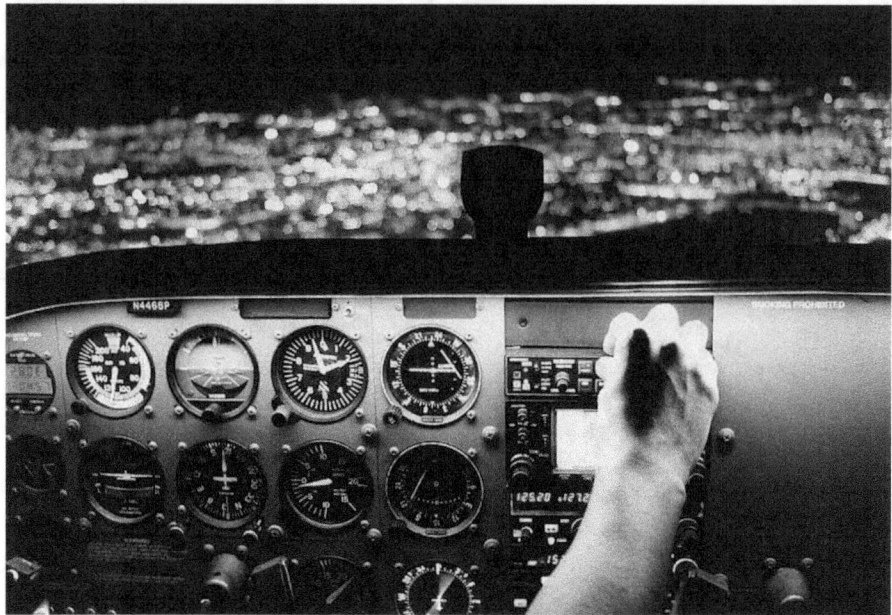

Figure 15: Cockpit view.

Counter-surveilling

While military agencies have led the development of aerial photography in a direction of total images useful for control, artists, to whom we owe the invention of the photographic medium itself, have worked toward the abolishment of this very control. Many contemporary artists and artist groups, in a continuation of the investigations first begun by pioneering aerial photographers Félix Nadar and Edward Steichen, raised their voices in protest against this new classified and covert aerial image culture. In order to critique this surveillance, artists have developed own countersurveillance practices. One such project is the Bureau of Inverse Technology's *BIT Plane* from 1997.[61] The artist, Natalie Jeremijenko, constructed a small plane which could be used to spy onto Silicon Valley. This twenty-inch plane, which may be seen as a prototype model for the fly-drone, has entered the very production center of the optical control technologies. Similarly, the Civil Counter-Reconnaissance group, led by the artist Marko Peljhan, has reverse-engineered military surveillance drones, and built their own drone system using a vehicle bought on the Internet.[62] In addition to these artworks, there are also projects by System77, Nicolas Schaffer (CYSP), The Surveillance Video Entertainment Network (SVEN), and others that engage in some form of drone counter-surveillance. Some

---

61   Bureau of Inverse Technology and Natalie Jeremijenko, 'Bit Plane', 1997, https://anthology.rhizome.org/bit-plane https://dronecenter.bard.edu/interview-natalie-jeremijenko/.
62   One of the interesting pieces, here, also is by the collective Apsolutno, who have exhibited, on *World Information.org* the audio piece derived from the black box of the NATO plane bombing Serbia, which they bought on the free market.

artists construct drones themselves, while others hack or reprogram already existing drones, and use these 'zombie drones' for alternative or even opposing purposes.[63]

In parallel to artistic counter-surveillance using actual drones, some artists also map drone positions from land, making visible what is otherwise invisible: the very presence and activity of drones in our societies.[64] Essam Adam Attia has created several works about drones and their use, including *Drone Zones*, *The Drone Campaign*, and *Children of Drones*. In *Drone Zones*, for example, Essam posted signs in the public spaces of New York City which warned of 'drone activity in progress', 'drone strike zones', and 'statutes enforced by drone'.[65] Essam, who served for three years in the army as a geospatial analyst before earning his BFA in photography, was even arrested by the NYPD's Bureau of Counter-Terrorism.

Other artists are also challenging the use of drones and drone-based aerial photography in their artworks. James Bridle in *Drone Shadows* (201-2015) produced a number of chalk drawings of drones on the streets of various cities, reminiscent of the temporary marks used to outline evidence at a crime scene, as a way to remind the public that drones are out there and up. above.[66] In another project, *Dronestagram* (2012-2015), Bridle used images from Google Earth in order to point out locations in which drone strikes were happening.[67] He also added data from the Bureau of Investigative Journalism, a nonprofit new organization based in London, in the image description.[68] On the other hand, an artist Christopher Csíkszentmi-hályi has reverse-engineered an unmanned roaming vehicle, so as to create what he calls the *Afghan Explorer*, to be deployed in the killing zones of the War on Terror in order to act as a global witness and overcome restrictions on the free press.[69] These artists and others are part of a broader discourse about the panoptic construction of the total image. And their artworks introduce questions about the reliability of these images and the ethics of their use, serving as counter-total image, its logical antipode.

Ethics on Distances

This new form of warfare is referred to as 'low-intensity conflict' because it is asymmetrical, and conducted from only the side of one group or territory. For this reason, the engagement

---

63   One such a case is a zombie drone or a drone which is hijacked by Skyjack or similar program, to be overtaken and lead by another agent, who can then commit crimes being uncaught. See: 'Hacking Drone Security', http://hub.jhu.edu/2016/06/08/hacking-drones-security-flaws/.

64   In addition to media artists, military agencies, such as those in Iran, have also hacked or reprogrammed existing drones.

65   He has also produced posters on the anniversary of the Constitution and Occupy Wall Street, warning that NYPD drone strikes are against civilians.

66   *Drone shadows* were produced in London, 2012 (produced with Einar Sneve Martinussen), Istanbul, 2012, Brighton, 2013, New York, 2013, Brisbane, 2013, Brixton, 2013, London, 2014, Berlin, 2015, Karlsruche, 2015

67   Trevor Paglen, *Dronestagram*, http://booktwo.org/notebook/dronestagram-drones-eye-view/.

68   Dronestagram, as opposite to Dronestagram, was used for sharing the most beautiful images made by drones, see: http://www.dronestagr.am/.

69   Christopher Csíkszentmíhalyi, *Afghan Explorer*, 2001. See: http://www.fondation-langlois.org/html/e/page.php?NumPage=365.

of the United States in Pakistan was often called a 'cowards' war'.[70] Noam Chomsky has written on this single-sidedness:

> Warfare has moved away from man-to-man combat, and is now dominated by deadly missiles, bombing campaigns and by the latest terrible weapons: drones, which are synonymous with terrorism and absolute impunity—they kill without the invading nation having to risk its own soldiers. It is a one-sided war; a video game for one side, the horror of destroyed villages, murdered individuals and mutilated bodies for the other.[71]

Central to the ethical issues which surround drone warfare is the question of whether or not the right to intervene someone else's life, someone who is not informed about the action, and who may not necessarily be given a fair court trial, the right to face their accuser, or the right of self-defense. That is, the person, persons, or population which is attacked may be deprived of their basic human rights. In this sense, a war conducted by drones appears not all that different from terrorism. The extended presence, in which a drone navigated by a person in one country is acting by the will of the person residing in another, leads to juridical complications. The chain of responsibility is broken. Pilot and commander are not necessarily in the same place. And how can a drone be held accountable for the actions of someone who is playing a game in a faraway land? New vision-killing technologies, which manipulate the perceptual distance between an armed force and their target, also diminish the physical distances which they represent so that those distances can be better navigated and controlled. Much like how cultures down through history have imagined their gods to view the world, such technologies present the Earth both with a flat surface and as immediately present.[72]

---

70   Stephen Graham, *Cities Under Siege: The New Military Urbanism*, London: Verso, 2011, xv.
71   Noam Chomsky, *On Western Terrorism: From Hiroshima to Drone Warfare*, London: Pluto Press, 2013.
72   Such a view can also be political, because the 'The hegemonic sight convention of visuality is an empowered but unstable, free-falling, and floating bird's-eye view that mirrors the present moment's ubiquitous condition of groundlessness'. Emmelhainz, 'Images do not Show', 137.

CHAPTER 3: IMAGE OF THE GLOBE

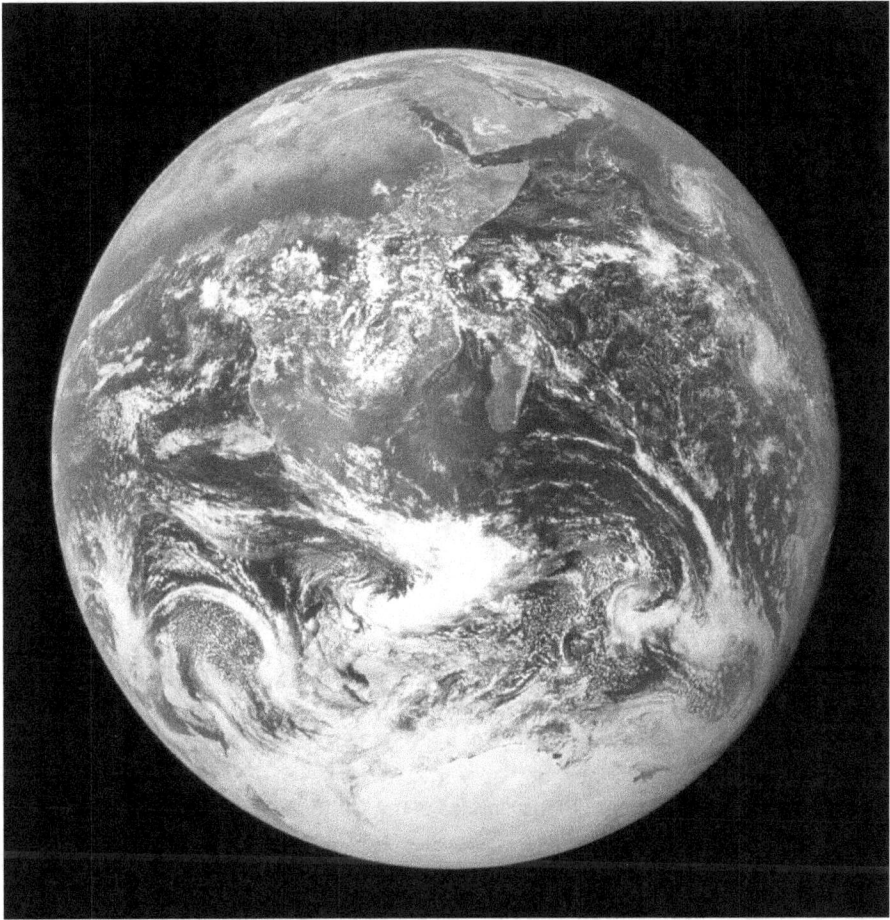

Figure 16: Eugene Cernan, Ronald Evans and Harrison Schmitt, Blue Marble, *1972.*

Widening the View

Historically, aerial photographs were the first media in which the total image which before had only been imagined in maps was actually realized. Aerial recording technologies afforded images which are compatible neither with photographs taken from the land, tied as they are to the horizon as their reference, nor architectural plans, with their perspectival illusion. Such high oblique aerial image did not include the horizon. In order to record the world from a distance science and technology would first have to achieve two innovations: technologies

for flight and powerful telescope optical systems.[1] Photography of the Earth from space led
to substantial changes in the use of the globe as a tool, by distancing from it.

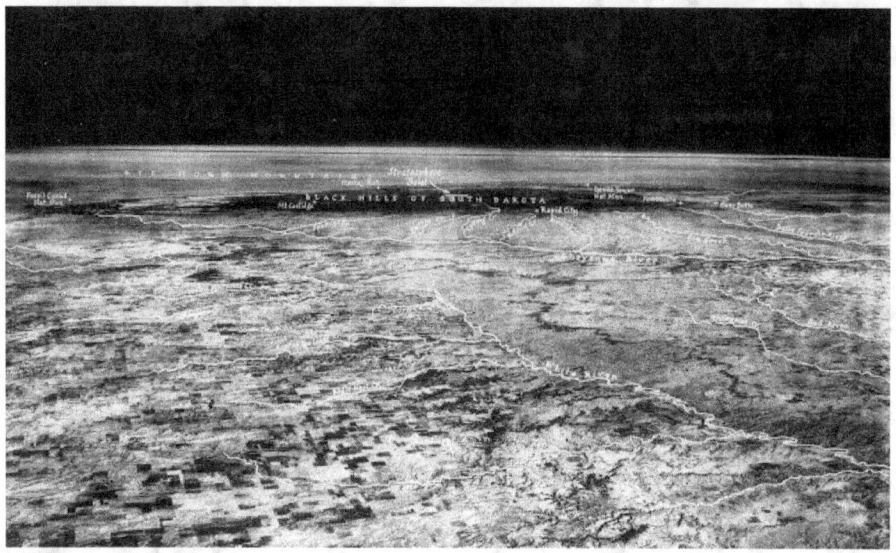

Figure 17: Capt. Albert Stevens' record from South Dakota, 1935.

This history begins with a photograph taken by American Army Air Corps officer and aerial
photographer Captain Albert Stevens in South Dakota on November 11, 1935 while flying
the Explorer II craft, which at the time set the world record of an altitude of 22,066 meters,
and the first image to depict the round-appearing horizon of the Earth. American astronaut
John Glenn was the next to record this surface of the Earth during the first American orbital
spaceflight of the Mercury-Atlas 6 in 1962. After this, astronauts recorded a number of
images that changed the way we see the planet, from *Earthrise* (1968), to the *Blue Marble*
or *22727* (1972), to the *Pale Blue Dot* (1990). Perhaps the most well-known of these images
is the black and white *Earthrise*, recorded by astronaut William Anders during the Apollo 8
mission on Christmas Eve of 1968, the first photo of the Earth from the Moon. It was taken
from distance of 45,000 km using a Hasselblad camera, 80 mm lenses, and 70 mm film
which had to be brought back physically from outer space to be developed. Almost twenty
years later, another iconic image, the *Pale Blue Dot* was taken, commissioned by astronomer
and author Carl Sagan, and recorded by the Voyager 1 upon leaving the solar system at a
distance from the Earth of more than 6.4 billion kilometers, capturing what Hannah Arendt
described as the story of our departure from the human condition. [2] In the years since, NASA

---

1   After Galileo Galilei's telescope, significant inventions would also include, for example, the refracting
     telescope as well as the astronomical revolving unit.
2   Arendt, 'The Human Condition'. Eventually, *Pale Blue Dot* was distributed by US president Lindon
     Johnson among world leaders. While the Soviets certainly pursued and made great achievements in
     their own space program, they did not record any image. See: Sagan, *Pale Blue Dot.*

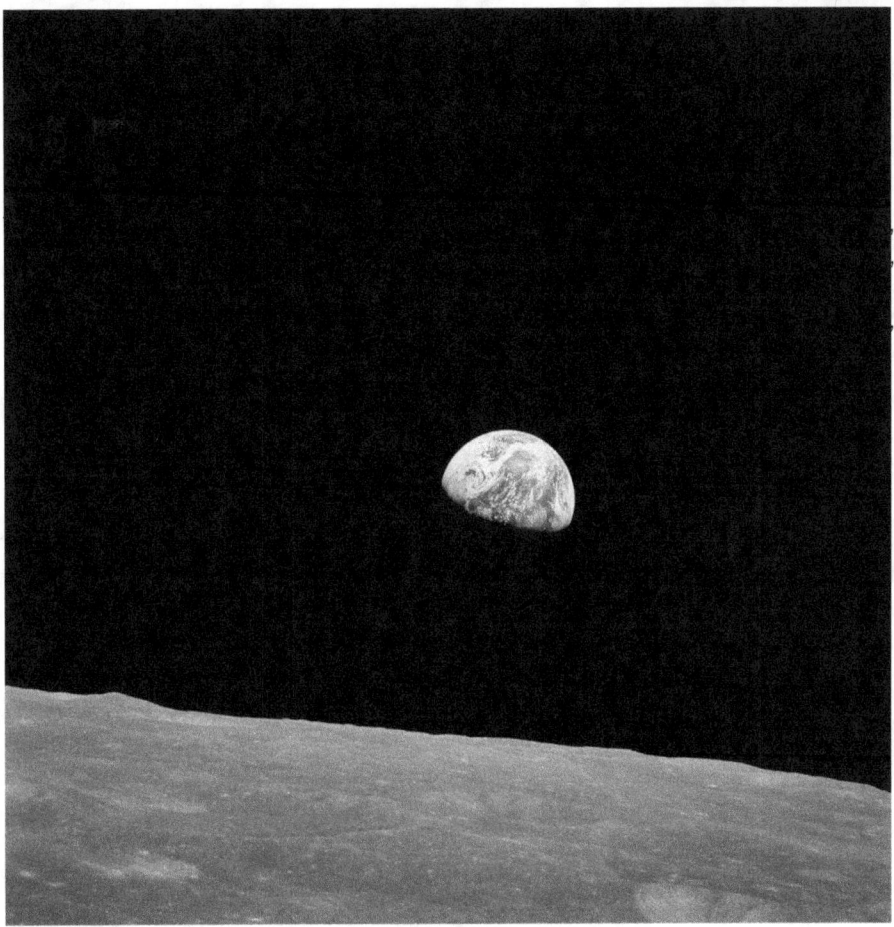

Figure 18: Capt. William Anders, Earthrise, *1968.*

Looking back on the evolution of spaceflight since the 20th century and of space photography since the 1960s, it is incredible what a profound impact these visuals, or more precisely these photographs, have had on our understanding of the mother Earth. Yet, flat Earth skeptics claim that these are just images, that none are true, and that none can be trusted. In fact, these images have indeed been recorded in such a way that a human could never see their subject using only their naked eye. These images dislocated the viewer from their place down on Earth, replacing the subjectively-viewed landscapes for transsubjectively- viewed maps.

3   Denis Cosgrove, 'Contested Global Visions: One-World, Whole Earth, and the Apollo Space Photograph',
     84.2 (June 1994): 270-294.
4   Lazier, 'Earthrise', 605.

Global world Splitting Apart

In the years since, these images of the Earth have been used again and again to the point where they have become a graphic icon. '[I]deas of globalization draw their expressive and political force' from these planetary images, Denis Cosgrove claims.[5] As John Pickles noted, 'The globe has served as an icon for expansive capitalism and nationalism'.[6] The principle representation for globalization is, of course, the image of a 'global earth'. While paradoxically, this icon of the Earth suggests both the globalist drive itself as well as how the achievement of globalism will undoubtedly come at a cost to the planet's biodiversity and ecosystem. Thus, Bill McKibben noted that we no longer live on the *Blue Marble* as pictured in 1972 but rather on an inhospitable planet.[7] Other authors also pointed out that the impact of humans on the planet is all the more visible from outer space.[8]

The destructiveness to the planet from industry which develops part and parcel alongside globalization is closely related to the theory of the Whole Earth, according to Cosgrove, as exhibited, for example, in *The Whole Earth Catalogue* by Stewart Brand printed from 1968 to 1971.[9] Through this *Catalogue*, Brand promoted a critical standpoint on how the idea of the globe should be implemented. Spaceflight has enabled the recording of the Earth as a sphere from the distant position of outer space, making the whole planet look like a miniature ball, almost a toy or some dummy model. Thus, late-20th century images of the Earth not only matched but illustrated Lovelock's thesis on Gaia as a self-sustainable system.[10] Not long after *The Whole Earth Catalogue*, as Bruno Latour criticized, even the Whole Earth theory itself was appropriated into environmental criticism. And the Earth has become a 'signifier for one collective existence', wrote Tobias Boes.[11] That is, images of the Earth have ceased to be only just iconic, and resemble that which they represents, the Earth itself, but have also become symbolic, encoded layer upon layer of culturally-learned interpretations and meanings.

---

5   Cosgrove, *Apollo's Eye*.
6   John Pickles, *A History of Spaces: Cartographic Reason, Mapping and the Geo-Coded World*, London: Routledge, 2003, 8.
7   He writes: 'Imagine we live on a planet. Not our cozy, taken-for-granted earth, but a planet, a real one, with melting poles and dying forests and a heaving, corrosive sea, raked by winds, strafed by storms, scorched by heat. An inhospitable place.' Bill McKibben, *Eaarth: Making a Life on a Tough New Planet*, London: St. Martin's Griffin, 2011.
8   Krewani, 'Google Earth'.
9   The iconic image of the whole Earth has been widely referred, and Whole Earth theory widely analyzed, by culturalists, including Stewart Brand's *Whole Earth Catalogue*, printed 1968-1971 in Sausalito, which was followed by *CoEvolution Quarterly* in period 1974-1984, and *New Whole Earth Catalogue* in 1980. Since then, Brand has further developed his early work in *Whole Earth Discipline: An Ecopragmatist Manifesto*, New York: Viking, 2009. Brand's works have also been recently revived through a spectrum of Anthropocene theories presented by Anselm Franke and Diedrich Diederichsen (eds) *The Whole Earth Catalogue: The Whole Earth California and the Disappearance of the Outside*, Berlin: Sternberg Press, 2013.
10   Lovelock, *Gaia*.
11   Tobias Boes, 'Beyond Whole Earth: Planetary Mediation and the Anthropocene', *Environmental Humanities* 5.1 (2014): 155-170. See Also: Yaakov Jerome Garb, 'The Use and Misuse of the Whole Earth Image', *Whole Earth Review* (March 1985): 18-25.

Global Connectivity

Finally, in addition to these two approaches to images of the Earth that have developed since the 1960s, One-world and Whole Earth theories, images of the Earth have become a symbol of our connectivity. This is due at least in part to astronomical imaging techniques which make visible the Earth in ways that humans cannot themselves naturally see, as well as astronomical imaging programs which are run over extended periods of time. For example, from 1959 to 1972, the Corona reconnaissance satellite program resulted in a number of panoramic images of the Earth which are classified still to this day. Since then, various space agencies all around the world have launched a huge number of unmanned satellites from the Earth's surface and into outer space which can directly record images of the Earth, including those not necessary within the light spectrum visible to humans, leading to new kinds of visual records. One of the longest running is the Landsat satellite program, launched in 1972, and jointly operated by the National Aeronautics and Space Administration (NASA) and the United States Geological Survey (USGS), which has been running since the early 1970s.[12] One of the best known of such imaging systems was the Advanced Research and Global Observation Satellite (ARGOS), launched in 1999 and terminated in 2003.

With the merging of systems for visual representation and data location, locating data occurred with the first GPS monitored by 24 satellites, three of which are needed to map the mobile device, by triangulation. In addition to these, more satellites for specific purposes, such as Ikonos or GeoSci, were used in order to produce what we know today as the 'digital globe'. Some of these projects include NASA's World Wind (2004), Virtual Earth by Microsoft, today a part of Bing Maps (2005), Earth browser (2008), to name but a few. Google Earth itself relies on images from the satellites of NASA and the USGS, including Landsat 8 and previously Landsat 7, as well as various aerial images and crowd-sourced GIS mapping platforms such as Panoramio, which incorporated millions of geotagged photographs which were also used in early days of Google Earth. Today, the images of the Google Earth are not crowdsourced, as they were at the beginning of the project, but directly recorded by satellite light detection and ranging systems. The ever less-and-less blue and green surface of the Earth is computed from images transmitted by low-orbit satellites only 800 kilometers distant from the surface. Google claims that these satellites based camera systems are focused on 15 centimeters, with positional accuracy less than 1 meter above the Earth's surface so as to maintain no visible loss to resolution.[13] Being so close, the satellites cannot supply one image of the whole Earth. Moreover, because of the curvature of the Earth, an image of the entire sphere of the Earth cannot be taken at once or even simultaneously. Therefore, Google muse use many images of the Earth taken from many places. Due to the high demands of this process of recording, to be up to date, images must be taken continuously across a three-year period. But this causes some images of some parts of the Earth to be asynchronous with others. The diachronic view of the images from Google Earth is further enhanced by its 'historical imagery' feature, which shows before and after sequences of this image record. Thus, while offering

---

12   For Landsat, an autonomous real-time ground ubiquitous monitoring system is employed. Its images are also used in today's Google Earth.

13   Google Answers: https://support.google.com/mapsdata/answer/6261838?hl=en.

a total image across space, this total image is segmented and assembled from substantially different images. Google Earth offers pictures from various time periods combined into a single representation of the Earth.

Earth as Symbol

As Stefan Helmreich sees the situation, in an application of Charles Sanders (C.S.) Peirce's semiotic triad, Google Earth is 'a mixture of representation forms. Indexical: satellite images. Iconic: road maps. Symbolic: nation state boundaries'.[14] The resulting total image is itself more of an aggregate image than an indexical photograph. Although we tend to perceive Google Earth as being indexical rather than aggregate. Once merged into Google Earth, however, these image records produce an illusion which does not fully provide an experience of three dimensions, as such. Indeed, Alexander Galloway wrote about how:

> [N]o longer will the viewer experience montage via cuts over time, proceeding from shot to shot, one must now "cut" (but in its opposite, as "suturing") within any given frame, holding two or more source images side by side which themselves will persist montage-free over much longer "takes" than their cinematic predecessors.[15]

Moreover, any information that is found to be missing from between images within this image composite are generated algorithmically.[16] They are mathematical computations produced out of many different systems for detecting light, from visible light to the infrared spectrum. Combining images from various times with maps, and merging them algorithmically, it creates a total image which is more fiction than document.

Travelling around Digital Globe

Today, composites images of the Earth such as virtual globes are more complex than being simply a set of joint or merged images. Google Earth now represents data for the entire globe of the Earth, a place we once understood and imagined only on the basis of our own person-al, subjective point of view. Thus, virtual globes such as Google Earth may alienate us from experiencing our own habitat. While in the early 16th century sailors first circumnavigated the globe, inspiring a renaissance in globe making, in the early 21st century virtual globes replace this idea of coming to understand the Earth through the visual and tactile exploration of its sphericity with travel inside of its imaging.

That is, these new digital models of the Earth allow the interactor or user to navigate within an image, from macro to micro and back again, from a wide view to the smallest detail, as shown in *Powers of Ten* mentioned in the Introduction. Through functions such as magnification

---

14   Helmreich, 'From Spaceship Earth to Google Ocean', 1222.
15   Galloway, *The Interface Effect*, 114-115.
16   For this purpose, some contemporary image processing systems include DSMAC (digital scene matching area code), which is used for image comparison, as well as DARPA's 'Mind's Eye', a kind of artificial intelligence known as visual intelligence (VI).

or zooming, a user can move close to or even inside the detail, which in turn produces the effect of movement through space, and thus an illusion of three dimensionality. Beyond these viewing options, several other kinds of interaction with the images are enhanced, such as the movements up-down, left-right, and forward-back.[17] Even so, more complicated motions such as combining left-forward are not available in the system. And rather than create a natural and embodied feeling of movement through a three-dimensional space, ultimately, the interaction feels unnatural and even 'robotized' because the flow is not smooth but rather broken into metered sequences or stages. The space represented by such an image, such as Google Earth or Google Street View, although it exists as a three-dimensional architecture, still consists only of many two-dimensional records. Thus, the space is actually sliced into layers, each of which is constrained to the apparatus of the screen.

Has the Globe Lost its Importance?

The Google Earth project is one of several digital projects for imaging the Earth in which some degree of animation serves as the interface by which people interact with the sphere.[18]

Yet such model of the Earth as a sphere no longer has the same function that it once did. Even when using projects such as Google Earth, we navigate an electronic galaxy not some global exploration.[19] We have at least to a certain extent outlived the usefulness of representing the Earth as a globe. Certainly, globalization has brought people into a greater degree of interconnectivity, making physical distances less and less relevant for work and home life. And with the iconization of images of the whole Earth, which in design and style make it appear flat, the representation of the planet as a sphere is rarely in daily use. By stepping back from the various processes of recording images of the planet, we have also excluded ourselves from the act of understanding our own habitat.

In order to explain how these total images have had a profound impact on our understanding of the very planet on which we live, in the Chapter 4 I will analyze two concepts, space and place, through a sociological framework, and apply these concepts to discussions from the field of geography and differences between the landscape and a map. Today, the Earth is no longer recorded from any one specific position in the universe, not even the most one of a drone pilot or space astronaut. New photographic technologies are automated. And these post-digital photographic devices assemble and compute a total image out of many other images. These images become 'hyperobjects', to employ Timothy Morton's term, a complex non-material structure that can have a significant impact on our lives.[20]

---

17 For the limitations of travel in Google Earth, see also: Hoelzl and Marie, *Softimage.*
18 Google Earth was developed from Earth Viewer 3D by Keyhole Inc, 2001.
19 Cosgrove, 'Contested Global Visions'.
20 Timothy Morton, *Hyperobjects*, Minneapolis: University of Minnesota Press, 2013.

CHAPTER 4: LANDSCAPES AND MAPS

Seeing and Imagining

Even given all of the differences between landscapes and maps, which are indeed substantial, both record an image of the world on a two-dimensional surface. Yet, philosophers often divide these ways of representing space as being conceptually opposed and contrasting.[1] And historians, in turn, apply this dualism to the history of Western art in order to categorize the landscape and map as emerging from irrational and rational drives, respectively. Further, until relatively recently, these visual representations have to a large extent belonged to the different disciplines of art and geography.[2] And, overall, when or where both are actually used in field of geography, the landscape serves the purpose of topography, as an arrangement of the natural and artificial surface shapes of land or sea, and the map serves the purpose of cartography, as a practice of diagrammatic representation of an area and its features such as cities and roads. Moreover, these two genres of images, the landscape and map, are interpreted by art historians as formative in the divide between realism and abstraction. Thus, the distinction between landscape and map in geography as well as art history also intersects and overlaps with the distinction between vision and visualization in visual studies.

	Landscape	**Map**
Geography	Topography	Cartography
Discipline	Arts	Geography
Visual studies	Vision	Visualization
Media	Photography	Drawing
Space studies	Place	Space
Subject-positioning	Author-centered; single-viewed	Audience-centered; multiple entries

Table 3: The dualistic split between landscapes and maps.

In the field of visual studies, this dualism between the landscape and map is attributed with even further connotations, as is perhaps most commonly exemplified by the distinction between photographic and drawing mediums. Yet, few authors define these distinctions in depth. Gilles Deleuze and Félix Guattari crucially define how these genre situate the viewer: 'A map has multiple entryways, as opposed to the tracing, which always comes back "to the same."'[3] In other words, the landscape relies most upon the subjective gaze of its creator, while the map relies most upon the subjective gaze of their user. But also, these genre categories are about fundamentally different things, as the landscape describes place, and the map describes space. Thus, the image of a landscape is self-referential and can be interpreted in

---

1   Although, as Gilles Deleuze and Félix Guattari noted: 'Have we not, however, reverted to a simple dualism by contrasting maps to tracings, as good and bad sides?' Gilles Deleuze and Félix Guattari, *Thousand Plateaus: Capitalism and Schizophrenia,* trans. Brian Massumi, Minnesota and London: Minnesota University Press, 1987, 13.

2   The science of geography was initiated in Antiquity, such as in the works of Ptolemy and Strabo. Historians describe Ptolemy as the founder of map-making and cartography, while Strabo as the father of the landscape.

3   Deleuze and Guattari, *Thousand Plateaus,* 2.

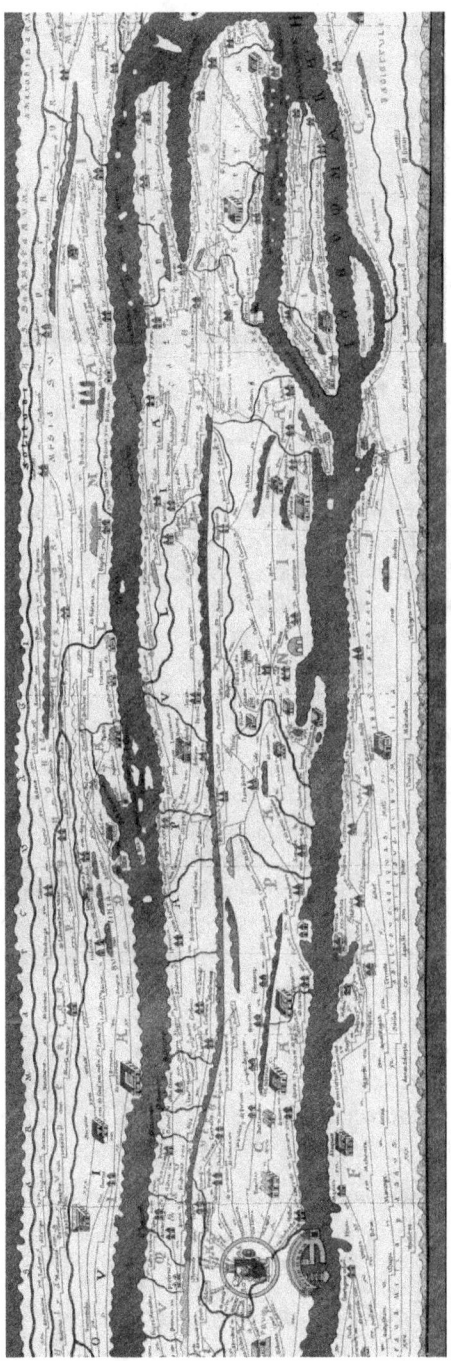

Figure 20: Monk of Colmar, Peutinger's Map, *1265. Rotated counter-clockwise 90 degrees.*

and of itself. Whereas the image of a map is externally referential and can only be interpreted in the context of that which it represents.

Landscapes and Maps as Preferences

Both the imaging practices for mapping and landscape have evolved alongside the advancement of technology. During each period in history there have been different capacities for the production of representations of space and place. But also, preference for specific types of representation shifted over time. So, in Antiquity, the Medieval Period, and the Renaissance, people overall preferred the map, while later periods, especially the 17th to 19th centuries, people were most fascinated with the colorful, dramatic, and romantic landscape.

Maps are the oldest abstract representations of space. And even today, children develop a cartographic literacy to one degree or another, whether through the study of geography in school or using applications on their smart phones. However, the first maps in Antiquity were more approximate than they were based on a system of measurement.[4] Part of the reason for this was that they did not serve the same purposes of navigation and orientation as maps do today, and because there was no widely agreed upon system for notation in maps.[5] For a long time, notation systems were flexible or unclear. But in order for a map to be a map, essentially, one needs to have an agreed upon and fixed measuring system, a set of rules for the composition, and consistent methods of reproduction. Thus, Denis Wood, John Fels and John Krygier claim that no maps existed before 1400, or maybe even 1500, at least in the sense that we understand the idea of the map today.[6] Even if some maps dated to Antiquity have been found, they served more of a decorative rather than a navigational purpose.[7] For the greater part of history, maps did not serve the purpose of navigating the world but to illustrate the way we humans conceive the world around us. Both the *ecumene* of Classical Antiquity as well as the *mappa mundi* of the Medieval Period represented the world which their creators thought as if it was the whole planet. Of course, at the time, the other parts of the Earth which we know about today had not yet been discovered. And, consequently, these maps depicted the earth as flat, and left out the *antoecumene,* opposite quarter of the earth, or southern half of the hemisphere.[8]

This 'whole world' theory is exquisitely recorded, for example, in the *Tabula Peutingeriana* or Peutinger's Table. This 6.74-meter-long panoramic scroll depicted a roster of the *cursus publicus* or road network which connected Constantinople to more than five hundred Roman cities and thousands of other sites.[9] The *Tabula* served to map the late Roman Empire to the

---

4   Tom Conley, *Cartographic Cinema*, Minneapolis: University of Minnesota Press, 2007.
5   This drawing, still, according to some presents merely a realistic drawing of the animal's spots, rather than a sophisticated abstract map.
6   Denis Wood, with John Fels and John Krygier, *Rethinking the Power of Maps,* New York: The Guilford Press, 2010.
7   Wood, Fels, and Krygier, *Rethinking the Power of Maps*.
8   Similarly, the first settlers' maps, according to Moore and Drecki, left unvisited areas blank. See: Antoni Moore and Igor Drecki (eds) *Geospatial visualization,* Berlin: Springer, 2013.
9   As the author is already mentioned Marcus Vipsanius Agrippa.

fullest extent possible at the time and revealed the spectacular size of the Roman's domain. Because of its layout, however, Peutinger's Table has remained one of the greatest enigmas of Roman cartography. During the Medieval Period, the *Tabula* was reintroduced and along with it the idea of the planet as flat. Of course, the world was not represented as a spherical globe in the Tabula, even though this reality already common knowledge for ancient Greek cartographers, but rather as flat plane.[10] Consequently, historians have interpreted Peutinger's Table as a sign of decay in knowledge about space from Antiquity to the Medieval Period.[11]

The Roman original *Tabula Peutingeriana* from Antiquity has either not yet been found or has not survived. What has been preserved is a Medieval copy made by a French monk in the town of Colmar around 1265. This copy references the original, which is believed to have been created between the 4th and 5th centuries CE during reign of the Roman Emperor Augustus.[12] As depicted in the *Tabula*, the geographic sites were constructed after the 4th century. And given the toponymic names for these sites, used in the manner customary during the Roman imperial period, the original map is usually considered to have originated at that time. In addition, because the toponyms are written in declinations, the map seems to have been revised in latter age, when these grammar rules as such had already been established.[13] Besides this, however, some of illustrations do in fact resemble the architectures found at the respective sites. For example, the landmarks of Rome, Constantinople, and Antioch are represented using columns or arches particular to that location. Most sites, however, are marked with far more generic icons. These consist of two general types: the house-like and courtyard-like. Although there is no legend explaining this categorization. Both types of icons, however, are drawn from a bird's eye or aerial view, as if seen from above, rather than not in the frontal or oblique view. Retrospectively, from our understanding today, such a viewpoint gives the map a visual aesthetic or style like that in aerial photography. The other information in the map is schematic, both simplified and symbolic. Cities and roads are laid out upon the flat surface, and the complexity of the Adriatic landscape it reduced to barriers set out in front of a traveler, as are the rivers and largest mountains ranges. Compared to the much older map, but also to contemporary maps, distances in the *Peutingeriana* seem to be approximate, as if the official measuring systems of Roman cartography, or the system developed by Hippodamus, was

---

10   Greek cartographers, as Anaximander (c. 610-546 BCE), Hecatus of Miletus (c. 550-476 BCE) in his *Ges Periodos* already used the circular representation of the known world, ecumene, while Erastosthenes (c. 276-194 BCE) used the system of parallels and meridians. In works by Posidonius (c. 150-130 BCE) there is a measure of circumference of the Earth, which was latter corrected in Strabo's (64 BC-24 CE) *Geographica*. Pomponius Mela went out of ecumene, anticipating the existence of the world outside of it to be discovered. Marinus of Tyre (c. 120 CE) invented equi-rectangular projection, allowing contemporary cartography. He also gave a shape of this world by referring to China and Fortunate islands. Ptolemy (c. 150) in his *Geography* used Marinus' system, calculating absolute distances.

11   Most of the maps from the Classical and Medieval periods, such as the Ptolomaic as Peutinger maps, with all earlier editions and versions lost to time, exist today only as some post-Medieval variant.

12   Konrad Peutinger was a German antiquarian who kept the map originally discovered by Conrad Celtes. Peutinger family has kept the map for hundreds a years until selling it to Prince of Savoy in 1714 who bought it for the public library in Vienna.

13   For further details, see: Benet Salway, 'The Nature and Genesis of the Peutinger Map', *Imago Mundi* 57.2 (2005): 119-135.

never consulted. Being entirely abstract rather than realistic, clearly the *Tabula Peutingeriana* represents knowledge of the land rather than the land itself. Thus, while resembling a map, it doid not rely on any known precise measure.

Indeed, the *Tabula Peutingeriana* is really neither a map nor a landscape because as a visu-al artifact it is imagined rather than either measured or observed. In other words, the map records temporal rather than spatial dimensions, indicating the geographic duration that a journey might take rather than the geographic length between the points being depicted.[14] Taking in consideration how the map represents only roads and various cities, it may even be assumed that it represents a kind of 'travelogue'.[15] This spatial distortion of the referential subject of the map, which presents more of an itinerary than a roadmap, may be due to the choice of the vehicle, such as a boat or a horse carriage.

After a time in the late Medieval Period and early Renaissance when maps were being repeat-ed and reprinted, an age of discovery, as well as of colonialism, exploration, and imperialism, brought with it a renewed interest in maps and map-making.[16] For example, in 1346 Fra Paolino da Venezia made *Civitas Venetiarum*, a map of of the city Venice, which in 1572 to 1617 led to the large cartographic project *Civitates Orbis Terrarum*, a great atlas edited by Georg Braun and illustrated by Franz Hogenberg. Published in six volumes, this atlas had 546 maps of different European cities, all of which simulated an aerial or bird's eye view which. at the time was inaccessible to humans. Yet, these maps had the purpose of representing a small area rather than a big region. Only in the 19th century, with the influence of the work of German geographers Alexander von Humboldt and Carl Ritter, did maps begin to locate a specific place within the context of a general space; that is, of the whole Earth.

Cartographic reasoning has been at the heart of the Western thought since the dawn of the age of discovery. Maps were the product of scientific discoveries but also imperial tendencies. By the time of 18th century, the surface of the Earth had been mostly discovered, leaving only a few places yet unknown. 'It is not a new terra incognita for explorers in colonial headgear. It is by no means a res nullius, ready to be appropriated', wrote Latour, describing that time.[17] Slowly each undiscovered country that had been vaguely represented in maps disappeared. With the loss of the sense of mystery surrounding these territories, the map primarily become a tool for navigation of the known world, rather than for illustration of the unknown world, and this remains its function today. With the closing in and completion of this total image of the world, cartographers went on to draw its ever-smaller details and, as Virilio notes, the map

---

14   Another itinerary map from this era is the *Itinerarium Antonini,* which lists places and distances.
15   If we compare this map to a recent project of mapping by Space Humanities on Stanford, giving us
      possibility to understand the travel in Roman era, a difference of time-map and map on time (in real
      space) comes obvious. Namely while time distort the Peutinger's map, the map of the Stanford project
      is the precise one provided by geometry, only being furnished with historical data. Still, while we can
      imagine travelling on Peutinger's map, it is more likely we will understand and learn objectively what it
      was during the Antiquity with Stanford map.
16   Andrew Pettegree, *The Book in the Renaissance*, New Haven: Yale University Press, 2011.
17   Bruno Latour, *Down to Earth: Politics in the New Climatic Regime*, Cambridge: Polity Press, 2018, 78.

began more and more to be copied rather than created, with the landscape as a genre again becoming a more frequently employed means for the representation of space.[18]

At the time when more attention was being given to the details in maps than map-making itself, the interest in the map was replaced by interest in the landscape. The image of the landscape occurred on an iconographic or symbolic level already by the 15th century. Still, it took a few centuries for the landscape genre to flourish. And only between the 17th and the 19th century did the landscape become a dominant art genre. With the Industrial Revolution, however, landscape painting became more and more important, as if a harbinger of the world-scale problems which this progress would lead to.[19] In paintings by British artists John Constable and J.M.W. Turner, for example, a warning appears to have been issued about industrialization and the consequent pollution or, at least, the paintings can be interpreted this way in the light of history).[20] Unfortunately, the teachings of such landscape painters were not recognized until more recently, when the consequences of the coal industry among others has reached a tipping point. Today, in an time not only of climate change but of climate crisis, landscapes are frequently employed to depict the loss of nature, while maps can be used to demonstrate the changes in the environment which have been introduced by humans show the destruction and intrusions of industry into this land.

The last moment in history in which the landscape held vital importance in the visual arts and for visual representation coincided with the invention of the photograph, which itself was a consequence of the Industrial Revolution of the 18th and 19th centuries. With the invention of camera technology, the photographic medium achieved greater and greater significance in the arts, relegating the painterly genre of the landscape to 'Sunday painters' in the open air. Indeed, Denis Cosgrove claims that as a visual genre in the 19th century the landscape was again replaced by the map, at least in part because it was in this moment that visual tools other than painting become capable of naturally and realistically depicting the immediacy and intimacy of place.[21] By the end of the 19th century, both photographic as well as aerial technologies were developed, which would lead to their fusion in the next century.[22] Edward Casey thus named this era 'the age of world picture,' referring to Heidegger's theme of the 'world image', a concept which is paraphrased in the title for this book.[23]

Today, the entire surface of the Earth is continuously photographed from the air. As Siegfried Kracauer wrote in 1928, 'This equation is not made without good reason. For the world itself

---

18   Paul Virilio and Sylvere Lotringer, *Crepuscular Dawn*, Los Angeles and New York: Semiotext(e) and MIT Press, 2002, 53

19   Gombrich analyses how even in the 16th century, the landscape it preserved the features of innovation in technology. See: Ernst Gombrich, *Norm and Form: Studies in the Art of the Renaissance, Volume I: Norm and Form*, London: Phaidon Press, 1994.

20   Edward Casey, 'Between Geography and Philosophy: What Does It Mean to Be in the World?', *Annals of the Association of American Geographers* 91.4 (2001): 683-693.

21   Denis Cosgrove, *Social Formation and Symbolic Landscape*, Madison, WI: University of Wisconsin Press, 1984.

22   Cosgrove, *Social Formation*.

23   Casey, 'Between Geography and Philosophy'.

has taken on a "photographic face"; it can be photographed because it strives to be absorbed into the spatial continuum'.[24] The consequence of such over-photographing is that today there are no secret or unexplored territories left on Earth. Satellites used by Google discover some previously hidden part of the world on the daily basis.[25] Or, as Virilio writes, 'There are eyes everywhere. No blind spot left. What shall we dream when everything shows visible? We'll dream of being blind'.[26]

Yet, even such photography is conditioned by maps and map-making practices and processes, as I will analyze in Chapter 5. Many maps today do not prove a direct correlation between physical measures of the land, instead representing it symbolically. Schematized, they simplify and reduce the information into what the author of the map, whether an individual or institution, deems to be the most important, which in turn leads to maps which are embedded with a priori interpretations. And moreover, they are adapting to the user, diminishing distinction by which landscapes used to depict places while maps spaces.

The development of maps has in recent years significantly accelerated in comparison to the development of landscape during the same time-period.[27] But cartography as we have known it no longer exists. Cartography has become emancipated from the role of the human to become an autotelic activity. Today, many types of maps are being implemented, including aggregated, data, geo-, and raster maps, which do not represent the world as it is experienced, measured, or lived by humans but some interpretation of information about this world. In other words, the cartographic reality is no longer directly connected to a single geographic reality. And there are so many maps online, each tailored to a specific need, or by a particular investor, leading the viewer to some product or purpose. We have arrived at an era of over-lapping visual geographic material, due to mapping and photographing services, included in most mobile gadgets from phones, watches, laptop, to even cars. There are more maps, and more photographs, of the same place existing. The same place is found over-represented in many systems at once. Multimodal images have further distorted our visual conception of reality by producing multiple and different maps referring to the single place.[28]

---

24   Kracauer, *The Mass Ornament*, 59.
25   Because of Google introducing Google Earth Engine, a cloud-based, planetary-scale computing platform for environmental and geospatial analysis, many countries have complained about the military secrets being accidentally revealed. Through the satellite images on Google Earth, everyday people have even seen places such as detention centers for refugees and asylum seekers, classified airports, and sentries training at secret military compounds. See for example: 'Google Maps Update Accidently Reveals Secret Military Sites', *ZDnet*, https://www.zdnet.com/article/google-maps-update-accidentally-reveals-secret-military-sites/; 'Taiwans Darkest Military Secrets Revealed Google Maps', *SCMP*, https://www.scmp.com/news/china/military/article/2186351/taiwans-darkest-military-secrets-revealed-google-maps?li_source=LI&li_medium=section-top-picks-for-you.
26   Louise Wilson, 'Interview with Paul Virilio: Cyberwar, God and Television', http://ctheory.net/ctheory_wp/cyberwar-god-and-television-interview-with-paul-virilio/.
27   McKenzie Wark, *Virtual Geography: Living with Global Media Events,* Indiana University Press, 1994. Thus, Buci-Glucksmann thus invites for a formation of yet another gaze, that would be in capacity to bridge the great divide of real and virtual, the "meta-gaze', 'which bears the modalities of the exercise of its execution and exhibits its syntax'. Buci-Glucksmann, 'Icarus Today', 61.
28   Cartwright, *Multimedia Cartography*.

Susan Sontag once warned, hyper-photographing reality or photographing it to an excessive or exaggerated, extent, can lead to our complete detachment from it.[29] Following Sontag's line of thinking, we may now ask ourselves: what is the consequence of our hyper-mapping and hyper-photographing of reality? Thirty years ago, Henri Lefebvre asked: how many maps do we need to understand a single place? [30] As the number of maps for a single place today grows exponentially, authors as such as Gunnar Olsson and Tom Conley claim we are living in the age of the 'cartographic reason.'[31] The data-driven characteristics of contemporary culture demonstrate the pervasiveness of what James Elkins term the 'post-medieval mapping gaze,' whereby people fail to learn how to see for themselves the infrastructure of the geography around them.[32] Other authors note that we are today even fixated on such a 'cartographic gaze.'[33] This overabundance of maps leads to general crisis of representation for the Earth, which in turn produces a 'cartographic anxiety', and, ultimately, according to what Flusser heralded as the 'end of cartography.'[34]

Space and Place

The crucial difference between the landscape and map, as already noted by Deleuze and Guattari, is in the positioning of the viewer. With the landscape, the position of the author is often repeated by the viewer. But there is no such view that can be repeated with the map. Thus, the landscape indicates the place of an actual viewer, while the map depicts the space for many potential viewers. Such concepts are useful because they demonstrate the role and significance of the social formation behind our ideas of environment and habitat. Ideas about place, however, from a sociological perspective, are commonly defined as being immediate and therefore localized. In contrast, space is always and necessarily defined as something at once elsewhere and everywhere. From a sociological perspective, ideas about space and place are informed by our social unconscious as communicated through the language and images which frame our cognition.[35]

---

29   Sontag, *On Photography.*
30   'How many maps, in the descriptive or geographical sense, might be needed to deal exhaustively with a given space, to code and decode all its meanings and contents? It is doubtful whether a finite number can ever be given to this sort of question. [...] We are confronted not by one social space but by many indeed, by an unlimited multiplicity or unaccountable set of social spaces.' Lefebvre, *The production of spaces,* 85.
31   Gunnar Olsson, *Abysmal: A Critique of Cartographic Reason,* Chicago: University of Chicago Press, 2007; Tom Conley, *Cartographic Cinema,* Minneapolis: University of Minnesota Press, 2007.
32   Elkins, *The Poetics of Perspective,* 135.
33   Christine.Buci-Glucksmann, *L'oeil cartographique de l'art,* Paris: Gallilee, 1996.
34   Vilém Flusser, 'Das Verschwinden der Ferne', *Arch plus* 111 (1992): 31–32.
35   In other words, place belongs to the domain of epistemology, of the immediate experience, while space belongs to the domain of ontology, as the possibility of even the most unspecific existence. Simultaneously, the idea of space is necessarily connected to ideas on the level of metaphysics, such as religion or ideology. Consequently, place has been dealt with mostly in terms of sociology and psychology, while space was a subject of the disciplines given the highest place in Plato's hierarchy of knowledge; mathematics, architecture, poetry, but also politics. Sociology is a discipline which compares and bridges the space and place.

The distinction between concepts of space and place in sociology is commonly attributed to French sociologist Michel de Certeau.[36] Place is what there is and physical space is what could be.[37] Pierre Bourdieu further elaborated upon this distinction.[38] And by 1996, he had reformulated his theory, defining the distinction between the communal and geographic spaces, attending to a more abstract level of meaning than with his original materially-based definition.[39] Bourdieu's division departed from the strictly physical definition of space to the one based on the experience of living (in a society). Bourdieu, as a sociologist, was focused on ideas of communal space. This he defined as an interpretation of the real or geographical space, formulated through the ways in which a certain population captures their belief systems through perception and production in order to produce a coherent and consistent meaning of their own habitat.[40] This amplified the distinction between communal and physical spaces, where communal space is based on the immediate experience of some place, and physical space is based on a variety of possible experiences of the same place. Yet, through his analysis, Bourdieu pointed out the interaction between the communal and physical space in general.

Urban sociologist Henri Lefebvre, who succeeded Bourdieu, also distinguished between space and place, and termed these 'conceived space' and 'perceived place' or the 'represented space' and the 'lived place' (or maybe even 'livable', as a place having a capacity to be inhabited), providing a direct link between space, place, and their representation.[41] Furthermore, Lefebvre distinguished between the representations of space and representational space or, in terms from my analysis, the image of the space and the space of the image, which correspond to the distinction among the conceived versus perceived (or lived) space.[42] Lefebvre's ideas about representational as well as abstract space would have a considerable influence for visual studies, and especially the differentiation between two main geographic genres: landscape and maps. While landscapes show an excerpt of the view of the author in the space, which is defining the place, maps lays down the space without placement of the author and have to be used in the placement of the audience. Still, with new technologies it is the precise place of the audience which is being mapped in an abstract space.

---

36   Michel de Certeau, Luce Giard, and Pierre Mayol, *The Practice of Everyday Life, Volume 2: Living and Cooking*, trans. Timothy J. Tomasik, Minneapolis, MN: University of Minnesota Press, 1998, 117-118.
37   De Certeau et al, *The Practice of Everyday Life*.
38   See: Pierre Bourdieu, 'Social Space and Symbolic Power', *Sociological Theory* 7.1 (1989): 14-25.
39   Pierre Bourdieu, 'Physical Space, Social Space and Habitus', *Rapport* 10, Institutt for sosiologi og samfunnsgeografi Universitetet i Oslo, Oslo, 1996.
40   Although society has changed since Bourdieu's writing, especially regarding non-national colonization inside Western communities, I will continue to use his theory of consummation of space as directly connected to terms I use concept of gentrification. This, in terms of the previously, given example meant – replacement of the old population with a new one.
41   Henri Lefebvre, *The Production of Space*, trans. Donald Nicholson, Smith, Oxford: Blackwell Publishing 1991.
42   Lefebvre, *The Production of Space*.

The Frame and the Space

In visual studies, space is a more of an abstract construct, particularly in discourses about photographic representation, whereas place is a more of a concrete instance, in terms of the precise geophysical location of a photographic shoot.

The photographic medium, because it can represent the landscape with precision, further complicated the space-place distinction. Photography cannot record anything else but a place, and yet a photograph can refer to the existence of space. At the conclusion of the photographic process, an image is realized which is a concrete object. Despite this, however, the relationship between image and place is not realized materially but referentially. Thus, the epistemic value of the photograph, as Jonathan Cohen and Aaron Meskin defined, is derived from the distinction between the general space of photographer and the specific place of the photograph, also known as egocentric and allocentric space.[43] The distinction between such kinds of spaces is important in order to understand the truth claim of the photograph. That is, while it is true that when a viewer looks upon a photograph what they see is a scene which a photographer has already seen, it does not represent an actual place, because the egocentric view of the photographer is already more than the allocentric view in a photograph.

These distinctions can be further applied to analyze the space of the object (the actual physical space being presented in the image), space of the author (the original perception of some actual physical landscape), and space of the viewer (the different real place where the image is experienced), as I have defined in my previous work.[44] I will call these spaces the real, experience, and visual or, in other terms, the actual, perceived, and represented, so as to define three different ways in which the Earth has been described. The first level of space, the real-actual, is independent; the second, the experiential-perceived, is characterized by its consumption and the perspectival view; while the third, the visual-represented, has been located by that view, which it re-experiences. Here, the author has some information about the real-actual space which they represent, while audience has some idea about space of the space the author represents, but also his own place. So, the author of an image 'sees' only a section of the view of the space, which he transfers to the audience. Each of the subsequent spaces carries elements of the previous one, and they are being framed by the perspectival view of two places; the one the author finds inside and the one the audience finds inside.

	Space	Limit
Object	Real / actual	
Author	Experienced / perceived	Position in space
Viewer	Visual / represented	Frame

Table 4: Analysis of three spaces in photography.

---

43   Jonathan Cohen and Aaron Meskin, 'On Epistemic value of Photographs', *Journal of Aesthetics and Art Criticism* 62.2 (2014): 197-210.
44   Peraica, *Fotografija kao dokaz*.

In 'ordinary' photography, as I will here refer to photographs which are produced in the course of our everyday activity, the audience sees only the section of space which was in front of the author. This section of space is determined by the author's choice, the type of photographic lens, as well as exposure settings. This is a small section of some place, about which the author can know much more than is shown in the photograph. Thus, contrary to the three types of spaces, there are only two types of places, because the object and an author or photographer reside at the same place, which becomes important particularly in remote photography. While both places, that of the object and that of the author, are located in the same place, the author's place is commonly not visible to the audience, but has to be reconstructed, whether through perspectival analysis or some other visual methodology. Therefore, the place of the author is not represented but only trajectory, defined through the transmission of the characteristics of the author's place to the audience's space. Because of this, an individual of the audience can produce completely different meanings based on numerous other factors such as her or his social and political contexts. If the perspectival analysis or visual method is successful, the author's place and audiences' space may come into alignment.[45] But, while the place of the author can only ever be two-dimensional rather than three-dimensional to the audience. Perspective is constrained by the fact that the audience cannot put their head into the picture, as Cohen and Meskin claim, and turn around to see what was behind the view of the author at the moment of recording. The audience ends up only being able to vaguely estimate spatial relationships surrounding the author according to their own personal and subjective perception.

In contrast to maps, photographs represent a certain place, which is also made by an author and interpreted by the audience. The place described in a photograph is not filtered through the technology of the camera in the same way as a map is filtered through the visual language and iconic vocabulary of the map-maker. This might be one reason that photography has since its earliest days been transformed in order to become more like maps, the development of which I will analyze in Chapter 5.

William Cartwright and his coauthors valorize the distinction between the space presented in a map and the place depicted in a photograph.[46] He claims that the location of the user of a map still does not produce a located space, because dot produced on the crossroad of the orthogonal lines is not a territory, as dot is basically single-dimensional.[47] This difference between a specific place and a general space becomes even clearer when dealing with the non-places which emerge with post-digital photography in the age of total images.

Such non-places, consumed through strategies of over-mapping such as Google Earth, lack the signature and specificity necessary to be determined as particular places.

---

45   Sometimes the two gazes can overlap, as the author's and viewers' gaze, still, as mentioned in analysis of the Medieval images. And in some cases viewer's view can be situated from the inside of the image space, thus having only a section of the author's space.
46   William Cartwright, Michael P. Peterson, and Georg Gartner, *Multimedia Cartography*, Heidelberg: Springer, 1999.
47   Cartwright, Peterson and Gartner, *Multimedia Cartography*.

Media Spaces

With new media, especially the rise of the digital media, these theories about space and place can appear over-simplistic, as Doreen Massey has already noted, because place is constructed through an understanding of space.[48] Indeed, the dualism between place and space turns out to be quite limiting. The complexity of the space in post-digital photography emerges, in principle, from a divide between the space as it is represented and the place which has in some way been broadcast or transmitted into this space. Such a simultaneity, with its vague origin, trajectory, and destination, leads not only to a 'middle' space negotiated by the audience or user, but also to a proliferation of multiple spaces. It is therefore crucial to revise our definitions of space and place, through the analysis of the complex, assembled spaces which today are nevertheless generated from actual recordings of specific places.[49]

For our definition of virtual space, Henri Lefebvre's definition of abstract space is important as is the manner in which abstract spaces is produced in relation to real space. This includes the historic, military, urban, and economic narratives within these spaces which in turn can make abstract spaces more complex and thus, at least to a limited extent, more real.[50] Supported by Lefebvre's distinctions between the conceived and the perceived, the represented and the lived, contemporary media epistemology suggests that we do perceive virtual space as if it is real. And we do not disregard the knowledge that it is being transmitted. Rather, we live in both virtual and real space simultaneously.[51] Thus, W.J.T. Mitchell distinguished between the virtual space that is transferred by a media and the unmediated 'feeling' of a place in reality.[52] That is to say space is epistemological while place is phenomenological, space is conceived while place is perceived. Yet, today space that is constructed around place, or digital space, is perceived as being integral to our life experience as well.

Aside from the precise placement of the viewer onto the map, there is yet another distinction of the new images – the question of the author which is now not placed into own, separate

---

48 Doreen Massey, John Allen, and Phil Sarre, *Human Geography Today*, Cambridge: Polity, 1991.

49 Christopher Tilley has mapped even more spaces, according the way they are experienced: somatic space, perceptual space, existential space (as social), architectural space, and cognitive space, for example. Tilley, Christopher Tilley, *A Phenomenology of the Landscape: Places, Paths and Monuments, Explorations in Anthropology*, London: Berg Publishers, London, 1997. And Michael Dear defined how 'the entire panoply of place-based contingencies involved in photographic production […] incorporates; […] - The place of production, which incorporates both the specific site of photography […]; - The production of place, including the narrative and compositional aspects of the image, as well as the spatial techniques employed by the image-maker […]; - The place of presentation, referring to the image and its mode of presentation […]; and […] - Reception in place, what happens to the image when it is released to the world of consumption'. Michael Dear, 'Creativity and Place', in Michael Dear, Jim Ketchum, Sarah Luria, and Doug Richardson (eds) *GeoHumanities: Art, History, Text at the Edge of Place*, London and New York: Routledge, 2011, 11.

50 A class struggle, Lefebvre noted, can exist within an image, representing space, in the way of its basic coding by the author as well as in the communal practice of reading. Lefebvre, *The Production of Space*, 210.

51 This obscuring of the line between the real and virtual has come the most visible in post-humanism, in which digital space has been recognized and acknowledged as reality, as it is been experienced as one.

52 Mitchell, *Landscape and Power*.

place, but can reside also in the audience space, which now co-creates the map by its use. Besides, the creator can also be nonhuman. Such is the total image made using artificial intelligence. Artificial intelligence is conditioned by biology, perception, or society the way human intelligence. And artificial intelligence does not interpret photographs from within the framework of the 'human photographic condition', as I have defined it in the Introduction. That is, the computation of these machines is not based on the distance from the scene, view angle, or individual frame which determines how the photographic medium is necessarily subjective. Moreover, place as such does not exist to artificial intelligence because any the concept of dimensionality would not be related to a physical place but rather to an overlay of space as an objective or pseudo-objective category. Therefore, to an artificial intelligence, all places are seen at once in so far as many places are computed or aggregated together.

CHAPTER 5: DATAFIED LANDSCAPES AND LOCATED MAPS

Maps and Photographs

The difference between the up-in-the-air photograph and the map is not as great as the difference between the map and the down-to-the-ground landscape. Indeed, aerial photography and map making have much more in common. Both genres of image depict the world without visibly having either a particular subject's view angle or even a general human view angle. Given the similarity between aerial photographs and maps, some authors, such as Anthony Vidler, claim that both image genres have their foundation in the representation of the human view from above.[1] Aerial photography, because it is free from the constraints of human existence on the surface of the Earth and perspective systems which are relative to this way of being, provides a big picture which functions topographically while appearing cartographical. And Christine Buci-Glucksmann also defined such an 'Icaro-cartographic' view by asking: 'Does the cartographic eye of the earth already reveal to us a truth that the Icarian eye of a technologically programmed world would conceal from us?'[2] An 'Apollonian perspective is implicit in Ptolemaic cartography's positioning of the observer at sufficient distance to see the spherical Earth', wrote Denis Cosgrove.[3] The media evolution of an image genre in which aerial photography and map making are combined was so rapid and intense that Fred Moffit named it an era of 'aero-photographic mapping'.[4] In this chapter, however, I will show how the small differences between aerial photographs and maps changed with their dataification.

Yet, at the very beginning of the implementation of aerial photography, map making and photography were still being treated as distinct practices. For instance, the map and photograph were used not only to represent space bellow, but also for mutual testing how space was being represented. During the First World War, the aerial view or bird's eye view was still a novel experience. Only a very few soldiers, being also aviators, ever actually went into the wild blue yonder and climbed high into the sun. And most of these soldiers were not yet accustomed to the view. They required additional support for their own eyes, in terms of some proof for the correlation between the location on the map and the location which they saw while they were flying. For this reason, so as to double check the reality of their own perception, some pilots sketched maps on the palms of their hands. Soon after WWI, aerial photography began to be combined with map making independent of human verification that the map and the photograph in fact reference the same information.[5] The principle motivation for combining

---

1   Anthony Vidler, 'Terres Inconnues: Cartographies of a landscape to be invented', *October* 115 (Winter 2006): 13-30.
2   Buci-Glucksmann, 'Icarus Today', 60.
3   Cosgrove, 'Contested Global Visions', 271.
4   Fred H. Moffit, 'A Method of Aerophotographic Mapping', *Geographical Review* 10 (November 1920): 326-338.
5   There can be different types of maps of the same battlefield in war, produced by different armies; field sketch, blank topographic map, trench maps, intelligence map, practical artillery positioning map, strategic map, each being used by different military order.

these image genres, at least in the armed forces, was not only to control the space represented, but also to correct this data through the reciprocal testing of each form's accuracy. And across the 20th century, with the acceleration in their use by the military, these two image types have become increasingly merged.[6]

After a time of acclimatization to an aerial view which combined ways of seeing from both photograph and map, further similarity between two image genres become clear. When comparing aerial photography to ordinary photography, the photographer has fewer choices for how they do the recording, such as less possible view angles, and even more objects on which to focus. By reducing the range and variety of subjective aesthetic choices in how the photographer can represent the landscape, aerial photography shifts from an aesthetic framework to a practical and utilitarian purpose.

Even so, there are differences between aerial photographs and maps. When comparing aerial photographs to map making, for example, there are no scales in aerial photography which provide a ratio between the distance in the image and the distance on the ground. This makes spatial distortions in the image less clear at a first glance because they have no metric parameter. And such distortions produce 'noise' in our interpretation of our own habitat. At least, this was a problem until the image genre became digitized, and aerial photographs could incorporate the kind of measurement systems that have long been included with maps. While in the early 20th century aerial photographs may have looked like maps but did not function like maps, since the 1950s with the digital turn, the possibility of full integration between aerial photography and map making became possible.

Datafication of Geography

The first experiments with imaging techniques which would lead to digital map making were already being undertaken after WWII. Yet it took many years for these techniques to become fully functional. And the mid-20th century wave of simultaneous digitization and datafication had a strong influence on our image of the world, regarding both photographs as well as maps, profoundly changing these image genres and, ultimately, even connecting them.

The first pre-digital experiment with mapping was undertaken in the project *The Streets of London* (1944) by the British company Nextbase. The *Glasgow Online Digital Atlas* soon followed. The first digital map was in ASCII format, with its code representing English characters as numbers, with each letter. Assigned a number from 0 to 127 in a reductive schema.[7] However, it took many years for interactive maps to be developed. In 1978 the *Aspen Movie Map* project by MIT introduced the streets of the city of Aspen to the audience using photographs. With CD technology, the *Digital Chart of the World* (DCW), a comprehensive digital map of the Earth based on the United States Defense Mapping Agency's (DMA) operational navigation chart, was developed. Still, the first years of implementation of digital maps were dedicated to the digitization of analogue media through a process of scanning, as in the *World Factbook* by the

6   Siegfried Kracauer, 'Photography', *Critical Inquiry* (Spring 1993): 433.
7   See: Cartwright, Peterson, and Gartner, *Multimedia Cartography.*

Central Intelligence Agency (CIA). Desktop and web publishing led to further developments for the map. Although only with Web 2.0, which emphasized user-generated content, ease of use, a participatory culture, and interoperability for end users, did digital cartography begin to develop. And today there are plenty of new techniques for mapping, from as augmented vision to tele-cartography.[8] Beyond such techniques, there are cartographic games, like the *Magellan* board and video games. The digitization of maps, along with satellite photography, has also been integrated into projects such as Google Earth, Google Maps, and Google Street View, which are accessible through mobile devices.[9] These projects, launched since 2001, 2005, and 2007, respectively, support users as they explore the Earth with comparatively realistic images which combine maps and photographs.

GiS

Another key invention for contemporary digital geography is the Geographic Information System (GIS), a computer system designed to capture, store, analyze, and present data related to spatial or geographic data about positions of various entities or objects on the Earth's surface. Utilizing systems like GIS in their analyses, the field of Geographic Information Science (GiScience or GiS) was established on the methodological and theoretical grounds of psychogeographic strategies for exploring urban environments. Historically, the field emerged from the Situationist International (SI) organization of social revolutionaries, prominent in Europe from 1957 to 1972, and made up of avant-garde artists as well as intellectual and political theorists. Already in the mid-20th century, in their work, aerial photography and maps were being fused together, as for example by Guy-Ernest Debord in his *Introduction to a Critique of Urban Geography* (1955) which, as Anthony Vidler notes, preserved the fundamental roles of both maps and photographs in the combined works, as with his collaged map of Paris (1956).[10] William Bunge in *Fitzgerald: Geography of a Revolution* (1971); as well as the Experiments in Art and Technology (E.A.T.) Datascape (1966-1970), an exploratory tool for humanities scholars in social history for exploring the intersection between art and non-art contexts followed.[11] And by the 1990s, GIS technology had evolved into a practical software.[12] Beyond applied GiScience, art-based researchers have also developed a number of experimental methods, such as the tactical cartography of the Paris-based conceptual art group Bureau D'études, or Mapping Contemporary Capitalism (MoC) by the editors of *Mute Magazine*, among others.[13] The psychogeographies of the mid-20th century included 'attempts to

8   See: Cartwright, Peterson, and Gartner, *Multimedia Cartography*.
9   Denis Cosgrove, *Geography and Vision: Seeing, Imagining and Representing the World*, London: I. B. Tauris, 2008; Cosgrove, *Apollo's Eye*; W.J.T. Mitchell, *Landscape and Power*, Chicago: University of Chicago Press, 2002.
10   See: Anthony Vidler, 'Terres Inconnues', *October* 115.1 (2006): 13-30.
11   This included artworks by Andy Warhol, Nam June Paik, Robert Breer, Merce Cunningham, John Cage, Robert Rauschenberg, and Robert Whitman, among others.
12   For example such software is: ESRI's ArcGIS, CARTO, mapbok.
13   For an overview, see: Michael F. Goodchild, 'Twenty years of progress: GIScience in 2010', *Journal of Spatial Information Science* 1 (2010): 10.5311/JOSIS.2010.1.2

record and represent the grain and patina of place through juxtapositions and interpretations of the historical and the contemporary, the political and poetic, the discursive and sensual'.[14]

In the GiScience of today, in addition to quantitative projects, there are also qualitative projects. These projects are used to present a critical geography in which new methods are applied to mapping services which might, for example, provide a better life quality. There are also feminist and queer geographic information systems.[15] The FOAM Map, for example, allows the exploration of various community-verified registries of crowdsourced places.[16] The 'network image', as Virilio them, today has a capacity to convey various rich information.[17] To describe such maps, which are made not only from spatial but other kinds of information, the term 'deep map' is commonly used.[18] The pioneering *Spatial History Project* at the Center for Spatial and Textual Analysis (CESTA) at Stanford University, for example, supports the development of such deep maps. In one of their projects, researchers use GIS technology to create a layered history of Rome, updating the cartographic masterpiece of ancient Roman topography, the *Forma Urbis Romae*, published in 1901 by archaeologist Rodolfo Lanciani. While the 13th century *Tabula Peutingeriana*, described previously, showed how many post-Roman cultures imagined the Roman Empire at one point in time, the 21st century *Forma Urbis Romae* shows how the city of Rome changed over time from the retrospective vantage point of today.[19] The outcome of such works from Stanford's *Spatial History Project* have not only informed the fields of visual studies and visual history, but improved how space is being visualized, leading to new kinds of interaction.[20] Other such projects which implement a critical geography include artistic projects like GPS Art by Michael Wallace, who drives around on his bike as it is tracked with GPS in order to outline various figures on a map, or the *Tangible Disaster Information System* developed by the Tangible Media Group at MIT, a collaborative tool. For planning disaster measures based on simulations using GIS.[21] And there are those which are based on crowd sourcing and social networks. Such artistic experiments show that control is

---

14   Mike Pearson and Michael Shanks, *Theatre/Archaeology*, London: Routledge, 2001, 64-65.
15   See: Matthew H. Wilson, *New Lines: Critical GIS and the Trouble of the Map,* Minneapolis: University of Minnesota Press, 2017.
16   'Foam Map', https://www.foam.space/map.
17   'Technical images arise in an attempt to consolidate particular around us and in our consciousness', writes Flusser in *Into the universe of technical images,* 16. Adding that the role of such images is to grasp the ungraspable, visualize the invisible, among others. 'People no longer group themselves according to problems, but around technical images', he wrote. Flusser *Into the Universe of Technical Images,* 5.
18   Trevor Harris gives a number of criteria for deep maps, they should be; '1. Large to contain all data, 2. Should be slow, 3. Sumptuous, or multilayered, 4. Multimedia, 5. Should contain graphic, time-based and database media/systems, 6. Require engagement of insiders and outsiders, 7. Bring together amateur and professional, artist and scientist 8. Are possible by digital, 9. Will not seek authority and objectivity as ordinary cartography, but will be negotiated, 10. Will be unstable'. David J Bodenhamer, John Corrigan and Trevor M Harris, *Deep Maps and Spatial Narratives*, Bloomington and Indianapolis: Indiana University Press, 2015.
19   'Spatial History Project', http://web.stanford.edu/group/spatialhistory/cgi-bin/site/project.php?id=1063.
20   This type of spatialization is often used in analysis of novels, especially adventurous. Susan Piedmont-Palladino, 'Intelligent Cities', in *National Building Museum*, 2011, 36-41.
21   'Disaster Simulation', https://tangible.media.mit.edu/project/disaster-simulation/.

not the only possible outcome for digital mapping, but that new tools can also be developed for the betterment of society.

Space and GIS

GIS has introduced large change in the way we orientate by using maps, so for example the navigation feature for Google Maps employs the reader of the map no longer has to navigate wander on the map, in the search of the place. Maps have long been thought of as objective, in large part because they are made in a Cartesian space and with location descriptors. But an element of subjectivity was still involved, because such maps were used by viewers who were engaged in 'reading' them, and who located themselves in relation to both the map and the world. Today, however, place is represented not by a coordinate system but rather the system's coordinates, which automatically position the viewer in relation to the data.[22] This re-introduction of the specific into the genre of the map is not only because Google Maps and other mapping systems turn our spaces of imagination into a concrete, unique, and physically precise place.

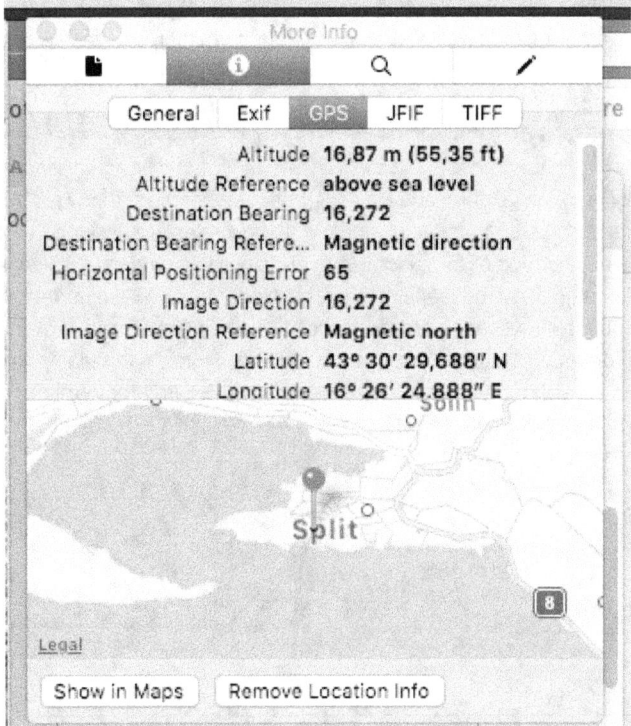

Figure 21: GPS information in photography (screenshot).

22   McKenzie Wark, *Molecular Red: Theory for the Anthropocene*, London: Verso, 2015.

As a consequence of the Geographic Information System, at least according to Alberto Toscano and Jeff Kinkle, local placement has become privileged over general picture in the post-digital era.[23] When using such geoprocessing, such as with the free-to-use and easily accessible proprietary web application Google Maps, the user becomes caught up in a passive logic within a system that self-organizes around them while allowing only a portion of the Earth to be visible. We use devices to locate ourselves in maps and photographs which are taken not from a human perspective down on Earth but from an eye-in-the-sky perspective up in the air. In so doing, however, they deprive us from the process of placing ourselves in the larger geographic area, which we would need in order to understand the geographic specification, as we are being placed by the system, not our own action of the navigation.

While conveying a great deal of information, becoming total, all information are situated and particular around placement of the user loosing insight into a total image. Geo-positioning triangulation, aerial photography, and images of outer space have all lead to a cartography which is far from the ground, producing total images, while simultaneously tracking the user.[24] Contemporary geographic imaging and representing technologies, contrary to drawings on palms of pilots, may pinpoint our location in a map, by the use of the global navigation satellite system (GNSS), global positioning system (GPS), and geographic information systems (GIS) which together provide geolocation and time information to a receiver anywhere on or near the Earth.

Tagging Landscapes

With each new technological means for geographic abstraction, the ways in which we represent space and place changes substantially, as new roles are assigned to the landscape and its parts which serve not to depict but to classify. New modes of visual representation, when applied in map and landscape making, have changed how we understand our habitat as well. These days, landscapes are highly coded with linguistic and symbolic information. Geographic information systems, designed to capture, store, manipulate, analyze, manage, and present spatial and geographic data, also allow users to create interactive queries to analyze spatial information, edit data in maps, and present the results of these operations, adding non-geographical data to place.[25]

23   Toscano and Kinkle, *Cartographies of the Absolute.*
24   Antoni Moore and Igor Drecki, *Geospatial Visualisation,* Berlin, Springer, 2011.
25   K.C. Clarke, 'Advances in Geographic Information Systems', *Computers, Environment and Urban Systems* Vol. 10 (1986): 175–184; V. Maliene, V. Grigonis, V. Palevi ius, and S. Griffiths, 'Geographic information system: Old principles with new capabilities' *Urban Design International.* 16.1 (2011): 1-6; Goodchild, 'Twenty years of progress: GIScience in 2010'.

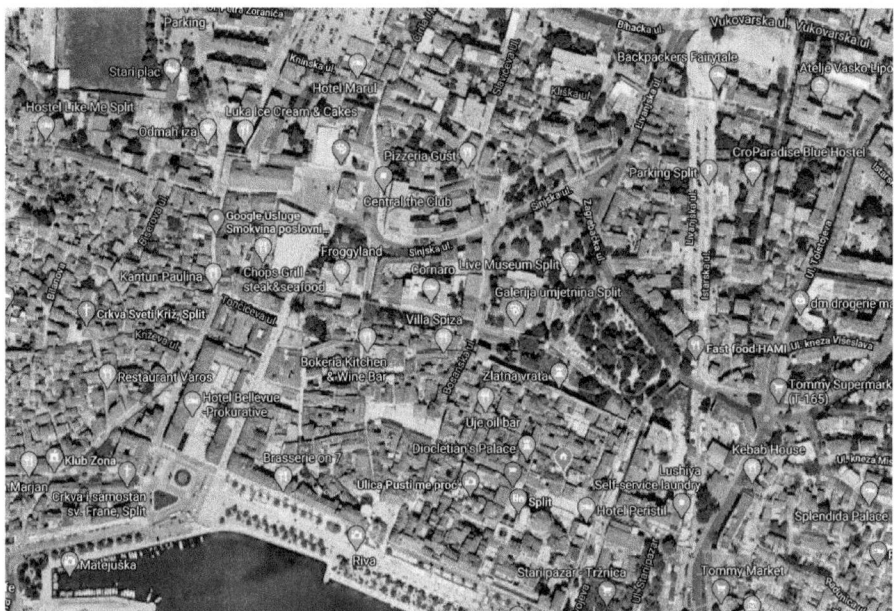

Figure 22: Hyperimage with place tags (screenshot).

Since of now, turning them into complex image-text collages. Name-tags are attached to photographs, making them complex collages. Such place names or toponyms, according to Matthew Johnson, 'continue to be an invaluable source of information, particularly in the topographical information they provide,' as it is possible to reconstruct ideas, narratives, purposes and values a society that made a certain map, out of the toponymic names on the map.[26] Mapping over a photograph is often even accompanied by crowdsourced data tagging, with crowd tagging and over-tagging. Using the navigation feature in the Google Maps application, a user of the map now moves through a dynamic system of explanation, rather than simply wandering the streets of a city or the hills of a wood in search of a place. These practices of naming and renaming are interesting because they indicate the specific meanings which become attached to the places on a map.[27] Crowd-sourced name-places are also available as GIS tools on platforms.[28] A number of users can crowd-name the same location producing a cacophony. So, for the artwork *The City Formerly Known as Cambridge* (2008), the artist Catherine d'Ignazio (known as kanarinka) held a series of thirteen events in which she invited members of the public to rename the public spaces in the city of Cambridge, Massachusetts, collecting over 300 new names for crowd-sourced maps.[29]

---

26   Matthew Johnson, *Ideas of Landscape,* Oxford: Blackwell Publishing, 2007, 142.
27   Growing with contemporary age, see 'Geonames', https://www.geonames.org/. Geonames contains nearly nine million toponyms. Besides historical and geographical analysis, also a comparative linguistic analysis is possible.
28   'Openstreet Map:', https://www.openstreetmap.org/.
29   Kanarinka, 'The City Formerly Known as Cambridge', http://www.kanarinka.com/project/the-city-formerly-known-as-cambridge/kanarinka. 'The City Formerly Known as Cambridge is a useless map by

Neither Maps nor Photographs

The post-digital age has lead to more interactive maps, bringing with it different kinds of interactivity and user-orientation, such as the browseability of fixed maps (while at the same it is possible for users to navigate aerial or street-view photographs as well). In the post-digital era, thus, map and landscape are merged as data are introduced into another map. Moreover, different types of maps are merged with the landscape, which carry not only information on place and space, but also spatially organized information, as geo-positioning and geolocation which effectively maps the user.[30] By merging landscapes and maps, precise places with spaces, and direct visions with visualizations, all previously strictly divided spatial descriptions are merged, and in a way – confused. Qualities of two previously separate genres fuse, and in a way mutually contaminate.

Fusing together this enormous amount of data, some of which are also maps, the medium as photography loses its vagueness, by which something that necessary exists is not the place we necessary recognize. Being precise and deictic, photographs are obliged to represent and lose the artistic vagueness characteristic for the medium. Among such data, geo-mapped photographs play a large deal, as they are simultaneously while used for mapping the road, used for targeting and evading the privacy. Today, most photographically based images are automatically encoded with location data. Maps situate photography in place which can be tracked and found. Today most of the cameras automatically precise the place via GPS, while GIS mapping can be introduced to mobile phones, already traced by satellites. Once set on the network such images directly produce data that can be used in order to engage many actions, even the complicated ones of satellite tracing.[31] Such new total images connect the devices to the internet, even acquiring an Internet Protocol (IP) address, and with direct implementation of GPS and GIS technologies, superimpose traceability of to ordinary human visual control.

Along with GPS features, both photographs and maps are incorporated into new location and tracking devices. With GIS technology maps are not general anymore, but user-orientated and situated, while with GIS and GPS data in photographs, we are precisely placed in space. Visualization of maps destroyed the original vision of evidence in photograph. At the same time maps started mapping users, not the territory. Simultaneously, with implementation of new location technologies maps become localized, losing their stabile general purpose, as being organized around dynamic directions, itineraries, or routes, which refer to only a section of the map. It is the map that mocks the viewer showing something that can never be seen. To the other hand, introducing location technologies into images produces a new sense of the targeting. What changes in particular with maps, is - their visuality and it is two parallel tendencies that mark the development: the de-visualization of maps, as tools of visualization by their change into systems that self-organizes around the act of use, rather than being visually constantly present and absorption of photographs into yet one of the layers of maps. A map is not only sequenced and de-visualized in its peculiar abstract sense. While map

---

      the Institute for Infinitely Small Things. Michael, *GeoHumanities*.

30   Susan Sontag, *On Photography*, London: Penguin Books, 1978.

31   Also Yahoo Maps, OpenStreetMap, Bing Live Map.

becomes a hypermap, containing many strata of information as layers, landscape produces a place into a hyper-place, merging various visual information.

Still, by merging with maps, photographs which were standing for particular yet usually not necessarily known places to the audience become very precise, geo-mapped places. Now, with the merge between photograph and map, these hybrid forms teeter between realism and abstraction. They are again, as Peutinger's map, neither-map-nor-landscape, and thus also; neither real-nor abstract. Yet, the problem of mixture is not in its vagueness, but for forms that cannot be easily defined.

Strict division between map and landscape, which has existed for over two thousand years, has all but vanished under these new geographies. Yet, despite the introduction of aerial photography and digital maps, bringing once split reality closer, especially by dataification, the divide between the map and landscape persist. With Google Earth Engine, for example, the divide between the map and landscape is still profound and applied to different projects, Google Maps and Google Earth, respectively.[32] While allows the viewer to sliding aside the orthogonal view for about five degrees, which maintains maintaining fixed shadows, allowing travel through streets, and 360-degree view, Google Maps combines flattened abstract street organization with Google Earth satellite image, as well as photographs uploaded by the user community. While these image genres have been partially integrated with new techniques for visually representing the world we live in, this has changed the way we use maps and landscapes as well.[33] To have a view that is cartographic and realistic the user must change layers or switch the platform in toto.

Double Coding

Bringing formally together far and close, map and landscape, space and place, contemporary technologies are diminishing clarity of binaries, often organizing human systems of thought. Thus, simultaneously as diminishing differences in the geographical binary, the new amalgamation leads to the same effect in visual and socio-political ones. A double coding occurs in new genres of images which are neither maps nor landscapes but a kind of coded text. This double coding may be analyzed using nine parameters set forth by Katherine Hayles for describing the differences between printed and coded texts.[34] First, coded texts are dynamic images. Second, they include both analogue and digital coding. And thus coded texts simultaneously include coded as well as natural languages. Consequently, third, they are not fixed, but mutable and transformable. Thus, fourth, they are generated through the fragmentation and recombination. Fifth, coded texts operate in three dimensions. And therefore, sixth, they are spaces to navigate. Seventh, they are written and are read in distributed cognitive environments and can be read only by cyborgs. Eight, 'with digital texts, the fragmentation is

---

32   'Google Earth Engine', https://earthengine.google.com.
33   When GIS become integrative, thus linking to sources such as Wikipedia.
34   Katherine Hayles, 'Print Is Flat, Code Is Deep: The Importance of Media-specific Analysis', *The Poetics Today* 25.1 (2004): 67-90.

deeper, more pervasive, and more extreme than with the alphanumeric character of print'.[35] And, in such a way, ninth, this information can be easier to manipulate. This shift between the printed and coded texts can also be applied to visual material, for instance, to the landscape and a map, but also to all of their potential layers of digitalization, such as analogue or digital maps as well as analogue or digital photographic landscapes.

Digital maps, which are more complex than analogue printed maps because they contain more information, in so far as the information which they contain is interactive and transforms according to the needs of the user, are also doubly coded: once by the computer and once by the user. Because of this double coding, and the consequent transformability of the map, the map can be manipulated. And the interpretation of digital maps becomes particularly tricky when photographic materials are employed in their production, given the epistemic power of such photographs. Although analogue photographs are not originally coded in the same way that digital photographs are, neither consists of the same kinds of discreet elements that both the language alphabet and cartographic symbols do, Hayles calls iconographic as bearing 'morphological resemblance to its referent', once fragmented, can be employed as a material in various manipulations too.[36] Likewise maps, in contrast to analogue photography, digital photography is discreet, consisting of equal basic elements, which are then computable. The pixel is the simplest metrical element. Because of this, large constellations of pixel structures may be more easily traced by photogrammetric software merging images. The merging of complex data does not just merge photographs and maps, but at certain stages in the process fuses them, using these as building material for a precise three-dimensional reality. Ultimately, of course, such digital photographs may still be printed on paper, as has been done with analogue photographs for nearly two centuries now. But having been reworked and distorted, even these photographs fail to provide a direct and undisturbed relation to the reality.

Manipulations Hayles mentions for texts also are applicable to photographs, as for example in photomontage. Photo montaged images are traceable in the analogue world, but less visible in the digital one. The initial coding of the photography has been set by aerial images, which tended to simulate a mapping view. Moreover, once merged with maps, photographs are not only as digital, but also as maps, becoming more complex systems. Such a double coding happens in all the cases where photographs are merged with maps, as in hypermaps, photomaps, orthophotos, and mapped photographs, I will analyze in the next chapter.

Post-digital aerial and satellite photography is not exclusively a photographic medium. Here, the photograph is but one layer of many. Or it is merely a visual style for the image. Whether part of the hypermap, orthomap, or photomap, the photograph is given a secondary role and value. It has lost its representative function. It has become a coded system. Even so, however, in comparison the visualizations of large datasets, photography fails to be authentically 'deep' in terms of an amount of information carried by it (if deep is to be taken as the authentic criteria of this age, as in deep space). Or, its 'depth' may consist of a mere resolution enlargement (such is the one in high resolution photography). These images display an enormous amount

---

35   Hayles, *Print is Flat*, 77.
36   Hayles, *Print is flat*.

of information, as well as offering both close and distant views and far breaking the barrier of the human vision. Besides, they are breaking the boundary of the human photography as offering the near and far, which was previously dividing the tele and macro photography.[37]

---

37   As the resolution of images constantly changes, the image with the highest resolution is a breakable border. At this point, in early 2019, the highest resolution recorded is the image of Mont Blanc, recorded in 365 giga pixels.

CHAPTER 6: COMPUTING PHOTOGRAPHS AND MAPS

Datascapes

Qualities of maps and landscapes have somewhat interchanged. Previously uncoded, landscapes have also become coded, carrying various types of information, not belonging to the realistic view, as landmarks, name-tags and various measures. Both landscapes and maps are today carrying a growing amount of data, in different layers. One could say that the landscape and map when placed together has become a datascape, in terms both of machine vision and data visualization. None of them are concrete but can also be just a set of data. Some of these Arjun Appadurai defined as 'five dimensions of global cultural flows that can be termed (a) ethnoscapes, (b) mediascapes, (c) technoscapes, (d) financescapes, and (e) ideoscapes'.[1] Each of them refers to a different type of the abstract landscape forming a context of life; habits, media, finances and ideology. Contemporary studies of such datascapes underline that data is not that distinct from the vision, although there is a substantial difference between processes of visualization and vision. As Steve F. Anderson notes, there is no longer a great difference between data and vision, capturing and looking.[2]

Like with the mappae mundi of medieval Europe described before, today's imaging technologies are used to compute, assemble, and overlap a variety of information into a single image. Consisting of many layers, they do not have any fixed visual layout, but are an abstract dataset, adapting to the user. Some of these layers, indeed, may be visually descriptive, as landscapes once were, especially when photography is being applied onto maps. Yet, new spatial data is not fully, but only partially visible. While being complex and inclusive, new total images of maps are merely possibly visible by the act of using of the map, or the act by which the map automatically maps the user, even without their knowledge. And moreover, the part of the set appears as invisible, thus counting more precise placement of the person in terms of relative distance to satellites, or by using GPS technologies, there is no need for visualization of the abstract space of the map. Thus, contrary to previous conceptions, today it is the general sense of the space that is lost, as the space becomes an aggregation of geographical or conceptual data.

Montaging Techniques

The combining of various materials in order to make a photo-like image is not a post-digital invention. Indeed, photomontage techniques, where the photographer combined several photographs into one, are as old as photographic technology itself. At first, the reason to produce such montages lay in the limitations of the photographic medium. The problem of slow

1   Arjun Appadurai, *Modernity at Large: Cultural Dimensions of Globalization* (Public Worlds, Vol. 1),
     Minneapolis: University of Minnesota Press, 1996, 33.
2   Steve F. Anderson, *Technologies of Vision: The War between Data and Images*, Cambridge, MA: MIT
     Press, 2017.

exposure time, for example, made it impossible to simultaneously produce images of the land and accompanying sky. In the late 19th century, photographers such as Oscar Rejlander and Henry Peach Robinson would combine several photographic negatives in order to produce one compact visual artefact in positive.[3] Results, overall, were consistent. Aside from combining negatives, photographers also used a number of post-production methods, such as retouch, shading, and tinting. Nevertheless, the merits of photomontage were often debated and criticized for distorting the truth claim of the photographic medium. And an idealistic duel between Realists and Pictorialists, who denied the obligatory realism of photography, marked the 19th century discussion about photography.[4] Photomontage was thus seen by many historians as a pictorial tool which destroyed the epistemic nature of photography, and made out of it yet another device for rhetoric and other literary figurations.

Geographic photomontage was used for the epistemic purpose of describing space. This contrasted with the deliberate use of photomontage for either rhetoric argument or poetical parable, as with the Pictorialists, or the use of this technique for political activism, as with Modernists such as John Hartfield, Hannah Höch, and others.[5] Such spatial descriptions were also amplified, as Rudolf Arnheim writes: 'The simple example of this innovation is the photomontage, which juxtaposes fragments of totally different spatial systems. The sizes of various pictorial objects can no longer be compared within the represented space'.[6] Yet not all photomontages led to impossible or unnatural descriptions of space. Some afforded great accuracy. And in the geographic information science of today, photomontage served the purpose of acquiring knowledge, not necessarily about reality itself, but rather about data and its many potential re-interpretations.

Proto-computational Methods

The oldest compositional method used to merge or, in a sense, compute photographs, is the panorama. Underlying the process of production of the panoramic image was the idea of seeing without being seen. In general, the object of ordinary panorama showed landscape and some portion of the sky. In the 19th century, the photographic imagination culminated with the innovation of the extended horizontal image of the panorama, which in the beginning were produced by painting and later photographically. The panorama evolved at the very moment that interest in landscape painting was slowly starting to fade away until finally, with the invention of the reproductive medium of photography, the landscape as an artistic and

3   See for example Henry Peach Robinson's *Figures in Landscape*, Gelligynan Series (photomontages), 1880.
4   See: Dawn Ades, *Photomontage*, London: Thames and Hudson, 1976; Robert Sobieszek, 'Composite Imagery and the Origins of Photomontage, Part I: The Naturalistic Strain', *Artforum* 17.1 (1978): 58-65; Robert Sobieszek, 'Composite Imagery and the Origins of Photomontage, Part I: The Formalist Strain', *Artforum* 16.2 (1978), 41-43; Richard Hiepe and C. A. Haenlein, *Dada: Photographie und Photocollage*, Hannover: Kestner-Gesellschaft, 1979.
5   See: Kristin Makholm, 'Strange Beauty: Hannah Höch and the Photomontage', *MOMA* 24 (1997): 19-23; John Heartfield, 'Photomontages of the Nazi Period', London: Gordon Fraser Gallery & Universe Books, 1977; Magdalena Dabrowski, 'Photomonteur: John Heartfield', *MOMA* 13 (1993): 12-15; Ades, *Photomontage*.
6   Rudolf Arnheim, 'Inverted Perspective in Art: Display and Expression', *Leonardo* 5.2 (1972): 125-135.

image genre was relegated to the amusements and crazes of the wealthy and elite.[7] Across the 19th century, panoramas became extremely popular, and many different panoramic forms were invented.[8] By 1870, the panorama and its variants were being mass produced and toured all over Europe. Audiences for the panorama, which at the time either remained largely in one place or had little experience travelling, even to nearby cities or to other places within their own home city, were fascinated by the way other places looked.[9] Indeed, as Walter Benjamin wrote, 'The interest of the panorama is in seeing the true city-the city indoors.'[10] He also noted:

> Just as architecture, with the first appearance of iron construction, begins to outgrow art, so does painting, in its turn, with the first appearance of the panoramas. The high point in the diffusion of panoramas coincides with the introduction of arcades. One sought tirelessly, through technical devices, to make panoramas the scenes of a perfect imitation of nature.[11]

At this historical moment, the emancipated masses of emerging societies had started to appropriate and recycle image genres that had long been reserved for the upper classes, producing from them a new kind of culture, a culture today known as popular culture. Panoramic images would eventually become a form of mass entertainment. But in those cases in which the panorama represented historical and archeological sites, its topographical and geographical aesthetic is undeniable, and it served to educate a population which, at that time, was still predominantly stationary in their habitat.[12]

With most early panoramic devices, a wide-angle view was achieved not by the audience moving their gaze in relation to the image, but by moving the image itself within the exhibition venue. Another type of moving panorama dates to the last few decades of the 18th century. Such a panorama was one of the first image genres to afford immersion within a total image. This immersion worked in one of several ways: either by moving the image mounted onto a panel around the audience, or by moving the audience standing on a stage inside the image.[13]

---

7   As Walter Benjamin described and categorized: 'There were panoramas, dioramas, cosmoramas, diaphanoramas, navaloramas, pleoramas, fantoscope, fantasma-parastases, phantasmagorical and fantasmaparastatic experiences, picturesque journeys in a room, georamas; optical picturesques, cineoramas, phanoramas, stereoramas, cycloramas, panorama dramatique'. Walter Benjamin, *The Arcades Project,* trans. Howard Eliand, Cambridge: Harvard University, Belknap Press, 2002, 527.

8   There were also a great number of more or less successful products which had to do with the original wide-scene view, such as the diorama, neoreama, cyclorama, eidophisikon, cosmorama, nahrama, phosporama, kineorama, myorama, sensorama, pleorama, mareorama, and more.

9   See Paul Mellon Sawyer, 'Panorama as a Global Landscape', *YouTube,* https://www.youtube.com/watch?v=ldLvpyoby-g.

10   Benjamin, Arcades Project, 532.

11   Benjamin, *The Arcades Project,* 5. Moreover, one of Parisian arcades is actually called the Panorama.

12   More on history of panorama: see Erkki Huhtamo, *Illusions in Motion: Media archaeology of the moving panorama and related spectacles,* Cambridge, MA: MIT Press, 2018; Oliver Grau, *Virtual Art: From illusion to immersion,* Cambridge, MA: MIT Press, 2003. See also: Wurzer, *Panorama.*

13   Type of latter panorama in which the public is freely moving is quite near the effect of the virtual reality. As Grau notes, distances are assumed rather than experienced, blurring the relationship between the image and real space, as naturally filling the observer's field of vision. Grau, *Virtual Art.*

These immersive techniques from panoramic photography would have a profound influence on later visual culture. In fact, the panorama anticipated virtual reality in one key respect: enlarging what is visible but doing so at a cost to the depth of the image. Because panoramic photography followed from the painted panorama, the image was made in a certain way. Firstly, the photographer rotated the camera around, with their own self as the axis, like the center point of a circle or semicircle, while photographing the world not which they might see at first glance, but which they saw while pivoting. Secondly, the full size of the objects in view were recorded within the picture plane. Objects were not visually cut. Thus, multiple images could be merged together more easily. And thirdly, the panoramic photograph had no central focus, distinguishing it from landscape painting, which may be created from a single vantage point.

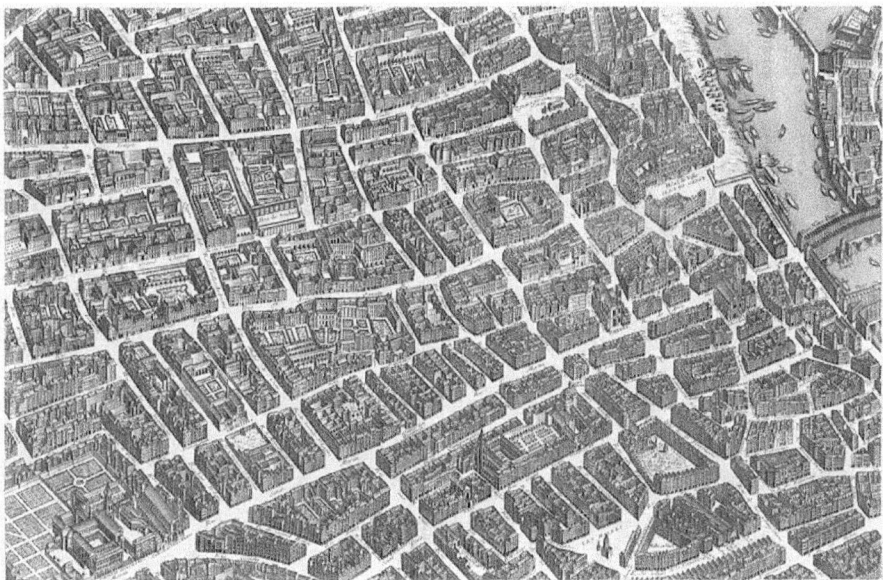

Figure 23: Turgot map of Paris.

With a panorama, the photographer described the space through a fluxing perspective, in contrast to the fixed perspective of the Renaissance. This movement introduced a cinematic experience to the experience of the photographic image which, at the same time, maintaining its frozen reality. There are a number of ways for a photographer or photographers to create such an image. Of course, these are besides pivoting on one's feet while taking the shot, as one might when using the 'pano' function of a smart phone camera today. According to Rob Towley, these panoramic techniques include: tiled constructions, planimetric, and diagrammatic, peripheral or rollout photography, and topological photography.[14] And each of these served a different purpose. In addition to these various ways of recording a panorama, there are also several ways to create overlapping images, such as the stereographic overlap (in which images are set in proximity to each other in order to construct the illusion

14   Rob Tovey, 'Photomaps: A Visual Taxonomy', *Visual Communication*, 17.2 (2018): 209-220.

of dimensionality) and sidelap or lateral overlap (in which images are placed one next to another).[15] While not yet computational, all of these techniques can be understood to be proto-computational method, advancing the consequential image scanning, as sectioning the image in equal sub-sections.[16]

Of these panoramic techniques, tiled constructions appear as complex panoramic images, while panoramas merge images in one row, tiled constructions do it in more. With a plani-metric image, the image is recorded via the strategic movement of the camera from the left to the right side, much like as with a scanner for a computer. With a diagrammatic image, on the other hand, the image is recorded through multiple perspective views to construct a flat diagram, which can produce quite a confusing effect, similar to the paintings of Cubism in the early 20th century. Each of these techniques may be applied for different purposes or to various extents. Aerial photographs, for example, consist of organized tiles of joined images. Photogrammetric images, in contrast, consist of a complex system of images which are merged one to another to make a three-dimensional object. Such photographs do not necessarily need to be photographed systematically, using neutral settings, or the same lenses. Rather, with the aid of computational photography and even artificial intelligence, diverse photographs can also be merged from archived sources of varying age and quality. For example, Bundler, software program written by Noah Snavely, is a structure-from-motion (SfM) system for unordered image collections, such as images from the Internet. It 'takes a set of images, image features, and image matches as input, and produces a 3D reconstruction of camera and scene geometry as output'.[17]

	MAP	PHOTO
MAP	Hypermap	Orthophoto
PHOTO	Photomap	'Deep photo'

Table 5: Provisory explanation of variants between photographs and maps.

---

15 When using stereographic, the parallax is 5-10 degrees, while with lateral overlap it must be larger, up to 30%.
16 Similarly, photogrammetric techniques may also be used to produce an objective viewpoint and obtain reliable information about physical objects and the environment. In photogrammetry, the photographer or photographic system fuses images together in order to produce a third dimension by employing several movements of recording: from up to down, meander (from outer to inner, in order not to step in), snake-shape (left-right and then rightst-left), and from distant to close. The recorded data is then assembled in alignment with how its author may choose to visualize the object, rather than how the object appears to vision.
17 'Bundler', https://www.cs.cornell.edu/~snavely/bundler/.

Orthophotos

Another way of computing images is to correct photographs according to or along with another visual, non-photographic material. Among the most known of such corrective computational or pre-computational photographic techniques is the orthophoto. An orthophoto is a 'planimetrically accurate photo image', or an image which functions like a map. And it can be used to visually depict the planet Earth in a way similar to using a camera with a telephoto lens and images which have been taken from an altitude or distance from the surface of the Earth of 45,000 km.[18] As such, it was not possible to record an orthophoto until the innovation of flying machines in the early 20th century.

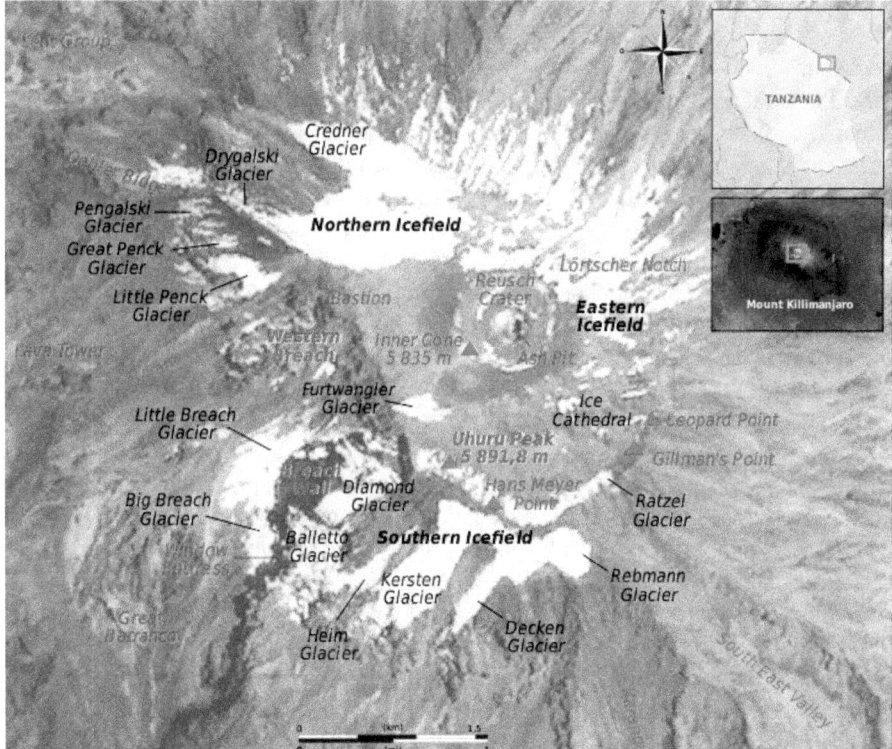

Figure 24: Geodaten Bayern, Orthophoto of Augsburg, 2012.

In contrast to panoramic photographs, which are recorded as a series of horizontal images, orthophotos are correcting photograph via orthographic projection, where all of the projection lines are perpendicular to the projection plane, in order to represent three-dimensional objects in two-dimensional space. Because this photographic image aligns with a map projection, it may be utilized to measure the true distances between features. Orthophotos do not indicate

18   The minimal distance to record the full image of the Earth is 35,786 kilometers.

a distance between the object and the subject as active perception, as there is no subject angle by which a distance can be metered, but depicts only distances on the surface of the image itself, standing for real place distances. Such an orthophotographic view is planimetric, in that it extracts only the horizontal position of features on the Earth's surface, and reveals these geographic objects, natural and cultural physical features, and other entities independent of elevation. Thus, orthophotographic techniques are used to correct the curvature of the Earth on a flat map.

Since the earliest beginnings of aerial photography, as described in Chapter 2, various mechanisms and methods have been used to correct the subjective human view with objective computational views. Aside from early efforts by Nadar and Batut, the first endeavor to automate orthophotography was in the 1920s. This coincided with several key innovations in cartography, including the stereo comparator, auto-stereography, auto-cartography, and aero-cartography. The first orthophotographic images were produced by 1931 by Otto Lacman, the author of a treatise on orthophotography.[19] But only after World War II was the orthophotoscope constructed, a 'photomechanical or optical-electronic device that creates an orthophotograph by removing geometric and relief distortion'.[20] Meanwhile, more and more photographic images were being geometrically corrected or 'ortho-rectified' so that the scale of the photograph would be uniform. Soon after, a matching projector, call an orthoprojector, was invented to assist in the production of accurate orthogonal projection. And the first such map to be converted from a photograph was taken in 1960, a map of the Union of Soviet Socialist Republics (USSR), which at that point presented a selection of the whole.[21] Most orthophotos today are made by using large-size cameras.[22]

Photomaps and Photorealist Maps

Orthophotographs made from photographic images can reference the Earth with greater accuracy than maps based on graphic prints could in the past. Yet, due to the intervention of computational processes, digital orthophotos (DOP) mask their origins in photographs while still retaining this realistic effect. Photomaps, in contrast, are actual cartographic products made on the basis of a photographic preparation. Photomaps have been produced for a long time. In the 19th and even 20th centuries, with the beginning of experiments in combining maps and photographs, photographic images would be covered with a thin sheet of paper and geographical lines would be traced over them. Later, such lines were carved directly into the material upon which the photograph was mounted. Then, the entire construct, photograph, map, and all, would be re-photographed in order to produce a new image. Today, however, a special kind of film is required to make a photomap, a type of film which is having equal

---

19   Otto Lacman, *Equalizer for non-flat terrain. Image measurement and aerial photography*, 1931, 10-12.
20   Definition of orthophotoscope from ESRI, https://support.esri.com/en/other-resources/gis-dictionary/term/d307b618-60b9-4efc-9afc-9c47918e54b4. Overlapping photographs scanned for the overlap, area is sequenced into smaller sections which are scaled.
21   Cartography in the USSR was so well developed as a field that they released maps of the entire world soon after the first orthophoto was taken. See: https://www.nationalgeographic.com/news/2017/10/maps-soviet-union-ussr-military-secret-mapping-spies/.
22   Cameras used today can record up to 450 megapixels in single shot.

density, so that lines can gradually be separated out according to scale. Usually such film is combined with reversal film, which can be used for large projections, recording the same images on both.

In addition to orthophotos and photomaps, there are also photographs which encompass some elements from map making, such as place or name tags, topographic borders or marks, or other geographic information. These photorealistic maps look more truthful and trustworthy than do photomaps, more objective, even like they are not coded, because of the seductive effect of the photographic image. However, here the photograph is also just a layer in a more complex system. And some photorealistic maps also have amplified elements, such as color or shape, which further distinguish them from photographs.

Hypermaps

Beyond the orthophoto, photomap, and photorealist map, all of which to some extent de-photographise some photographically recorded reality by diminishing the indexical or realistic effect of the photograph, there are other ways of preserving the post-digital photograph as an authentic carrier of geographical information. One such way is the hypermap. Hypermaps are systems of images which include many layers of information, some or none of which may be photographic in nature.[23] Viewers or users of a hypermap can therefore zoom into different areas of space or layers of information, which may connect to place-tags or other geo-information, a large amount of data which enhances the user's search return through a 'hypergeo model'.

Hypermaps are a hybrid between photograph and map which gain layers of information because of how they fuse these several kinds of mediation together. But hypermaps also loose information from these various media forms, including the indexicality of the photograph, as well as the precision of the map. This loss is most significant in relation to photography, because the photograph has to be corrected in order to simulate the flat, two-dimensional visual space of the map. Indeed, only the 'realistic effect' remains from the photograph in a hypermap which, according Rob Tovey, may be present in cartographic, scanned, diagrammatic, peripheral, and topological information.[24] Here, the vision and mediation of the photographic eye is combined with the visualization and abstraction of the cartographic gaze. But this simultaneity between photographic techniques and map making contaminates the overall epistemic value of the hypermap.

One of the most important kinds of information that is lost in this process of hybridization is the subjectivity of the author. In a hypermap, photographs are computed and merged in order to achieve a non-subjective view. Hypermaps and their depiction of absolute space erase the presence of the subject by failing to provide the viewer with any immediate information about the point of view of the image author. Moreover, the hypermap describes everything but the

23   Menno-Jan Kraak and Rico Van Driel, 'Principles of Hypermaps', *Computers & Geosciences* 23.4 (1997): 457-464.
24   Rob Tovey, 'Photomaps: A visual Taxonomy', *Visual Communication* 17.2 (2018): 1-12.

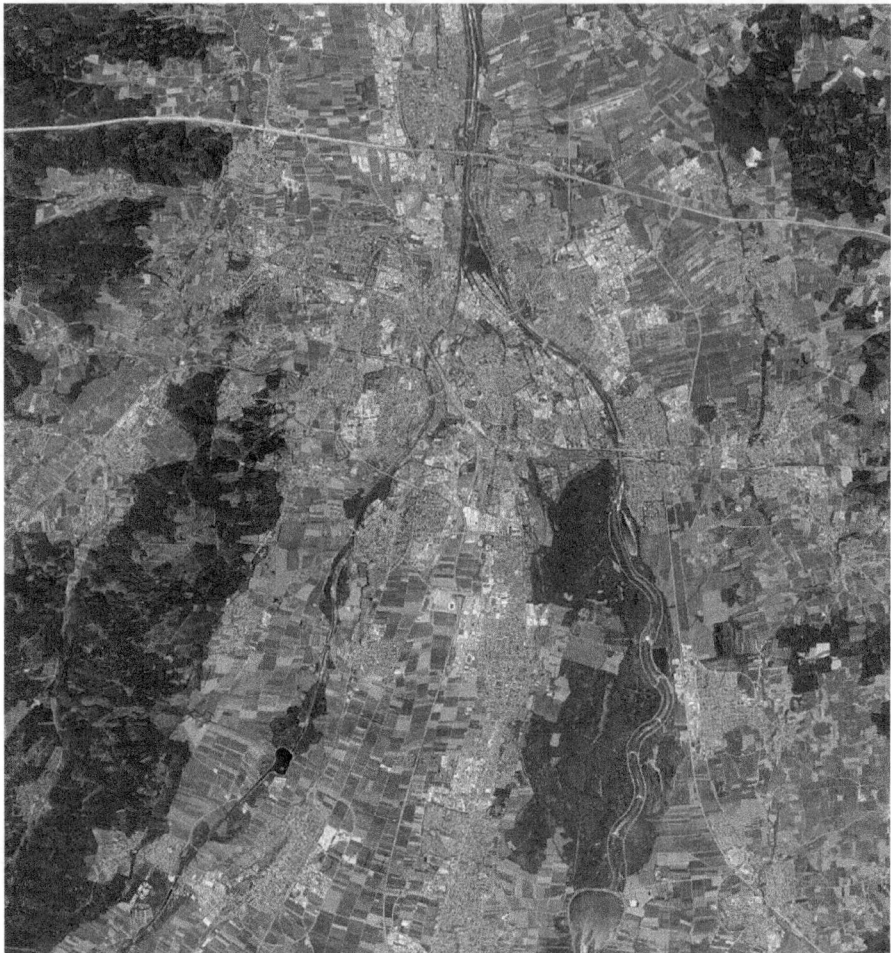

Figure 25: Mount Kilimanjaro Summit photomap.

subject, either by re-distributing the subject through the act of use, or by describing only the world around the subject, as if the total image is a donut and the subject is its absent hole.

'Deep Photo'

In addition to hypermaps, as well as other possible combinations of maps and photographs, there are systems which can be used to merge various layers of photographically-based imaging into a single view. These deep photographs are a kind of 'complex image', including more data than what is seen at the first place, to employ a concept by Oliver Grau.[25] And while not as axiomatic or transparent as basic photography, deep photos can in fact be

---

25   Oliver Grau, 'Images (R)-Evolution: Media Arts Complex Imagery Challenging Humanities and Our
      Institutions of Cultural Memory', *Leonardo Electronic Almanach* 20.2 (2014): 72-86.

used to attain an even greater degree of veracity in the objective depiction of reality. This is because the very process which is involved in creating such a total image eliminates the role of the subjective and thus interpretative. These images are recorded systematically and with precision. In many cases, they describe reality by measuring it rather than interpreting it. And this, in turn, supports more objective meanings.

Deep photography has many currently emerging subtypes. However, the categories for these are not yet stable enough for them to be distinguished as genres. In metrophotography and photogrammetry, however, various layers of information are embedded, such that they can be classified as a type of deep photography.[26] Perhaps the most significant characteristic of the deep photo is that it has a resolution far beyond that which naked human vision can itself be capable of achieving. Deep photos are merged from big data which has a photographic origin. So they have far more detail and description than ordinary photographs. For example, the largest deep photograph made by a single artist to date is *Mont Blanc Under Snow* by Filippo Blengini.[27] This 365-gigapixel assembly is made out of 70,000 individual photographs. The image offers the viewer a detailed close-up with better image quality than with those images taken by satellite.[28] With the previous record holder for 'largest image,' a 360-degree panorama of the city of London recorded from BT Tower, it is possible to see almost every house within the line of sight, but from a low oblique view.[29] For the low oblique, the camera has depression angle of about 60 degrees, showing only a relatively small area of the surface of the Earth, in perspective that is neither fully aerial nor landed human.

Among other methods of image computation and merging with non-photographic materials, deep photographs can also be made by overlapping the very same frame recorded across three or more different exposures. This process is usually known as bracketing. Through bracketing, the photographer repeatedly shoots the same visual scene, and with each shot alters the parameters of the exposure, such as white balance, or some other parameter. By so doing, the depth of field, exposure details, and contrast relationships may be manipulated. The recorded images, which are usually made with a camera fixed upon a tripod in order to stabilize the long exposure times which provide greater detail, are then superimposed over and under one another as layers within the same image. This produces an evenly sharp image that would otherwise be impossible to record. In addition, by taking multiple exposures, the photographer may choose those with the best quality, even without necessarily

---

26 Yet another form, which serves 3D construction metrophotography, or latter photogrammetry, being the latest of genres merging photographs with maps, are based on projective geometries, used in measurement of the architecture, while orthophoto merges analyses landscape in general. Rules for shooting images to be photogrammetrically. processed to have changed with the development of equipment, but in general they are recorded to be overlapped, in order of producing a higher precision.

27 Whereas the largest montaged image from multiple sources by this date is Pan Starrs, made out of 3 billion separate sources and in 2 petabyte size. See: https://www.ifa.hawaii.edu/info/press-releases/panstarrs_release/.

28 Recorded using a Canon 70D DSLR, a Canon EF 400mm f/2.8 II IS, and a Canon Extender 2X III on a special robotic mount.

29 This image consists of more than 48,000 images.

merging it with others. Such a practice was especially common in landscape and, most of all, architecture photography.

Today, this bracketing technique is an automated feature which is built into most if not all digital cameras, including the phone, tablet, and laptop cameras which are supported by high dynamic range (HDR) photography or Google Pixel. Bracketing can be used to alter more elements in an image than just the exposure and depth of field. Bracketing can be used to widen the field (such as in panoramic photography), change the image spectrum (multi-spectral images, a kind of hyper-photo), produce higher resolution (deep photography), create a parallax image (stereo-photography), and erase or generate objects (post-production). These are more or less the features of all so-called 'cognitive cameras', plenoptic cameras which through the programming of their functionality can be used to extract information out of an image sequence, rather than just conjoin images.[30] A plenoptic or light-field camera is defined by several key features and functions. Most essentially, it captures the light which emanates from a scene, including the intensity of light as well as the direction in which these light rays are travelling. This contrasts with other types of cameras, such as the analogue or digital camera, which primarily are defined by the medium with which they record, such as through a chemical process or onto a memory chip, respectively. Beyond this essential feature of light detection and tracking, the plenoptic camera has the same functionalities as other photographic cameras in terms of automatically producing a frozen image or sequence of images. And because the mechanism of such a camera works largely independently from human intervention, as with the loading and reloading film or the changing of settings, the time between taking pictures is shortened, which in turn leads to greater image stabilization (IS) and reduced blurring or noise. With the aid of plenoptic photography, an amateur photographer can produce images which appear as though they have been created by a professional photographer. In most digital single lens reflex (DSLR) cameras, images are computed on the micro, or data level, beyond either the vision or control of the camera user. Therefore, an amateur photographer often remains unaware of this process.

Today, post-digital photographs include a vast amount of photographic as well as non-photographic information which has been synthesized into a single visual artefact. Such artefacts cannot be seen all at once, which is certainly how photographs used to be perceived, but rather is user-directed in terms of which layer is looked at. In fact, the user creates the image through the very act of use, zooming in to see the narrow details, and zooming out as well as moving in various planar directions to see a wider picture. Such images are also compressed. And they have to be decoded or processed otherwise. For this reason, these photographs do not have a single meaning or message but a multitude of possible meanings and messages which are created by each user. It may be concluded, therefore, that the total image is a post-digital photograph which contains more visual data about some place than any single one viewer could naturally perceive on their own, whether in terms of the view angle of the camera or cameras, the wave-length of the light, or additional information such as maps, tags, and geolocations. Indeed, with the total image, we have entered into what Hito Steyerl

---

30   Jin-Li Suo, Xiangyang Ji, and Qionghai Dai 'An Overview of Computational Photography', *Science China Information Sciences* 55.6 (2012): 1229.

calls 'the age of post-representation' in which the world is simultaneously represented by many visual techniques.[31]

Dangerous Places and Comfortable Spaces

Commonly, images of the Earth or of the layers of its atmosphere which are taken from planes in the air can be photorealistic. But such images become more and more abstract when taken by satellites in space. As Bruno Latour notes: 'By looking at the satellite image we extract ourselves from our particular point of view, yet without, bouncing up to the bird's eye view; we have no access to the divine view, the view from nowhere'.[32] Different systems of coding and transmission are used with new technologies from radar to infra-vision. And the more the aerial view is coded, the less realistic is the image. Indeed, these new kinds of images do not at first sight appear to be as substantially coded as maps, because to one degree or another they still represent the Earth indexically, or at least with some factual connection, such as by incorporating aerial photographs. Even so, the overall lack of realism in such a total image, because it encompasses a view extended beyond that which the naked human eye could naturally perceive by using technology, in turn minimizes the viewers' obligatory relationship to the subject of the image. In erasing the place of the subject in the view, and thereby any possibility for the audience to relate to that subject, whether through abjectification or empathy, the total image becomes a symptom of the pathological forces in contemporary culture.[33] With everyday experience which is increasingly abstracted from the Earth through using and interaction with such images, whether you 'Choose Destination' or 'Explore Nearby' with Google Maps, or if you share where you are 'Traveling To' on Facebook, it becomes that much more difficult to connect with the concreteness of life. And this is the tragedy of such technological innovations as the deep photograph and computational methods.

With the innovation of aerial photography, it is the map that become real. But in turn, such photography also introduced an abstract vision, as abstracting from a human position. Reality, when perceived through several mapping tools, also becomes digital, James Bridle notes.[34] Today, the augmented or virtual space of maps which provides the user with an experience other than reality, in turn separates the user from the once-necessary process of verifying for themselves the reality which they perceive and navigate.[35]

The space in which we live today is a space which is computed, assembled, and multi-perspectival. Maps are no longer necessarily objective, because they are based on data, and at the moment in which a user views or interacts with the map, they are viewing or interacting with data this data that has already in some way gone through a process of selection and

31   Hito Steyerl, 'Digital Debris: Spam and Scam', *October* 138 (Fall, 2011): 70-80.
32   Bruno Latour and Emilie Hermant, 'Paris: Invisible City', Liz Carey-Libbrecht (trans.), 1998. http://www.bruno-latour.fr/sites/default/files/downloads/viii_paris-city-gb.pdf, 9. Section published as: Bruno Latour, 'Introduction: Paris – Invisible City: The Plasma', *Culture and Society*, Elsevier, 3.2 (2012), 91-93.
33   Dorrian and Poussin, *Seeing from Above.*
34   Bridle, *New Dark Age.*
35   Tim Mehigan, *Frameworks, Artworks, Place: The Space of Perception in the Modern World,* Rotterdam: Rodopi, 2008.

interpretation. As computed photographs and maps, once being closely tied to physical reality, have become yet another tool of visualisation, we have dived into virtual space. Neither
landscapes nor maps do necessarily mean a real place. They are not settled on one side
while reality on the other anymore, but everything is fully integrated inside the map, from
cars driving, over taxi services and apartment rentals, restaurant working hours. Both are
combining a part of material reality with the abstracted one. In many cases it is impossible
to split the cartographic reality from the geographical one.[36]

In parallel to a great precision of the place, a new generation of fully places that emancipated
from physical reality, such as virtual places are expanding our perception of the real space,
and overlapping with the real ones in many cases, changing their (also spatial) meanings, as
in augmented reality.[37] The world of today is a super-networked self-organizing datascape,
rather than a fixed reality. There are many interpretations of reality co-existing, each presented as a total and unique one. So, all images of it are distorted and our visual conception of
reality, by mapping it.

---

36   Bridle, New Dark Age.
37   Cosgrove, Social Formation and Symbolic Landscape, Cosgrove, Geography and Vision.

CHAPTER 7: PERSPECTIVAL LOSSES

Hyperimages are assembled from many computed and corrected photographs. Because of this, they lack any one specific point of view (POV) as well as angle of view (AOV) or field of view (FOV). In other words, the such images do not allow for the possibility of a subjective view. Rather, they are computed based on the differential parallax between stereoscopic pairs, or the apparent displacement of the position of an object, such as the Earth's surface, in respect to a reference point or system, when viewed from various positions of observation.

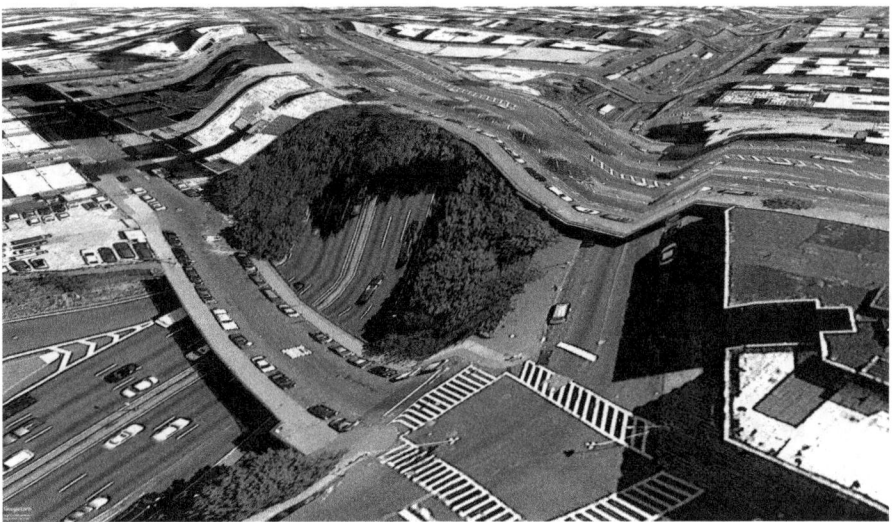

Figure 26: Clement Valla, Postcard from Google Earth - 40°50'41.94"N,73°54'42.33"W. *Courtesy of the artist.*

The combining of geographical and geological images, maps, and photographs is today mostly done automatically. Yet, problems arise from such computational techniques. Using artificial intelligence, many different and diverse images can be computed and combined into a total image. fuse can calculate and fuse many images to produce a map-alike imaging. Such AI-based software includes, for example, the NASA Ames Stereo Pipeline (ASP), which merges a large amount of satellite images; Skycatch, a drone image processing platform; and Altizure, a community for realistic 3D modelling; to name but a few.[1] Google Earth Engine also assembles together aerial photography, geological information system data, and satellite photography. Yet, problems arise from such computational techniques.

Machine vision, like human vision, has its own specific errors. What computer scientists call 'glitches' are often the result of some failure of a machine to execute the commands which we instruct it with, as machines have completely different way of operating than humans do.

---

1   'Stereopipeline', https://ti.arc.nasa.gov/tech/asr/groups/intelligent-robotics/ngt/stereo/; 'Skycatch', https://www.skycatch.com; 'Altizure', https://www.altizure.com

But artificial intelligence, because it is synthetic, does not automatically check for its own errors. Rather, AI can only detect errors in the imaging process through glitches in the image structure.[2] Clement Valla, an artist who catalogues errors in the computations of Google programs which combine different images, has demonstrated in his serial *Postcard from Google Earth*, how many such glitches may have certain visual features in common.[3] Valla's series of artworks embody what Keller Easterling once observed: that disruptions, dissensus, and discrepancy are all contradictions in the structure of space.[4] In Valla's art, Google's software is shown to have failed to recognize the pattern of a road or railway, building or bridge, having morphed such forms in accordance with the landscape. Therefore, Lawrence Bird concludes that:

> [I]t is not a coincidence that these images, which record elaborations and disruptions in the infrastructure of a city, also evince ruptures in its image. These images are sewn together by the machinery of Google Earth from multiple satellite images taken at different times.[5]

This total image is an image which is fractioned, segmented, sewn, and even partially invented. It does not form any unitary visual system. Or, as Angela Krewani writes, 'Google Earth disjoins the experience of a planet earth into fractured smithereens of planetary knowledge'.[6] Yet, it is not only that Google Earth which produces spatial deviations, but the employing photography without its original, linear perspective system. Computational photography, rather than serving as a tool for the analysis of space, actually produces a new category of space. This total image space exists independently of any given subject or subjective perception. And neither is it singular nor objective.

---

2   Facebook recently added software which is able to recognize deep fakes, which are created through a type of artificial intelligence called generative adversarial networks (GAN), by detecting glitches in these images of nonexistent people.

3   See, for example: Jessica Becking, 'Records of Representation: Clement Valla's Postcards from Google Earth', *Media Theory* 2.1 (2018): 307-315. Further, other artworks made using Google Earth demonstrate how the inspiration for representational art may include not only concrete reality, but also mediated supra-reality. A number of artists use visuals which are realistic, even indexical, from Google Earth. These artists include, for example, Benjamin Grant, who composes satellite abstractions on his blog and in his book *Overview*, as well as Mishka Henner. In the artworks of both of these artists, among others, the world retains its recognizable curvature but is flattened through the use of an aerial view angle. In contrast, Kenny Jacqui, whose artwork *The Agoraphobic Traveler* is based on capturing images from Google Street View rather than Google Earth, includes prints of photos taken with large open-air distances in a low oblique view of urban settlements. Therefore, unlike Grant and Henner, but like to the artwork by Trevor Paglen, Jacqui's art includes the curvature of a horizon.

4   Keller Easterling, *Extrastatecraft: The Power of Infrastructure Space*, London: Verso, 2014.

5   Lawrence Bird, 'Territories of Image: Disposition and Disorientation in Google Earth', in Steve Hawley, Edward M. Clift, Kevin O'Brien (eds), *Imaging the City: Art, Creative Practices and Media Speculations*, Bristol: Intellect, 2016, 19.

6   Angela Krewani, 'Google Earth: Satellite Images and the Appropriation of the Divine Perspective', in Solvejg Nitzke and Nicolas Pethes (eds), *Imaging Earth: Concepts of Wholeness in Cultural Constructions of Our Home Planet,* Berlin: Transcript Verlag, 2018, 58.

Medieval Perspective

Given of the complex, assemblage effect in some images, authors such as Clemena Antonova and Martin Kemp, among others, look to the perspectival systems of the Medieval Period in their analysis of perspective, and these are of crucial importance in the post-digital age. [7] Rudolf Arnheim terms such a perspective 'inverse perspective',[8] Clemena Antonova 'reverse perspective',[9] and John White 'divergent perspective'.[10] This perspectival system, in contrast to those which are more 'analytic' or 'synthetic', if the view is from above, has more in common with the 'complex' and 'oblique' view. [11] As most of these authors consider this type of perspective to have already existed since Greek scenography in Antiquity, but to have reached its peak in Byzantine and Medieval icons, it is often referred to as – Medieval perspective.

During the Medieval Period, namely, Christian thinkers commonly thought of God as the guarantor of the existence of space, including those spaces which are not immediately perceivable, such as spaces in the past or at a distance. Therefore, for visual representations, various spatial views had to be conjoined in order to produce a space as would be viewed both by God and humans, which in turn introduced into images both past and distant spaces through the logic of assemblage. This perspective system, also known as 'orthodox isometric', shows the parallels of an object as diverging into the distance, thus allowing the viewer to see both sides of an objects. In orthodox isometric perspective, the artist or image-maker depicts objects which are farther away as larger in size and closer objects as smaller. In many instances, the so-called 'rule of the bottom' is applied as well, whereby objects which stand on the ground are depicted as either larger in the foreground or smaller in the background of the image. Finally, the scene is often viewed from an elevated or even eye-in-the-sky position, and it is this in particular which connects Medieval Perspective to the aerial photography of today.

In the pre-linear perspective systems of the Medieval Period, distortions or glitches are most visible when there are straight lines in the composition, such as with the building architecture of an urban scene. This perspective, according to Lev Zhegin, produces distortions in the view like that those which occur when looking through a telescope or barrel.[12] Also known as 'Byzantine perspective', in this inverse or inverted perspective system, straight lines curve into concave ones, while convex lines become straight lines, according Fernando C. Casas. [13]

---

7   Clemena Antonova, 'On the Problem of "Reverse Perspective": Definitions East and West', *Leonardo* 43.5 (2010): 464-469.
8   Arnheim, 'Inverted Perspective in Art'.
9   Antonova, 'On the Problem of "Reverse Perspective"'.
10   John White, *Birth and Rebirth of Pictorial Space,* Cambridge, MA: Belknap Press, 1987.
11   Yet, some authors criticize the imposition of a Western, linear perspective, because as the criteria of definition of visual representation preceding its era, as well as the norm that any representation is necessarily realistic.
12   Zhegin from Antonova. See: Clemena Antonova, *Space, Time and Presence of the Icon, Seeing the World in the Eyes of God,* Martin Kemp (pref.), London and New York: Routledge, 2010.
13   Fernando C. Casas, 'Flat-Perspective Sphere', *Leonardo* 16.1 (Winter 1983): 1-9.

This so-called curvilinear perspective is when straight lines do not meet but foreshortening exists in all directions. According to White, Leonardo da Vinci defined this perspective in his now-lost manuscript *Discorso*, at least as the story was told by Benvenuto Cellini.[14] Although James Elkins argues that Leonardo's descriptions could also have matched three-point linear perspective.[15] With this perspective system, the image is perfectly projected onto the sphere of the eye, given that the shape of the inner eye is concave too, leading Erwin Panofsky to conclude our vision is spheroid or tunneling. [16] Images, namely fall on the retina that is concave, producing a subjective, perspectival view which is then convex. (And this is also what happens in representations of the planet by the Flat Earthers. compose such a shape, a convex shape is transitioned into a flat shape.)

Linear Perspective

Medieval perspective is usually contrasted with linear perspective, which creates an illusion of depth on a flat surface through a system of parallel lines or orthogonals which converge in a single vanishing point on the composition's horizon line. Inverse perspective, because it is not truly systematic, is commonly described in contrast to linear perspective, which Arnheim also calls the 'illusionist doctrine'.[17] But were the perspective systems of the Medieval Period really perspective systems at all? Some art historians suggest that the perspective of the Medieval Period is but a 'twisted' or 'warped' representation of the way vision works. And some further deny the category of systems which might be called perspectival to the East. Such authors find that the reasons for the visible distortion of space in the Medieval Period rest upon the logics of iconographic symbolism and hierarchies of visual rhetoric, rather than an organized way of presenting. Whereas, as John Berger notes, the historical moment when linear perspective was introduced, given its basis in mathematics rather than in symbolism, also introduced a profane view into art, image making, and our representations of the world.[18]

According to Pavel Florensky, linear perspective is based on six conditions which are presumed to define reality.[19] First, the world itself is not organized as a Euclidian space and any space made through geometry is going to be different from the space which is actually seen. Second, there is no absolute point of view or center for perspective. Third, the way of seeing which is provided to the viewer in reality is binocular. Fourth, the viewer, or eye of the beholder, in reality is fluxing not fixed like it is in an image. Moreover, fifth, while an image

14   White, *Birth and Rebirth of Pictorial Space*.
15   White, *Birth and Rebirth of Pictorial Space*; James Elkins, 'Did Leonardo Develop a Theory of Curvilinear Perspective? Together with Some Remarks on the "Angle" and "Distance" Axioms', *Journal of the Warburg and Courtauld Institutes* 51 (1988): 190-196.
16   Erwin Panofsky, *Perspective as Symbolic Form*, Christopher S. Wood (trans.), New York: Zone Books, 1996.
17   Arnheim, 'Inverted Perspective in Art'.
18   John Berger, *Ways of Seeing*, New York Penguin, 1972, 16. Also, Haraway has named it 'God's trick'. See Donna Haraway, 'The Persistence of Vision', 1997; *The Visual Culture Reader*, Nicholas Mirzoeff (ed.), London: Routledge, 2002, 678-684.
19   Pavel Florensky, 'Reverse Perspective (1920)', trans. Wendy Salmond, in Nicoletta Misler (ed.), *Beyond Vision: Essays on the Perception of* Art, London: Reaktion Books, 2002, 197-273.

is static, the world itself is not. And finally, all psycho-physiological processes are excluded from linear perspective, as he writes:

> The eye looks motionlessly and dispassionately, the equivalent of an optical lens. [...] Moreover, this looking is accompanied by neither memories, nor spiritual exertions, nor recognition. It is an external-mechanical process, at the most a physio-chemical one, but in no way is it that which is called vision. The whole psychic element of vision, and even the physiological one, are decisively absent.[20]

During the Renaissance, an artist could apply linear perspective in an image in order to describe both the scene as well as the position of the narrator. When viewed from the vantage point of the narrator, the scene is then seen all at once, perceived by the audience as being fixed and having existed prior to the action itself of viewing the artwork. Linear perspective, since its development in the Renaissance, has consisted of the geometric projection of three dimensions onto a two-dimensional plane. This, in turn, has supported the mathematization and, consequently, the rationalization of observed space. Such a view has been further revolutionized by the invention of new techniques and tools. For example, as Friedrich Kittler describes, in the mid-18th century the ruler invented by Alsatian Johann Heinrich Lambert, today known as 'Lambert's ruler', assisted in the calculations of perspective for scenes of the open landscape.[21]

Technical Perspective

Already in Antiquity, optical research was initiated to orient to measure reality, reaching its peak with the discovery of Renaissance perspective, and at least being mechanical realized with the invention of photography. Although it was not the camera obscura itself, which was the direct precursor of the photographic camera, but rather camera lucida and lanterna magica, used as perspectival tools, which first offered a geometrically correct translation of reality.[22] The photographic camera itself would be more accurate than any previous tool as aperspectival device. Soon after the invention of the technology and the medium, photography was accepted as a more perfect way of seeing than even human vision which itself suffers from parallax confusion, overlapping images received through two eyes as sources, producing a third one. Monocular vision of the camera presented the *finnisage* of development of visual representational media. Because of its monocularity, photography had a high capacity for representing a three-dimensional reality without additionally coding it, as it would by producing yet another set of symbols.

However, there are also significant differences between the pictorial perspective of a painting painterly and mechanical perspective of the photo camera. A painted image can lose per-

---

20   Florensky, 'Reverse Perspective', 263.
21   [Friedrich Kittler, *Optical Media,* Anthony Enns (trans.), Cambridge: Polity Press, 2009, 94-96.
     According to Kittler, this ruler was a tool which assisted in calculating the perspective of any open view of the landscape.
22   Berger, *Ways of Seeing.*

spective for various reasons, Rudolf Arnhem analyses, such as if the painter lacks skills, has chosen not to adopt the canon of fundamental principles and general rules, has a perceptive error, paints only what they think they see, or has an unusual angle of view. [23] But such distortions to the perspective do not so easily happen with the creation of a mechanical image. Unless the photographer intentionally creates some distortion or other, images taken with a camera will all record relatively the same reality. Yet, what is recorded may still not impact the beliefs of the photographer, so if the photographer thinks that they have recorded UFOs, there may be no way to employ the image to contest this belief.

Photographic metrology, or the science of measurement in photography, is defined by at least three elements: the depth of the field, the ordering of planes, and the metric or proportion of the composition. Beyond any the interpretation of the angle of view, together these elements can convey to the viewer the relationship between objects in the image, as well as the relative distance to the subject or photographer from their position in space. And all three elements, distance, plane, and measurement, can be modified or even distorted through the use of various lenses. Still, there are many differences between this perspective which is recorded by a camera and that which is produced by the eye. One key difference, as Vasco Ronchi elaborates, lies in the fact that the photographic camera is set in front of the eyes but not necessarily having neutral lenses (although 50 mm lenses are often taken to be a model of neutral sight).[24]

View from Above

The aerial view has changed our perspective on the world. Since the beginning of perspective systems in Western culture during the Renaissance, as Antoine Bousquet remarks, two different perspective systems have been developed: a linear and a military perspective, with a military perspective supporting the aerial view.[25] Linear perspective was based on the representation of architectural structures within a geometrically-designed space, like with Renaissance paintings in which all lines meet at the vanishing point. In contrast, military perspective was based on the second perspective depicted space the way two parallel lines stay parallel and thus they never meet, like with a surveying map. This was the perspective system of the aerial view, Bousquet claims.[26] It contained neither infinite points nor straight lines and has only a single plane.[27] From down on the ground, space was seen like a pyramid, with the biggest plane that of the Earth's surface, and the smallest plane that of the Earth's sky or atmosphere. Whereas from up in the sky, perspective was reversed, with the biggest plane the sky, and the smallest the surface. Further, in the absence of architecture, which frames the space, this view could not include the measurement of distance. Thus, from the aerial view, the observable world had no depth of the field, order of planes, proportional rules, or a view angle. In other words, the Earth become approximate and unmeasurable.

---

23   Arnheim, 'Inverted Perspective in Art', 125.
24   Vasco Ronchi, 'Perspective Based on a New Optics', *Leonardo* 7.3 (Summer, 1974): 219-225.
25   Bousquet, *The Eyes of War*, 36.
26   Bousquet, *The Eyes of War*.
27   Bousquet, *The Eyes of War*.

There are further elements which distinguish the aerial view from linear perspective. Linear perspective is defined by both a horizon and pictorial vanishing point. While horizon exists in reality, the vanishing point, which does not exist in the real world, but it is tied to the image space where serving the simulation of the third dimension on the flat surface. Without a horizon, it is difficult to determine vanishing point as well as the relative distance between the subject and the horizon. But in aerial photography, the vanishing point is independent from the horizon, or the horizon is completely missing. Often, the viewer's eye is even located below the horizon line, which distorts the perspective.[28]

	MAPS	LAND PHOTO	ORTHOPHOTO
SPACE DESCRIPTION	Space	Place	Larger space
VIEWER POSITIONING	Distributed	Fixed	Distributed
CONSTRUCTION	Discreet	Compact	Compact
VISUAL CHARACTERISTIC	Abstraction	Realism	Realism
VISUAL STUDIES	Visualization	Vision	Vision

Table 6: Comparison of qualities which characterize maps, land photographs, and aerial photographs.

Photographic Polyperspectivalism

While photographic technology in and of itself is a perspectival machine, the medium also enabled artists to experiment with perspective. In the 19th century, the first polyperspectival experiments were conducted by the Pictorialists, who montaged several photographs together in order to produce complex stories such as simulating the existence of ghosts. The most famous mechanics or 'monteurs' in photographic technology, however, remain Eadweard Muybridge, Etienne-Jules Marey and, around the same time or just a bit later, Harold Edgerton with his stroboscopic photography. Both Muybridge and Marey used photography to analyze time.

---

28   Such a view is frequent in panoramic photography, where the focus for the photographer as well as the audience is on the clearness of the land rather than the infiniteness of the sky.

Although, each did so in their own distinct way. Muybridge, for example, used a set of twelve cameras to analyze the movements of an animal or human in sequence, by shooting with multiple cameras, which he distributed in space. Whereas, Marey used multiple exposures to produce an effect of simultaneity. These experiments directly led to the development of photogrammetry (through the construction of the multiplexing camera, like the one Muybridge used) as well as deep photography (through sub-sequential same-frame recording)., Félix Nadar also combined multiple images which had been recorded in sequence while on the move, in order to create the most total image possible in the day of the Earth as seen from the air. But while Muybridge's and Marey's images were organized around the spatial third dimension (the movement of the subject through space), Nadar's revealed the fourth dimension of the space-time continuum (the polyperspective simultaneity across time).[29]

Because of their polyperspective simultaneity, Nadar's aerial photographs had a direct influence on the birth of Cubism.[30] These images taken up in the sky broke with the Renaissance system of organizing the image-space down on the ground into linear perspective. Artists working in this style depicted objects in their artworks 'relatively [...] from several points, no one of which has exclusive authority'.[31] Theses Cubists, especially Analytical Cubists, used polyperspective to bring different views of the subject, whether objects or figures, together within a single composition. This resulted in images which appear to be fragmented or somehow abstracted. Through such polyperspectivalism, a different perspective is applied to each object. Through a simultaneous view, here the author and their subjectivity were abstracted out of and away from the image.

Around the same time as the Cubist art movement, experiments with computing the image were also being conducted by photographers such as Laszlo Moholy-Nagy, Man Ray, and Christian Schad.[32] Indeed, since Cubism, many artists across the late 20th and early 21st centuries have investigated the role of perspectival systems in the photographic medium, interrupting, manipulating, or even reversing the process of image-making in some way, in order to explore the potentials and possibilities of perspective. These experiments perhaps culminated with the rise of computational photography in works by Herbert W. Franke, and Sonia Landy Sheridan, among others. And today, in the post-digital era, as computational photography flourished, this polyperspectivalism supports the innovation of total images which encompass many different points of view.[33]

---

29   Space-time continuum is also shown in Cubism, while fourth dimension in dynamism by Duchamp or
      Futurism by Balla. See: Linda Dalrymple Henderson, 'Four-Dimensional Space or Space-Time? The
      Emergence of the Cubism-Relativity Myth in New York in the 1940s', in Michele Emmer (ed) *The Visual
      Mind II*, Cambridge, MA: MIT Press, 2005, 349-398.
30   Other influences on the birth of Cubism included Einstein's theory of relativity, Minkowski's theory of the
      space-time continuum, and non-Euclidian geometry.
31   Henderson, 'Four-Dimensional Space or Space-Time?', 362.
32   For a brief history of these experiments, see: Gottfried Jäger, 'Generative Photography: A Systematic,
      Constructive Approach', *Leonardo* 19.1 (1986): 19-25.
33   Both definitions may be missing the point for two reasons; 1. As they define reverse in regard to the
      linear perspective, presupposing its existence, as well as the knowledge on it. 2. Presupposing that
      the Byzantine perspective had a systematic rule, as linear had. This argument was stressed by Martin
      Kemp and Clemena Antonova, in 'Reverse perspective' historical fallacies and an alternative view, in

'New Medievalism'

The total image, while it is a derivative of photography, does not satisfy any of conditions for linear perspective, as set by Florensky.[34] Total images deny the absolute point of view, the center of perspective introduces more or many viewpoints distributed along the surface, and most commonly the viewer cannot stay fixed to the scene, and the image is anything but static.[35] As a direct consequence of this merging of a vast amount of photographic imagery and data, the polyperspectivalism is being revived. There are many simultaneous views, and they are all dynamic. One single reality may be experienced in a multitude of ways, which in turn produces multiple realities, each providing a coherent picture. Because the basic sense-data interface with polyperspectival systems is produced by visual sense data which has been detached from the other senses, a feeling of immersion in this reality is provided to the viewer or interactor.

Prior to the Renaissance, in non-linear perspectives space was chaotic. Still, a new polyperspectival space is not inconsistent and incoherent as a space Panofsky recognizes as once was Medieval.[36] Besides, the perspective of the total image is not a priori eternal, transcendent, or unchangeable without points of reference or parameters of space, like in the Medieval Period. Rather, the total image is computed out of many parts or pieces; it is assembled.[37] This new polyperspectivalism gives birth as well to a pseudo-philosophy, in which knowledge both objective and neural is understood to be relativistic. Like reverse perspective in the Medieval Period, linear perspective in the Renaissance, absolute perspective in the Baroque, and the mechanical perspective of photographic technology beginning in the 19th century, the assemblage logic of polyperspectivalism logic in the post-digital era characterizes and constrains our capacity for understanding the world. In such total images, the techniques which are used to correct many original photographs in the process of composing one single image of the Earth as seen from above, also dismiss the role and importance of subjectivity and relativity. As Martin Jay notes, even before our entrance into the post-digital, 'If postmodernism teaches anything, however, it is to be suspicious of single perspectives, which, like grand narratives, provide totalizing accounts of a world too complex to be reduced to a unified point of view'.[38]

In the Renaissance, the centering of images from the viewpoint of the subject also indicated the rising significance of the self and of the individual. And in the post-digital era, the separation of images from subjects may very well suggest the rise of a new amalgamated, generic, or homogeneous selfhood. Thus, from all of the elements which characterize the total image, perhaps most important is the re-distribution of multiple perspectives into a polyperspectival

---

Michele Emmer, *Visual Mind II*, Cambridge MA: MIT Press, 2005, 349-399.

34 Florensky, 'Reverse Perspective', 1920.

35 There are a few more conditions, added by Oscar Wulff, that define the reverse perspective, one of which is the inclusion of the viewer inside of the space, as a part of the pictorial space, as for example also in selfies or 360-degree panoramas. See Wuff in Antonova, *Space, Time and Presence of the Icon*.

36 Panofsky, *Perspective as Symbolic Form*.

37 Merleau Ponty writes about the '"baroque" proliferation of generating axes for visibility in the duplicity of the real'. Merleau Ponty, *Visible and Invisible*, Northwestern University Press, 1969, 60.

38 Jay, *Downcast Eyes*, 545.

view. Through this process, post-digital photography loses the mechanical perspective which describes not the view angle of any one single subject, but in fact returns to a way of seeing from before the invention of linear perspective. For example, panoramic images are made through recording a series of photographs with overlapping borders. And aerial images are made through recording a series of photographs with orthographic correction. Viewing such images can even cause dizziness or even more serious neurological effect.[39]

As many authors of perspective theory have emphasized, perspective is not merely a system for visual representation, but also a system of understanding the world, a discourse unto itself. According to Cristoforo Landino, for example, perspective is 'part philosophy and part geometry,' used to not only to inform our representation of space, but to influence our ideology about place as well.[40] Since Plato's allegory of the cave, optical principles and perspectival tools have served to create paradigms of explanation within the context of ideological production, as has been analyzed, for example, in photography and cinema through Marxist theory as well as contemporary theories of the apparatus.[41] Essentially, through a given perspective system, the viewer accepts the position which someone else has created, identifies with it, and accepts its gaze, even if that gaze is misogynistic or racist, for example. Still, whereas the viewer can resist the fullest absorption into cinematic experience, doing so with intense virtual realities becomes more difficult, and this is why some virtual perspectives out of total experience may become total explanations, as theories of flat earth.[42]

---

39   Commonly explored as neurological problem in aviation.
40   Cristoforo Landino as quoted in Margaret Iversen, 'The Discourse of Perspective in the Twentieth Century'. *Oxford Art Journal* 28.2 (2005): 191–202
41   Sarah Kofman, *Camera Obscura: of Ideology*, Athlone Press, 1998; Jean-Louis Baudry and Alan Williams, 'Ideological Effects of the Basic Cinematographic Apparatus', *Film Quarterly* 28.2 (1974-1975): 39-47.
42   Laura Kurgan refers to assemblage function of the trace in writings by Vil m Flusser. Laura Kurgan, *Close Up at a Distance: Mapping, Technology, and Politics*, MIT Press, 2013.

CHAPTER 8: POLYOPTICON

Spinning Around

Google Earth Engine, related products such as Google Maps and Google Street View, and other aerial, panoramic, and satellite image mapping programs have opened the door to an era of total surveillance or so-called 'deep imaging'.[1] Alike maps, photographs today have become a navigable space, as it no longer presents a fixed place. The ancient dream of being able to see the world like the gods has been realized in the total image. There are many correlations between the view in the contemporary aerial photography of the post-digital age and in the historical perspective systems of the Medieval Period; that is, between the folkloric, mytho-logical, and religious concept of the omnipresent eye, and the interventionist concept of the evil eye. And especially during times of nation-state interventionism, these views are used to manipulate an economy, people, or society.[2] During the 19th century, for example, two models of control were conceived: the panopticon and the peep show. The panopticon, which in a sense also imprisoned the guards, began as an architectural blueprint for prisons, based on an idea of control through presence and visibility. It was first sketched by Samuel Bentham and published in a book by his brother Jeremy.[3] After the invention and implementation of the panopticon, peep show marked the second such surveillance model, in which the observer was positioned outside of the system, thus was invisible to the object monitored. The principle difference between the two was the position of the observer. With the panopticon, a design for institutional buildings such as prisons which consist of a rotunda with an inspection house at the center, control is achieved from above and inside of the system. Whereas with the peep show, an exhibition of pictures viewed through a small hole or magnifying glass, control is achieved from outside while freely moving about.

With the birth of aerial photographs, these two ways of seeing, one from the inside of an architectural construct, and one from the outside, were merged. With aerial images the observer is having a full control of the area under it, as in panopticon, yet, he is not locked down into a building of a prison. Prison keeper is having an immediate insight into much wider reality than the one being represented by the author of the image and imagined by the perception of the audience.

The ideas of space which are being represented in today's aerial, drone, and satellite post-dig-ital photography may to a certain extent be like the ideas of space defined in the mythologies of Antiquity and in the religion of the Medieval Period. But this technology is far from all-seeing (omnipresent) or all-knowing (omniscient). Instead, it allows various agents to simultaneously observe, monitor, and control others. As this technology becomes more readily available and cost effective, it also becomes more open, allowing a range of user greater access to

1   Trevor Paglen, 'Homepage', http://www.paglen.com/.

2   Jennifer Stob, 'Detournement as Optic: Debord, Derisory Documents and the Aerial View', *Philosophy of Photography* 5.2 (2013): 19-34.

3   Bentham writes in *Panopticon: The Inspection House* written as a series of letters in 1787.

the technology, and with fewer and fewer constraints or restrictions on its use. For example, drone may be used by a private citizen to invade another's privacy. The popular use of this technology, in turn, leads to questions concerning its legality, especially in terms of the privacy and property. On a daily basis, American citizens and non-citizens are being surveilled by drones in the USA, and not only by the military or state, but also by private individuals.[4] And artists also use drones in their art, as with John Carlucci and Brandon LaGanke of Ghost + Cow who in their art-porn project *Drone Boning* filmed people having sex from the air.[5]

For this distribution of monitoring devices, contemporary paradigm of control is more distorted, fragmented, and simultaneous than Bentham's panopticon or Foucault's panopticonism. Bruno Latour defines it as 'oligoptic organization', consisting of numerous small chunks that do their small surveillances.[6] The key difference between Foucault's panopticon and Latour's oligopticon lies in whether the data is centralized or decentralized. Merging both together, in what Zygmunt Bauman defines as 'liquid control', is the simultaneous implementation of the synopticon defined by Thomas Mathiesen and Foucault's panopticon, producing something as a polyopticon, which simultaneously surveilles at small and at large.[7]

Machine Gods

As today 'corporations replace the Christian churches as the primary source of aerial integration', the system of airplanes, drones, and satellites is also polycentric.[8] In the post-digital era, the forces of the universe which humans have previously attributed to deities, gods, or other spiritual beings, are more and more being attributed to machines. Indeed, one could perhaps go so far as to say that machines are becoming gods in the minds and hearts of many if not most people, and that humans have dethroned god, and replaced him with a machine. The acts of surveillance and judgement are just some of these god-like powers, which humans previously attributed to some god or other, and presently attribute to aerial photography. But the total image does not emerge from a natural way of seeing which has evolved gradually through use over time.

Rather, the machine gaze behind the total image has replaced the metaphysical 'eye in the sky' which previously belonged the exclusively to the domains of folklore, mythology, and religion, by taking up a point of view from the higher dimensions of the stratosphere and outer space, from which it achieves a kind of total seeing. Such a gaze affords multiple operations, with a capacity for a 360-degree view, telephoto zooming by astronomical units, and focus

4   See, for example: The Electronic Frontier Foundation's *Map of Domestic Drone Authorization*, https://fusiontables.googleusercontent.com/embedviz?viz=MAP&q=select+col2+from+1WuTyH62PmUF97oxo6IreT1BL_aw9HJN5pocwmwg&h=false&lat=44.08758502824518&lng=-85.5615234375&z=4&t=1&l=col2&y=1&tmplt=2.
5   See John Carlucci and Brandon LaGanke (Ghost + Cow), 'Drone Boning', http://www.droneboning.com.
6   Bruno Latour, *Reassembling the Social: An Introduction to Actor-Network-Theory*, Oxford: Oxford University Press, 2007.
7   Zygmunt Bauman, *Liquid Modernity*, Cambridge: Polity Press, 2000.
8   Barney Warf and Santa Arias, *The Spatial Turn: Interdisciplinary Perspectives in Human Geography*, New York: Routledge, 2009, 114.

simultaneously at far and near distances. Imaging systems today differ from those yesterday primarily in regard to the type of surveillance which is being established.[9] For example, it has now become possible to zoom in and out of a map almost instantaneously, and to almost synchronically experience both panoptic and synoptic vision.

Unmanned photography, getting rid of the human as the first, named, author (the one that presses the button) and leaving him the function of the second author working behind (as the creator or the programmer of the apparatus), tries to remain itself in the objective place, reducing any trajectory and abstract distortion of the located and situated object's space. The author now infiltrates or invades the audience space, while the image space manipulates the audience through the illusion that they are having an exchange or interaction with the author. Further, each individual of the audience is continuously being mapped and datafied by the system itself, generating new content around about their place. Moreover, systems for the viewing and monitoring of others have been perfected, and now have come into the hands of the masses, who share their own as well as others' private data without a second thought.

Viewer Tracked

Yet, contemporary surveillance seems to be at least partially voluntary, as humans provide a great deal of this information themselves. And in the Quantified Self movement, which is fast gaining popularity, all data is provided voluntarily. As Matthew H. Wilson notes, 'Quantification, as an interoperable, proprietary system that fashions habits and surveils for the purpose of competition, is life lived under spectacle'.[10]

The subject in the post-digital era is not whole unto themselves, in the eye of a machine, but rather consists of discreet elements such as number of steps, calories lost, weight, height, time spent online, DNA, pin codes, passwords, facial features, and on. Healthcare applications such as pedometers and cardiograph heart rate monitors for smart phones or smart watches at once connect us to and dissociate us from our own bodies. And with the increasing use of web mapping services and applications, we are losing our primordial connection to the Earth. Although these may situate us within our environment, we have no big picture, no navigational instinct. In each of these systems, the place is over-produced. That is, the same location is covered by views from satellite, GPS trackers for cars, and mobile trackers for personal devices. We live in a time where the majority of our devices, which extend the functions of our perception, also serve to locate us as dots within a Cartesian coordinate system. While previously maps were placing oneself on the space by the act of use, now the map places the users without their knowledge, simultaneously providing seducing total images of space.

---

9   Latour defines the oligopticon in contrast to the panorama: 'Whereas oligoptica are constantly revealing the fragility of their connections and their lack of control on what is left in between their networks, panoramas give the impression of complete control over what is being surveyed, even though they are partially blind and nothing enters or leaves their walls except interested or baffled spectators'. Bruno Latour, *Reassembling the Social*, Oxford: Oxford University Press, 2007, 188.

10 Matthew H. Wilson, *New Lines: Critical GIS and the Trouble of the Map*, Minneapolis: University of Minnesota Press, 2017.

Not only personal data but also real-time is transmitted through our devices to various track-ers, broadcasting GPS information to cellular stations and to internet servers. Indeed, data has become more valuable than even oil in the post-digital age. After the 2018 scandal with Cambridge Analytica, which harvested personal data from social media in order to manipulate election outcomes for various clients, it has become clear that data is itself a currency. Game applications on social networks provide our data to commercial companies, for example.[11] And today, it is even possible to exercise surveillance on oneself, whether with a 24-hour webcam or using satellite imagery.

Systems collect more data on us than ever before. Consequently, surveillance has been modified into 'dataveillance' organized around discursive practices.[12] As Manuel deLanda writes in his analysis of work by Gilles Deleuze:

> Non-discursive practices of visual surveillance and monitoring, performed in build-ings specifically designed to facilitate their routine execution, sort the raw materials (human bodies) into criminal, medical, or pedagogic categories; and discursive practices, like those of the criminologists, doctors, or teachers who produce a variety of conceptual categories, consolidate those sorted human materials, giving prisons, hospitals and schools a more stable form and identity.[13]

The era of visible totalitarian organization, marching soldiers, not-that-invisible secret services following, arresting and interrogating citizens has passed. As totalitarianism reaches the space beyond visibility, such as the micro and macro, but curiously enough skip over being visible in everyday life.

Tracked by the Image

Post-digital photography may also be function as a system of control through the view or views which they afford. In historical original photography, the direction for the transaction of value flowed from the author through the photograph to their audience. That is, the photographer depicted and framed the content of the image which was then interpreted by the viewer. In contemporary post-digital photography, however, the image value is neither unidirectional nor interactive. Rather, the author of the image is the audience itself, with the content of the image depending upon the choices made and data given by the viewer. In other words, the audience has become part of the image in so far as they are voluntarily or involuntarily recorded while interacting with the images on some device. And the age-old distinction between the space of the author, the space of the object, and the space of the audience has become porous and blurred. There almost seems to be a certain inverted relation by which the amount of totality

---

11   The information being sent out by 24 satellites, allowing precise location of a mobile phone between three of them.

12   Roger A. Clarke, 'Information Technology and Dataveillance', *Communications of the ACM* 31.5 (1988): 498–511.

13   deLanda, *Assemblage Theory*, 38-39.

of the image influences on the loss of the particular picture; the more total image it is offered, lesser the capacity for the picture-view.

CONCLUSION: SO, THE EARTH IS FLAT...?

Assembled Perspective

Our ideas about the Earth, and about both our space and place in relation to the world, changed with the innovation and introduction of each new imaging technology, from the map and landscape, to various globes, to today's post-digital photography. Starting with the balloon-mounted photographic apparatus in the 19th century, and continuing with air, drone, and satellite imaging in the 20th and 21st centuries, post-digital photographs of our home planet, like those which constitute Google Earth or virtual globes, are not captured but rather assembled. By the time they reach our eyes, these images have been adjusted, with the density, opacity, saturation, and transparency of the output images much transformed from the input images or original real-world source images. These images have also been layered with other images, as well as information such as maps and tags, with all of these many layers have been flattened together. And, perhaps most significantly, these images have been corrected, frequently in terms of their perspective, using a polyperspectival system which affords multiple, simultaneous points and angles of view, in order to make a more total image of the Earth by combining human and machine vision.

The view which is constructed through these post-digital photographs of the Earth is total, at least in so far as that it extends the function of human vision, such that we can explore the whole of our world by the use of this technology, and from a perspective or view that the constraints of our bodies and eyes could not achieve. Yet, while this space may at first sight appear to be systematic, and to represent space with the linear perspective found in the architectural plans, drawings, or paintings of the early Renaissance, it is aggregated out of countless perspectives. This totality is, thus, not homogeneous. It is assembled. The total image is composed out of many different parts, which automatically or algorithmically combined into a whole, across various angles, distances, and perspectives, each with their own respective interpretations and subjectivities. It is not the world unique, total sphere, but as a fragmentary experience, rather cartographically and with different borders which are not existing on the planet, as viewed from above. And it is changing with each new use.

The quantity and kind of information which is contained in any post-digital photograph of the Earth makes it impossible to see this total image all at once. As James Bridle rightly notes, 'The aggregation of complex systems in contemporary networked applications means that no single person ever sees the whole picture'.[1] Thus, despite the sheer volume of total images which exist in the post-digital age, when compared and contrasted to the pictures of the planet in Antiquity and the Medieval Period, we are actually losing any totalizing view or perspective. In the total images of today, there is in fact no totality. Instead, space and place as they are represented are more fragmented than ever before. Through such technology, the audience, interactor, or viewer can only experience and come to know the world as if it is a broken vase, that has pieces lost or missing, and having no idea of what the object actually looks like, also

---

1   Bridle, *New Dark Age*, 40.

no possibility for piecing it together. As Fredric Jameson argues, this almost schizophrenic *decentering* and *dispersion* of the subjective view also brings alienation.[2] And such a growing inability and incapacity to locate for ourselves a place in the world plays an important part in the burgeoning systematic failure of a globalized society to preserve culture, heritage, and personhood between all its differences and diversity.[3]

Assembled World

A major problem for post-digital contemporary perception is that the world appears sequenced, as it is visually indeed assembled, more over it appears overly close, so no distance needed in order to construct a perception is possible. This fractioned appearance reintroduced along with the total image is a concept of absolute space and New Medievalism, elaborated in the Introduction and Chapter 8.[4] The theory of assemblage is often used to analyze perspective and space in the various forms of images from the Medieval Period, Modernity, and their combination in the post-digital age. Yet, in addition to being applied by philosophers in their analysis of more general, cultural. patterns, assemblage logic has many variants when applied to media: from bricolage to collage and from photomontage to filmic montage. Gilles Deleuze and Félix Guattari, followed by Manuel deLanda and Saskia Sassen, have theorized on assemblage in a wider context.[5] Following Deleuze and Guattari's famous theorizing on assemblage, deLanda introduced the model of an 'abstract machine', which he applied in his theory of society and which, in turn, Sassen applied to practical concepts.[6] With these analyses, the focus of contemporary theories of assemblage have shifted from material and medial processes in visual culture to a political and social perspectives. These social theories of assemblage are now being practically applied in the analysis of the hybrid geographies which combine maps with photographs. Here, concepts such as 'territorialization' and 'deter-ritorialization' refer to the degree of indexicality between the total image and the reality which is being represented.[7]

---

2   Fredric Jameson, *Postmodernism, or, the Cultural Logic of Late Capitalism*, Durham: Duke University Press, 1991, 413.

3   Many places on the Earth are being erased from maps. According the artwork of Columbian-born American filmmaker Maurizio Arango, being part of the project *Victims Symptom* I have curated which only used few concepts of victimology to show how the number of victims is being reported in media, there are many places of the planet which are erased from media maps. They are not being reported thoroughly even in cases of events with large fatalities. See: Ana Peraica, *Victims Symptom: PTSD and Culture*, Amsterdam: Institute of Network Cultures, 2009.

4   Grau, *Virtual Art*.

5   Deleuze and Guattari analyze assemblage in territorial, statist, capitalist and nomadic layer, as well as their amalgams, in a constant change of predicate logic functions. deLanda furthermore is defining parts of the assemblage as coded, arbitrary and variable, contrary to stratum. Deleuze and Guattari, *Thousand Plateaus*; Saskia Sassen, *Territory Authority, Rights: From Medieval to Global Assemblage*, Princeton, NJ: Princeton University Press, 2008; deLanda, *Assemblage Theory*.

6   deLanda, *Assemblage Theory*; Sassen, *Territory Authority, Rights*.

7   Throughout *Anti-Oedipus*, Deleuze and Guattari analyze various types of deteritorialization, from relative to absolute. See: Gilles Deleuze and Felix Guattari, *Anti-Oedipus: Capitalism and Schizophrenia*, Minneapolis: University of Minnesota Press, 1984, 130-149 and 192-200.

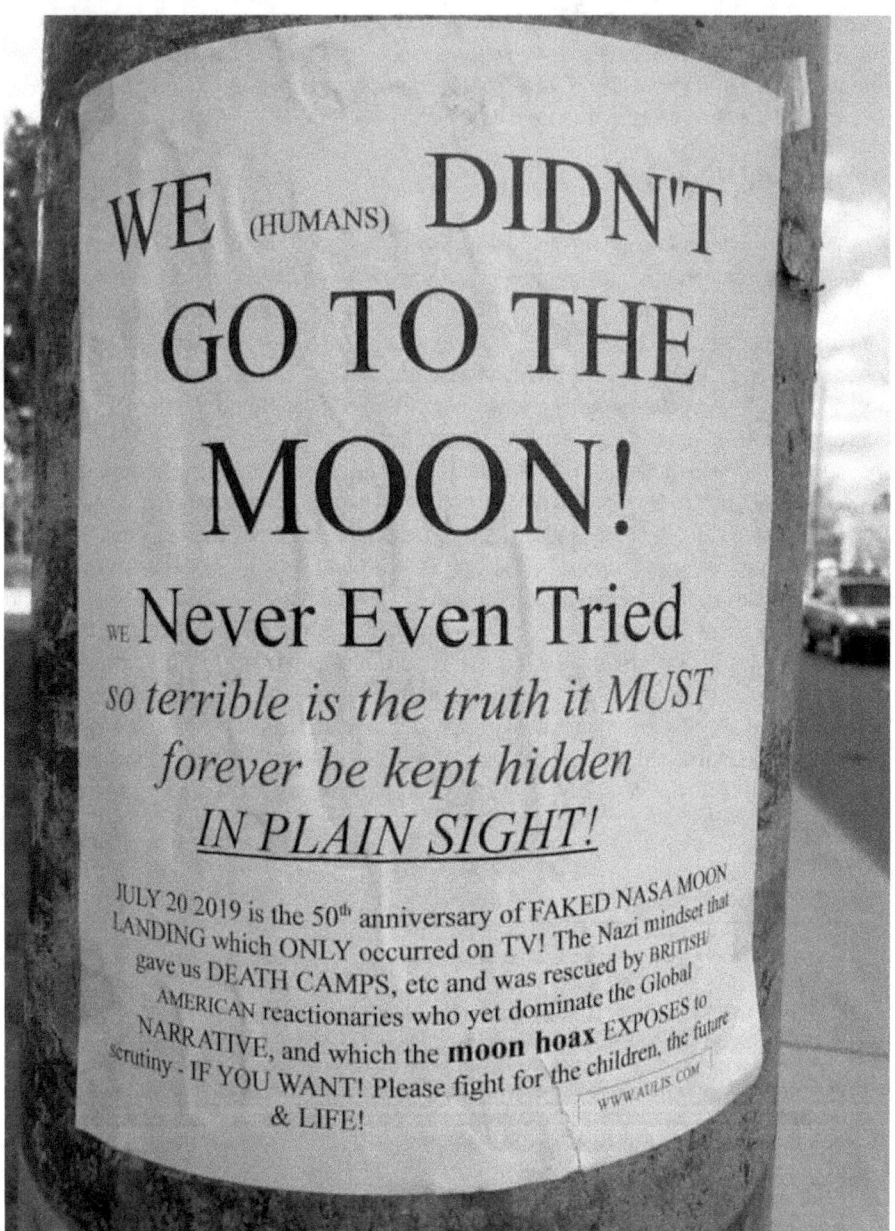

Figure 27: We Have Never Been to the Moon, street poster and internet meme.

The Loss of the Common World

In the real world, such processes of fragmentation also are progressing. For example, more and more countries are withdrawing from international organizations, such as with the USA and Israel leaving the United Nations Educational, Scientific and Cultural Organization (UNESCO) in December 2018, and the UK leaving the EU in January 2020. Yet, at the same time we have never lived in time having more total consequences. While the whole Earth and people all over the world are impacted by climate change and the climate crisis, not everyone shares the total view of the planet. As Timothy Clark writes, 'No-one sees the Earth globally and no-one sees an ecological system from nowhere'.[8] Indeed, even the governments and corporations in both larger or smaller nations which occupy a particular territory behave as if they are isolated rather than connected to the whole. But whatever fate is made by the human species will be the grand master narrative produced, claims Clive Hamilton.[9] None will be spared. At least regarding global warming, as Hamilton writes, 'there are no more enclaves'.[10] Enclaves, uncontaminated by the virus that is the confidence of one group in their own dominion over another group, will vanish. And if the difference and diversity in humanity is further dispersed and distributed, then this will be at least in part due to the seduction of a total image of the world, an image which does not provide a real picture of how things are, but an image which we construct according to our own attitudes, beliefs, and desires.[11]

Loss of Place

In addition to a loss of totality in the total view in the total images of the post-digital age, the idea of place is being lost; that is, place is being overproduced, becoming redundant. With the datafication of geography and programmability of images in terms of integrating a realistic effect, the impetus for us to use technology in order to achieve better and better estimation and identification of the real-world geographic locations for objects has led to another function in the combination of map and landscape: the need to capture places.

But does the precision of this location in turn lead to a loss in our sense of place? There are several recent changes of human conditions which today shape our belief of reality, framing it down to a small scale. Overall, humanity is losing its physical contact with the surrounding world. We have lost our joy, which is characteristic of children and scientists alike, in simply observing nature, the way Aristotle did in what I described as his 'argument from experience', which is characterized by naïve realism and interpreted in the framework of limited knowledge. In previous eras, this curiosity has led each of us to learn, sometimes completely on our own and independent of any given education, about phenomena such as the horizon of the Earth, the movement of the Earth around the sun which is made visible in changes to the shadows of objects, the turning of the seasons which can be seen in movements of the

---

8   Timothy Clark, *Ecocriticism on the Edge: The Anthropocene as a Threshold Concept*, New York: Bloomsbury, 2015, 18.
9   Clive Hamilton, *Defiant Earth: The Fate of Humans in the Anthropocene*, New Zealand and Australia: Allen and Unwin, 2017, Chapter 3, unpaginated.
10   Hamilton, *Defiant Earth*, Chapter 2, unpaginated.
11   Hamilton, *Defiant Earth*, 54.

constellations in the night sky, and solar as well as lunar eclipse and their various shadows. In addition, there are agricultural and urbanization factors which limit our access to nature and influence this detachment. The human race has cultivated more than half of the planet, in many places making views of the horizon literally inaccessible. Today, in or near cities, there is also light pollution, and the sky is obfuscated with smog, to such an extent that the stars may not be visible at all. Because of the speed of transport and communication technologies, even the very idea of the space as existing from a departure to an arrival point has all but disappeared. Paul Virilio thus observed that here 'depth no longer includes the visual horizon, nor the vanishing point of perspective', but rather speed becomes the most essential and important dimension.[12]

Time is essential element in our perception of the world which is in front of us. Our eyes move to analyze the space, not only in terms orthogonals but also depth, by focusing on various distances. The interface, as a temporary form-image, is also connected to our understanding of time as well as of space. The speed of the signal through the Internet or from a television network, as well as the speed with which this signal is carried through the device itself, has a temporal quality. This, leads to progressive disappearance of space-time, providing no illusion that the Earth is a sphere and that, hypothetically, one could travel around it endlessly, thereby introducing not only the idea of the finiteness of the planet but also the finiteness of the view. And again, according to Virilio, the speed and acceleration towards instantness have destroyed fixity of both the space and its visualizations.[13] In addition they have set the place in motion, so it is impossible to capture it. It is not that our four-dimensional world, with its three dimensions of space (height, width, depth), as well as the temporal dimension, is thereby fixed or flattened, but it has sliced into layers in which it has been decoded, and such layers do not describe general categories.

Reality Effect

The subjective view angle of humans, and thus the human condition as well, is radically dismissed in total images also because the trustworthiness and truthfulness of these images cannot be verified. Consequently, the very concept of the view angle, as it has been understood in Western culture and thought for the past five hundred years, is disappearing right before our very eyes.

As such, the total image is at once convincing and dangerous. Jean Baudrillard was right: with the image, reality disappears.[14] Instead, indexicality in the total image is merely a realistic effect or style which is applied to the image by the layering of photographs. Through the computational processes of artificial intelligence which combine multiple photographs together, as well as many other kinds of information, the photograph loses its original indexi-

---

12 Virilio, *Lost Dimension*, 66.
13 Virilio, *Lost Dimension*, 140.
14 He writes: 'This is also true of geographic and spatial exploration: when there is no longer any virgin territory, and thus one available to the imaginary, *when the map covers the whole territory, something like the principle of reality disappears.*' Jean Baudrillard, *Simulacra and Simulation*, Sheila Faria Glaser (trans.), Ann Arbor, Minnesota: University of Michigan Press, 1994, 123.

cality, or at least the indexicality takes on more of a symbolic quality, as the indexical realism of photography is being merged with the data systems of mapping. In post-digital photography, the connection between the image and its reference, such as between Google Earth and the Earth itself, is based more on indirect resemblance than direct relation, as has already been suggested by Baudrillard.[15] By confusing the chain of custody for photographic evidence from firsthand witnesses, human or machine, its credibility in relation to space becomes lost. Thus, indexicality in the total image no longer serves as proof to the viewer that the something being represented actually exists in reality, as has long been the role of indexicality in photography.

And it only because of this effect, as Allen Carlson notes, that we are 'picturing and perceiving nature as if it were a landscape painting, as a grandiose project seen from a specific standpoint and distance'.[16] Photographic realism is just one element in the total image. As I have described across the proceeding chapters, in many if not most instances, photographs become just one layer of material out of many within a complex system. In fact, in many cases the outcome of this process does not make visible any photograph at all. In photomaps, for example, photographs are first added and later discarded. In photomontage, they are stretched or merged. And in orthophotography, they are corrected so that their scale is uniform. Indeed, more often than not, photographs camouflage more complex data. When integrated into maps, however, and both corrected and layered, the photograph becomes less of a medium and more of a style for providing a realistic effect. The photograph is appropriated for the total image because of its visual qualities which carry or convey the natural world to the eye in a way which we recognize as being like our own human way of seeing. Consequently, as an epistemic genre, photography today has acquired a secondary value beyond the indexical. Indeed, the medium has become a 'slave' to our culture of hyper-visualization as it is used less for itself and more in more for complex interpretations of reality. Indeed, it is as if the photographic medium has been 'hacked' and opened up to intrusion from a 'virus' of substantially different media types, whether map, landscape, globe, or just raw data.

The consequences of utilizing photography for its realistic effect in our representations of the world may be far reaching. By introducing complex, non-mimetic models of reality, we distance ourselves from reality even further. The post-digital photographic reality has by now become completely un-checkable, leading even to the production of landscapes which have no relation to reality at all. As Trevor Paglen addresses the issue, 'As "landscape" in art has moved far outside the frames of painting and photography, a lot of artists are turning towards geography for methodological and analytic inspiration'.[17] Today the landscape exists no longer as an object but as something abject. Rather, our relationship to these new datascapes, at least in terms of cognition, is projective. That is, this landscape itself is a projection of our selves. And each of these projections is individual. []{#_Toc30753600 .anchor}Today, total images of the Earth no longer help us to learn about the world. Rather, they function as a

---

15   Jean Baudrillard, *The Evil Demon of Images*, Sydney: The Power Institute of Fine Arts, 1987.
16   Allen Carlson, 'Appropriation of the Nature Environment', in Alex Neil and Aaron Ridley (eds), *Arguing about Art, Contemporary Philosophical debates*, London: Routledge, 155-166.
17   Michael Dear, 'An Interview with Trevor Paglen', in *GeoHumanities: Art, History, Text at the Edge of Place*, Michael Dear, Jim Ketchum, Sarah Luria, Doug Richardson. Routledge, 2011, 24.

barrier between us and the planet, an illusion, which breaks us away from our own human processes of discovery, exploration, and navigation. As with other images of the Earth taken from the air and from space, which some people believe are proof that the surface of the planet is flat, in the post-digital age the total image serves not only to explain our habitat, but to falsely stabilize its ever dynamic and shifting qualities.

BIBLIOGRAPHY

Books and Articles

Abbott Abbott, Edwin. *Flatland: A Romance of Many Dimensions*, pref. Thomas Banchoff, New York and Dover: Princeton University Press, 1993.

Ades, Dawn. *Photomontage*, London: Thames and Hudson, 1976.

Alberti, Leon Battista. *On Painting*, Cambridge: Cambridge University Press, 2011.

Anderson, Steve F. *Technologies of Vision: The War between Data and Images*, Cambridge, MA: MIT Press, 2017.

Andrew, Shryock and Daniel Lord Smail, Timothy K Earle. *Deep History: The Architecture of Past and Present*, Berkeley, Los Angeles and London: University of California Press, 2011.

Antonova, Clemena. 'On the problems of "reverse perspective": Definitions East and West', *Leonardo* 43.5 (2010): 464-469.

Antonova, Clemena. *Space, Time and Presence of the Icon, Seeing the World in the Eyes of God*, pref. Martin Kemp, London and New York: Routledge, 2010.

Appadurai, Arjun. *Modernity at Large: Cultural Dimensions of Globalization* (Public Worlds, Vol. 1), Minneapolis: University of Minnesota Press, 1996.

Arendt, Hannah. *The Human Condition*, Chicago, University of Chicago Press, 1998 (1958).

Arnheim, Rudolf. 'Inverted perspective in art, display and expression', *Leonardo* 5.2 (1972): 125-135.

Baudrillard, Jean. *Simulacra and Simulation, The Body, In Theory: Histories of Cultural Materialism*, University of Michigan, 1994.

Baudrillard, Jean. *The Evil Demon of Images*, Power Institute of Fine Arts: University of Sydney, 1987.

Baudrillard, Jean. *The Gulf War did not Took Place*, Sidney: Power Publications, 2012.

Baudry, Jean-Louis and Alan Williams, 'Ideological Effects of the Basic Cinematographic Apparatus', *Film Quarterly* 28.2 (1974-1975): 39-47.

Bauman, Zygmunt. *Liquid Modernity*, Cambridge: Polity, 2000.

Becking, Jessica. 'Records of Representation: Clement Valla's Postcards from Google Earth', *Media Theory* 2.1 (2018): 307-315.

Benjamin, Walter. *The Arcades Project,* Howard Eliand (trans), Cambridge: Harvard University, Belknap Press, 2002.

Berger, John. *Ways of Seeing,* London: Penguin, 1972.

Bermingham, Ann. *Landscape and Ideology,* Los Angeles: Berkeley University Press, 1986.

Berry, David and Michael Dieter. *Postdigital Aesthetics: Art, Computation and Design,* London: Palgrave Macmillan, 2015.

Bird, Lawrence. 'Territories of Image: Disposition and Disorientation in Google Earth', in: *Imaging the City: Art, Creative Practices and Media Speculations,* Steve Hawley, Edward M. Clift, Kevin O'Brien (eds), Bristol, Intellect books, 2016.

Bishop, Ryan and John Phillips. *Modernist Avant-Garde Aesthetics and Contemporary Military Technology,* Edinburgh, Edinburgh University Press, 2010.

Blumenthal-Barby, Martin. 'Cinematography of Devices': Harun Farocki's Eye/machine, *German Studies Review* 38.2 (2015): 329-351.

Bodenhamer, David J. and John Corrigan, Trevor M Harris. *Deep maps and spatial narratives,* Bloomington and Indianapolis: Indiana University Press, 2015.

Boes, Tobias. 'Beyond Whole Earth: Planetary Mediation and the Anthropocene', *Environmental Humanities* 5 (2014): 155-170.

Bourdieu, Pierre. 'Social Space and Symbolic Power', *Sociological Theory* 7.1 (1989): 14-25.

Bourdieu, Pierre. 'Physical Space, Social Space and Habitus,' *Rapport* 10, Oslo: Institutt for sosiologi og samfunnsgeografi Universitetet i Oslo, 1996.

Bousquet, Antoine. *Eyes of War: Military Perception from the Telescope to the Drone,* Minneapolis: University of Minnesota Press, 2018.

Bredekamp, Horst. *Image Acts: A Systematic Approach to Visual Agency,* trans. Elizabeth Cregg, Berlin: De Gruyter, 2017.

Bridle, James. *New Dark Age: Technology and the End of the Future,* London and Brooklyn: Verso, 2018.

Buci-Glucksmann, Christine. 'Icarus Today: The Ephemeral Eye', *Public* 18 (1999): 53–77.

Buci-Glucksmann, Christine. *L'oeil Cartographique de l'Art*, Paris: Gallilée, 1996.

Buckminster Fuller, Richard. *Operating Manual for Spaceship Earth,* 1969, http://design-sciencelab.com/resources/OperatingManual_BF.pdf.

Bury, Michael. 'The Meaning of Roman Maps: Etienne Duperac and Antonio Tempesta', in *Seeing from Above: The Aerial View in Visual Culture*, London: IB Tauris, 2013, 26-46.

Carlson, Allen. 'Appropriation of the Nature Environment', in *Arguing about Art, Contemporary Philosophical debates*, Alex Neil and Aaron Ridley (eds), London: Routledge, 155-166.

Cartwright, William and Michael P. Peterson, Georg Gartner. *Multimedia Cartography*, Heidelberg: Springer, 1999.

Casas, Fernando C. 'Flat-Perspective Sphere', *Leonardo* 16.1 (1983): 1-9.

Casey, Edward S. *Earth-Mapping*, Minneapolis: University of Minnesota Press, 2005.

Casey, Edward. 'Between Geography and Philosophy: What Does It Mean to Be in the World?', *Annals of the Association of American Geographers* 91.1 (2001): 683-693.

Chadwick Clanton, Elaine. *Flat Earth for Dummies 101: Definition of Dummy: Indoctrinated in Globe from Birth*, Elaine Chadwick Clanton, 2018.

Chamayou, Gregoire. *A Theory of the Drone,* trans. Janet Lloyd, New York: The New Press, 2015.

Chomsky, Noam and Andre Vltchek. *On Western Terrorism, From Hiroshima to Drone Warfare*, London: Pluto Press, 2013.

Clark, Kenneth. *Landscape into Art*, Boston: Boston Press, 2015 (1963).

Clark, Timothy. *Ecocriticism on the Edge: The Anthropocene as a Threshold Concept*, London: Bloomsbury, 2015.

Clarke, K.C. 'Advances in Geographic Information Systems', *Computers, Environment and Urban Systems* 10.3-4 (1986): 175-184.

Clarke, Roger A. 'Information Technology and Dataveillance'. *Communications of the ACM* 31.5 (1988): 498–511.

Cohen, Jonathan and Aaron Meskin. 'On Epistemic value of Photographs', *Journal of Aesthetics and Art Criticism* 62.2 (2014): 197-210.

Conley, Tom. *Cartographic Cinema*, Minneapolis: University of Minnesota Press, 2007.

Cosgrove, Denis and Stephen Daniels. *The Iconography of Landscape: Studies in Historical Geography*, Cambridge: Cambridge University Press, 1988.

Cosgrove, Denis and William L. Fox. *Photography and Flight*, London: Reaktion Books, 2010.

Cosgrove, Denis. 'Contested global visions: One world, Whole Earth, and the Apollo space Photograph', 1994.

Cosgrove, Denis. *Apollo's Eye: A Cartographic Genealogy of the Earth in the Western Imagination*, Baltimore, Maryland: John Hopkins University Press, 2001.

Cosgrove, Denis. *Geography and Vision: Seeing, Imagining and Representing the World*, London: I. B. Tauris, 2008.

Cosgrove, Denis. *Social Formation and Symbolic Landscape*, University of Wisconsin Press. University of Wisconsin Press, 1984.

Couprie, Dirk L. *When the Earth was Flat: Studies in Ancient Greek and Chinese Cosmology*, Berlin: Springer, 2018.

Coward, Martin. *Urbicide: The politics of urban destruction,* Routledge Advances in International Relations and Global Politics, London: Routledge, 2008.

Creveld, Martin van. *The Age of Airpower*, New York: Publicaffairs, 2011.

Dabrowski, Magdalena. 'Photomonteur: John Heartfield', MOMA 13 (1993): 12-15.

Dahlberg, RE. 'The design of photo and image maps', *The Cartographic Journal* 30 (1993): 112-118.

Dale, P.F. 'Photomaps', *Survey Review* 21.160 (1971): 96-96.

Dalrymple Henderson, Linda. 'Four-Dimensional Space or Space-Time? The Emergence of the Cubism-Relativity Myth in New York in the 1940s', in Emmer (ed), *Visual Mind II*, Cambridge, MA: MIT Press, 2006.

Damisch, Hubert, *The Origin of Perspective*, Cambridge, MA: MIT Press, 1995.

Damisch, Hubert. *Noah's Ark: Essays on Architecture*, Cambridge, MA: MIT Press, 2016.

Damisch, Hubert. *Theory of the /c/loud*: Stanford, CA: Stanford Univ. Press, 2008.

Davis, Heather and Etienne Turpin (eds) *Art in the Anthropocene*, London: Open Humanities Press, 2014.

De Certeau, Michel, Luce Giard, and Pierre Mayol. *The Practice of Everyday Life. Vol. 2: Living and Cooking*, Timothy J. Tomasik (trans.) Minneapolis: University of Minnesota Press, 1998.

deLanda, Manuel. *Assemblage Theory: Speculative Realism*. Edinburgh: Edinburgh University Press, 2016.

deLanda, Manuel. *Intensive Science and Virtual Philosophy,* London: Bloomsbury Academic, 2013.

Dear, Michael and Jim Ketchum, Sarah Luria, Doug Richardson. *GeoHumanities: Art, History, Text at the Edge of Place*, London and New York: Routledge, 2011.

Deleuze, Gilles and Felix Guattari. *Anti-Oedipus: Capitalism and Schizophrenia*, Minneapolis: University of Minnesota Press, 1984.

Deleuze, Gilles and Felix Guattari. *Thousand Plateaus: Capitalism and Schizophrenia,* trans. Brian Massumi, Minneapolis and London: Minnesota University Press, 1987.

Dennett, Daniel. 'Descartes' Argument from Design', *The Journal of Philosophy* 7 (2008): 333-346.

Dorrian, Mark and Frederic Poussin (eds) *Seeing from Above: The Aerial View in Visual Culture*, London: I.B. Tauris 2013.

Easterling, Keller. *Extrastatecraft: The Power of Infrastructure Space*. London: Verso, 2014.

Edgerton, Samuel Y. *The Mirror, the Window, and the Telescope: How Linear Perspective Changed our Vision of the Universe*, Ithaca, New York: Cornell University Press, 2009.

Elkins, James, and Rachel DeLue. *Landscape Theory*, London and New York: Routledge, 2008.

Elkins, James. 'Did Leonardo Develop a Theory of Curvilinear Perspective? Together with Some Remarks on the "Angle" and "Distance" Axioms', *Journal of the Warburg and Courtauld Institutes* 51 (1988): 190-196.

Elkins, James. *The Poetics of Perspective*, Ithaca and New York, Cornell University Press, 2018 (1994).

Elsaesser, Thomas. 'The Future of "Art" and "Work" in the Age of Vision Machines: Harun Farocki', Randall Halle (ed) *After the Avant-garde: Contemporary German and Austrian Experimental Film,* Rochester: Camden House, 2009.

Emmelhainz, Irmgard. 'Images do not Show: The Desire to See in the Anthropocene', in Heather Davis and Etienne Turpin (eds) *Art in the Anthropocene, Encounters Among Aesthetics, Politics, Environments and Epistemologies*, London: Open Humanities Press, 2015.

Emmer, Michele (ed) *Visual mind II: Mathematics and Art*, Cambridge MA: MIT Press, 2005.

Florensky, Pavel. 'Reverse Perspective (1920)', in Nicoletta Misler (ed) *Beyond Vision: Essays on the Perception of Art*, trans. Wendy Salmond, London: Reaktion Books, 2002, 197-273.

Flusser, Vilém, 'Das Verschwinden der Ferne', *Arch+* 111 (1992): 31-32.

Flusser, Vilém. *Towards the Philosophy of Photography*, London: Reaktion Books, 2000.

Flusser. Vilém. *Into the Universe of Technical Images*. Minneapolis: University of Minnesota Press, 2011.

Franke, Anselm, and Diedrich Diederichsen (eds) *The Whole Earth Catalogue: The Whole Earth California and the Disappearance of the Outside*, Berlin: Sternberg Press, 2013.

Friedberg, Anne. *The Virtual Window: From Alberti to Microsoft*. Cambridge, MA: MIT Press, 2009.

Fuller, Buckminster Richard. *Operating Manual for the Spaceship Earth*, Zürich, Lars Müller, 2008.

Galloway, Alexander R. *The Interface Effect*, Cambridge and Malden: Polity, 2012.

Garb, Yakov Jerome. 'The Use and Misuse of the Whole Earth Image', *Whole Earth Review* (March 1985): 19-25.

Garrett, Gregory. *The Flat Earth Trilogy: Book of Secrets I*, Gregory Lessing Garrett, 2018.

Garwood, Christine. *Flat Earth: The History of an Infamous Idea,* New York: Macmillan Publishers UK, 2008.

Gombrich, Ernst. *Norm and Form: Studies in the Art of the Renaissance, Volume I: Norm and Form*, London: Phaidon Press, 1994.

Goodchild, Michael F. 'Twenty years of progress: GIScience in 2010', *Journal of Spatial Information Science* 1 (2010). doi:10.5311/JOSIS.2010.1.2

Graham, Stephan. *Cities Under Siege: The New Military Urbanism*, London: Verso, 2011.

Graham, Stephan. *Vertical: The City from Satellites to Bunkers*, London: Verso, 2016.

Grau, Oliver. 'Images (R)-Evolution: Media Arts Complex Imagery Challenging Humanities and Our Institutions of Cultural Memory', *Leonardo Electronic Almanac* 20.2 (2014): 72-86.

Grau, Oliver. *Virtual Art: From Illusion to Immersion,* Cambridge, MA: MIT Press, 2003.

Gregory, Derek. *Geographical Imaginations*, Oxford: Blackwell, 1993.

Gregory, Ian N. *Toward Spatial Humanities: Historical GIS and Spatial History*, Bloomington: Indiana University Press, 2014.

Grosscup, Beau. *Strategic Terror: The Politics and Ethics of Aerial Bombardment*, London: Zed Books, 2006.

Grusin, Richard (ed) *The Nonhuman Turn,* Minneapolis: University of Minnesota Press, 2015.

Haffner, Jeanne. 'Historicizing the View from Below: Aerial photography and the Emergence of Social Conception of Space', *UC Berkeley: The Proceedings of Spaces of History / Histories of Space: Emerging Approaches to the Study of the Built Environment*, 2010.

Haffner, Jeanne. *View from Above: The Science of Social Space*, Cambridge, MA: MIT Press, 2013.

Halle, Randall (ed) *After the Avant-garde: Contemporary German and Austrian Experimental Film,* Rochester: Camden House, 2006.

Halpern, Orit. *Beautiful Data: A History and Reason Since 1945,* Durham: Duke University Press, 2015.

Hamilton, Clive. *Defiant Earth: The Fate of Humans in the Anthropocene,* New Zealand and Australia: Allen & Unwin, 2017.

Harman, Graham. *The Quadruple Object*, Winchester and Washington: Zero Books, 2011.

Haraway, Donna. 'The Persistence of Vision', 1997. *The Visual Culture reader,* Nicholas Mirzoeff (ed) London: Routledge, 2002, pp. 678-684.

Hayles, Katherine. 'Print Is Flat, Code Is Deep: The Importance of Media-specific Analysis', *The Poetics Today* 25.1 (2004): 67-90.

Hayles, Katherine. *How Did We Become Posthuman?,* Chicago: University of Chicago Press, 1999.

Heartfield, John. 'Photomontages of the Nazi Period', London: Gordon Fraser Gallery & Universe Books, 1977.

Heidegger, Martin, 'The Thing' in Martin Heidegger, trans. Albert Hofstadter, *Poetry, Language, Thought*, New York: Harper & Row, 1971.

Heidegger, Martin. 'The Age of the World Picture', A.I. Tauber (ed) *Science and the Quest for Reality*, London: Palgrave McMillan, 1997, 70-88.

Helmreich, Stefan. 'From Spaceship Earth to Google Ocean: Planetary Icons, Indexes, and Infrastructures', *Social Research* 78.4 (2011): 1211-1242.

Hiepe, Richard and C. A. Haenlein. *Dada: Photographie und Photocollag*, Hannover, Kestner-Gesellschaft, 1979.

Hills, Alice. 'Deconstructing Cities: Military Operations in Urban Era', *The Journal of conflict studies* (Fall 2002): 99-117.

Hoelzl, Ingrid and Remi Marie. *Soft Image: Towards a New Theory of the Digital Image*, Chicago: Intellect, Chicago University Press, 2015.

Hookway, Branden. *Interface*, Cambridge, MA: MIT Press, 2014.

Huhtamo, Erkki, *Illusions in Motion: Media archaeology of the moving panorama and related spectacles*, Cambridge, MA: MIT Press, 2018.

Husserl, Edmund. *Foundational Investigations of the Phenomenological Origin of the Spatiality of Nature*, Edmund Husserl Shorter Works, Notre Dame, Ind.: University of Notre Dame Press; Brighton, Sussex: Harvester Press, 1981.

Iversen, Margaret. 'The discourse of perspective in the twentieth century', *Oxford Art Journal* 28.2 (2005): 191–202.

Jäger, Gottfried. 'Generative Photography: A Systematic, Constructive Approach', *Leonardo* 19.1 (1986): 19-25.

Jameson, Fredric. 'Cognitive Mapping', in Nelson, C. and Grossberg, L. (eds) *Marxism and the Interpretation of Culture*, Chicago: University of Illinois Press, 1999.

Jameson, Fredric. *Postmodernism, or, the Cultural Logic of Late Capitalism*, Durham: Duke University Press, 1991.

Jameson, Fredric. *The Geopolitical Aesthetic: Cinema and Space in the World System*, Bloomington: Indiana University Press, 1995.

Jay, Martin. *Downcast Eyes: The Denigration of Vision in Twentieth-Century French Thought*, Berkeley and Los Angeles: University of Chicago Press, 1999.

Jecu, Marta. *Architecture and the Virtual*, Bristol and Chicago: University of Chicago Press, 2016.

Johnson, Matthew. *Ideas of Landscape*, Oxford: Blackwell Publishing, 2007.

Joseph, Paul (ed) *SAGE Encyclopedia of War: Social Science Perspective*, Thousand Oaks, SAGE, 2016.

Kandel, Eric. *Reductionism in Art and Brain Science: Bridging the Two Cultures*, New York: Columbia University Press, 2018.

Kayasing, Bill. *We Never Went to the Moon: America's Thirty Billion Dollar Swindle*, CreateSpace Independent Publishing Platform, 2017.

Kemp, Martin. *The Science of Art: Optical Themes in Western Art from Brunelleschi to Seurat*, New Haven: Yale University Press, 1992.

Kenneth Clark, *Landscape into Art*, Boston: Beacon Press, 2015.

Kittler, Friedrich, *Optical Media: Berlin Lectures 2009, Cambridge:* Polity, 2012.

Kittler, Friedrich. 'Perspective and the Book', *Grey Room* 5 (Autumn 2001): 38-53.

Kofman, Sarah. *Camera Obscura: Of Ideology*, London: Athlone Press, 1998.

Kracauer, Siegfried. 'Photography', *Critical Inquiry* 19.3 (1993): 421-436.

Kracauer, Siegfried. *The Mass Ornament: Weimar Essays*, translated by Thomas Y. Levin, Cambridge, MA: Harvard University Press, 1995.

Krewani, Angela. 'Google Earth: Satellite Images and the Appropriation of the Divine Perspective: Concepts of Wholeness in Cultural Constructions of Our Home Planet', in *Imaging Earth*, Nitzke, Solvejg, Pethes, Nicolas (eds) Berlin: de Gruyter, 2017, 45-60.

Kurgan, Laura. *Close Up at a Distance: Mapping, Technology, and Politics*, Cambridge MA: MIT Press, 2013.

Latour, Bruno, *Reassembling the Social*, Oxford: Oxford University Press, 2007.

Latour, Bruno, and Emilie Hermant, 'Paris: Invisible City' Liz Carey-Libbrecht (trans), from 'Paris ville invisible: Paris: La Découverte-Les Empêcheurs de penser en rond', 1998, http://www.bruno-latour.fr/sites/default/files/downloads/viii_paris-city-gb.pdf.

Latour, Bruno. 'Introduction: Paris: Invisible City: The Plasma', *Culture and Society*, Elsevier 3.2 (2012): 91-93.

Latour, Bruno. *Down to Earth: Politics in the New Climatic Regime,* Cambridge: Polity, 2018.

Latour, Bruno. *Mreže, društva, sfere,* FUK, 2017.

Latour, Bruno. *Politics of Nature,* Cambridge MA: Harvard University Press, 2004.

Latto, Richard and Bernard Harper. 'The Non-Realistic Nature of Photography', *Leonardo* 40.3 (2007): 243-247.

Lazier, Benjamin. 'Earthrise: or, The Globalization of the World Picture', The American Historical Review 116.3 (2011): 602–630.

Lefebvre, Henri. *The Production of Space,* trans. Donald Nicholson-Smith, Oxford: Blackwell Publishing, 1991.

Lodder, Christina. 'Malevich, Suprematism and Aerial Photography', *History of Photography* 28.1 (2004): 25-40.

Lovelock, James. *Gaia: A New Look at Life on Earth,* Oxford and New York: Oxford University Press, 2000.

Lynch, Kevin A. *Image of the City,* Cambridge, MA: MIT Press, 1960.

Makholm, Kristin. 'Strange Beauty: Hannah Höch and the Photomontage', *MOMA* 24 (1997): 19-23.

Maliene V., V. Grigonis, V. Palevičius, and S. Griffiths. 'Geographic Information System: Old Principles with New Capabilities', *Urban Design International* 16.1 (2011): doi:10.1057/udi.2010.25.

Massey, Doreen, John Allen, and Phil Sarre. *Human Geography Today,* Cambridge: Polity, 1991.

McKibben, Bill. *Eaarth: Making a Life on a Tough New Planet,* New York: Henry Holt and Company, 2010.

McLaren, Peter and Petar Jandrić, *Postdigital Dialogues on Critical Pedagogy, Liberation Theology and Information Technology,* London: Bloomsbury, 2020.

Meece, Stephanie. 'A Bird's Eye View: Of a Leopard's Spots: The Çatalhöyük "Map" and the Development of Cartographic Representation in Prehistory', The British Institute of Archaeology at Ankara, 2006.

Mehigan, Tim. *Frameworks, Artworks, Place: The Space of Perception in the Modern World,* Amsterdam, Rodopi, 2008.

Kraak, Menno-Jan and Rico Van Driel. 'Principles of Hypermaps', *Computers & Geosciences* 23.4 (1997): 457-464.

Minton, Anna. *Ground Control: Fear and Happiness in the Twenty-First-Century City*, London: Penguin, 2012.

Mitchell, W.J.T. *Landscape and Power*, Chicago: University of Chicago Press, 2002.

Moffit, Fred H. 'A Method of Aerophotographic Mapping', *Geographical Review* 10 (November 1920): 326-338.

Moholy Nagy, Laszlo. *The New Vision: From Material to Architecture*, New York: Brewer, Warren and Putnam, 1932.

Monmonier, Mark. *How to Lie with Maps*, Chicago: University of Chicago Press, 1991.

Moore, Antoni and Igor Drecki (eds) *Geospatial visualization,* Berlin: Springer, 2012.

Morton, Timothy. *Hyperobjects*, Minneapolis: University of Minnesota Press, 2013.

Nadar, Félix. *When I Was A Photographer,* trans. Eduardo Cadava and Liana Theodoratou, Cambridge, MA: The MIT Press, 2015.

Nancy, Jean-Luc. *After Fukushima: The Equivalence of Catastrophes*, New York: Fordham University Press, 2014.

Nitzke, Solvejg and Nicolas Pethes (eds) *Imagining Earth: Concepts of Wholeness in Cultural Constructions of Our Home Planet*, Bielefeld: Transcript Verlag, 2017.

Olsson, Gunnar. *Abysmal: A Critique of Cartographic Reason.* Chicago: University of Chicago Press, 2007.

Otto, Lacman. *Equalizer for Non-flat Terrain: Image Measurement and Aerial Photography*, 1931, 10-12.

Paglen, Trevor. *The Last Pictures*, Berkeley, Los Angeles and London: University of California Press, 2012.

Paglen, Trevor. 'Operational Images', *E-flux* 59 (November 2014): https://www.e-flux.com/journal/59/61130/operational-images/.

Panofsky, Erwin, and Christopher S. Wood. *Perspective as Symbolic Form*, New York: Zone Books, 1996.

Parikka, Jussi. *A Geology of Media,* Minneapolis: University of Minnesota Press, 2015.

Paul, Christiane. *Digital Art*, New Haven: Thames and Hudson, 2015.

Paulsen, Kris. *Here/There: Telepresence, Touch, and Art at the Interface*, Cambridge, MA: MIT Press, 2017.

Pearson, Mike and Michael Shanks. *Theatre/Archaeology*, London: Routledge, 2001.

Peraica, Ana. *Fotografija kao dokaz*, Zagreb: Multimedijalni institut, 2018.

Peraica, Ana. *Culture of the Selfie: Self-representation in Contemporary Visual Culture*, Amterdam: Institute of Network Cultures, 2017.

Peraica, Ana. *Victims Symptom: PTSD and Culture*, Amsterdam: Institute of Network Cultures, 2009.

Pettegree, Andrew. *The Book in the Renaissance*, New Haven: Yale University Press, 2011.

Pickles, John. *A History of Spaces: Cartographic Reason, Mapping and the Geo-Coded World*, London: Routledge, 2003.

Piedmont-Palladino, Susan. 'Intelligent Cities', in *National Building Museum*, 2011, 36-41.

Ponty, Merleau. *Visible and Invisible*, Evanston: Northwestern University Press, 1969.

Reddleman, Claire. *Cartographic Abstractions in Contemporary Art: Seeing with Maps*, London: Routledge, 2018.

Riedl, Andreas. 'Digital globes', in W. Cartwright, M.P. Peterson, and G. Gartner (eds) *Multimedia Cartography*, Berlin/Heidelberg/New York: Springer, 2007, 255– 266.

Ronchi, Vasco. 'Perspective Based on a New Optics', *Leonardo* 7.3 (1974): 219-225.

Rotch, Abbott Lawrence. 'Benjamin Franklin and the First Balloons', *American Antiquarian Society* (April 1907): 259-174.

Russell, Jeffrey Burton. *Inventing the Flat Earth: Columbus and Modern Historians*, New York, Connecticut and London, Praeger, 1991.

Sagan, Carl. *Pale Blue Dot: A Vision of The Human Future in Space*, New York: Ballantine Books, 1997.

Salisbury, Brett, Dr. Lawrence Cohen, Dr. John Mack, and Captain Obvious, *Spherical Trigonometry for Dummies*, Createspace Independent Publishing Platform, 2015.

Salway, Benet. 'The Nature and Genesis of the Peutinger Map', *Imago Mundi* 57.2 (2005): 119-135.

Sargent, Mark, *Flat Earth Clues: The Sky's The Limit*, Booglez limited, 2016.

Sassen, Saskia. 'Women's Burden: Countergeographies of Globalisation and the Feminisation of Survival', http://www.columbia.edu/~sjs2/PDFs/womensburden.2000.pdf.

Sassen, Saskia. *Territory Authority, Rights: From Medieval to Global Assemblage*, Princeton: Princeton University Press, 2008.

Schwartz, Hillel. *Culture of the Copy: Striking Likeness, Unreasonable Facsimiles*, New York: Zone Books, 1996.

Scott, Clive. *The Spoken Image: Photography and Language*, London: Reaktion Book, 1999.

Sekula, Allan, 'The Instrumental Image: Steichen At War', *Artforum* 14.4 (1975): 26-35.

Shanken, Edward. 'Virtual Perspective and the Artistic Vision: A Genealogy of Technology, Perception and Power', *ISEA*, Rotterdam, 1996.

Shanks, Michael, *Experiencing the Past: On the Character of Archaeology*, London: Routledge, 1991.

Shearer, Rhonda Roland, 'From Flatland to Fractaland', *New Geometries in Relationship to Artistic and Scientific Revolutions Fractals* 3.3 (1995): 617-625.

Shuttleworth, Kaleb. *Planet or Plane?: A Debate of the 'Flat-Earth' Hypothesis*, unknown publisher, 2018.

Sloterdijk, Peter. *Spheres, volume 2, Globes: Macrospherology*, South Pasadena: Semiotext(e), 2014.

Sloterdijk, Peter. *Terror from the Air,* Los Angeles: Semiotext(e), 2009.

Sobieszek, Robert. 'Composite Imagery and the Origins of Photomontage, Part I: The Formalist Strain', *Artforum* 16.2 (1978): 41-43.

Sobieszek, Robert. 'Composite Imagery and the Origins of Photomontage, Part II: The Naturalistic Strain', *Artforum* 17.1 (1979): 58-65.

Söderström, Ola. 'Paper Cities: Visual Thinking in Urban Planning', *Ecumene* 3.3 (1996): 249–281.

Soja, Edward W. *Postmodern Geographies: The Reassertion of Space in Critical Social Theory*, London: Verso, 1989.

Sontag, Susan. *On Photography,* London: Penguin Books, 1978.

Steyerl, Hito. 'Digital Debris: Spam and Scam', *October* 138 (Fall 2011): 70-80.

Stob, Jennifer, 'Detournement as Optic: Debord, Derisory Documents and the Aerial View', Philosophy of Photography 5.2 (2013): 19-34.

Sumira, Sylvia. *Globes: 400 Years of Exploration, Navigation, and Power,* Chicago and London: University of Chicago Press, 2014.

Suo, Jin-Li and Xiangyang Ji, Qionghai Dai. 'An overview of computational photography', *Science China Inf. Sci.* (2012): 1229-1248.

Tabborn, Eric. *PROOF: Does God say the Earth is Flat?: Ending the Debate between the Flat Earth vs. the Globe*, publisher unknown, 2018.

Tilley, Christopher, *A Phenomenology of the Landscape: Place, Paths and Monuments, Explorations in Anthropology*, London: University College London, Berg Publishers, London, 1997.

Toscano, Alberto and Jeff Kinkle. *Cartographies of the Absolute*, Alresford: Zero Books and John Hunt Publishing, 2015.

Tovey, Rob. 'Photomaps: A Visual Taxonomy', *Visual Communication* 17.2 (2018): 209-220.

Vidler, Anthony. 'Terres Inconnues: Cartographies of a Landscape to Be Invented', *October* 115 (Winter 2006): 13-30.

Virilio, Paul and Sylvère Lotringer, *Pure War*, Los Angeles, Semiotext(e), 1984.

Virilio, Paul and Sylvere Lotringer. *Crepuscular Dawn*, Los Angeles and New York: Semiotext(e) and MIT Press, 2002.

Virilio, Paul. *Open Sky,* trans. Julie Rose, London: Verso, 1997.

Virilio, Paul. *The Lost Dimension*, trans. Daniel Moshenberg, New York: Semiotext(e), 1991.

Virilio, Paul. *The Vision Machine,* Bloomington and Indianapolis: Indiana University Press, 1994.

Warf, Barney and Santa Arias. *The Spatial Turn: Interdisciplinary Perspectives in Human Geography.* New York: Routledge, 2009.

Wark, McKenzie. *Molecular Red: Theory for the Anthropocene*, London: Verso, 2015.

Wark, McKenzie. *Virtual Geography: Living with Global Media Events*, Bloomington: Indiana University Press, 1994.

White, John. *Birth and Rebirth of Pictorial Space*, Cambridge: Belknap Press: 1987.

Wilson, Louise. 'Cyberwar, God and Television: An Interview with Paul Virilio', *CT Theory*, http://ctheory.net/ctheory_wp/cyberwar-god-and-television-interview-with-paul-virilio/.

Wilson, Matthew H. *New Lines: Critical GIS and the Trouble of the Map*, Minneapolis: University of Minnesota Press, 2017.

Wittgenstein, Ludwig. *Tractatus Logico Philosophicus*, London: Routledge, 2001.

Wood, Chris. *Sudden Justice: America's Secret Drone Wars (Terrorism and Global Justice)*, Oxford: Oxford University Press, 2015.

Wood, Denis and John Fels, and John Krygier. *Rethinking the Power of Maps*, New York: The Guilford Press, 2010.

Woodward, David and RB Harley. *The History of Cartography, Volume 1: Cartography in Prehistoric, Ancient and Medieval Europe and the Mediterranean*, Chicago: University of Chicago Press, 1987.

Wurzer, Wilhelm, *Panorama: Philosophies of the Visible*, London and New York: Continuum, 2002.

Zylinska, Joanna and Kamila Kuc (eds) *Photomediations,* Open Humanities Press, 2016.

Zylinska, Joanna. *Nonhuman Photography*, Cambridge, MA: MIT Press, 2017.

Exhibitions

'Movable borders: Here comes Drones', Furtherfield Gallery, London, 11–26 May 2013, http://www.furtherfield.org/programmes/exhibition/movable-borders-here-come-drones.

'Once is Nothing: Drone Art Exhibition', Interacess, 17 February–2 April 2016, http://interacess.org/exhibition/once-nothing-drone-art-exhibition.

'The Sky Is Also a Map', http://interaccess.org/exhibition/sky-also-map.

'Ctrl+Space: Rhetorics of Surveillance from Bentham to Big Brother', ZKM, Karlsruhe, 2001, http://ctrlspace.zkm.de/e/.

'Exposed, Voyeurism, Surveillance and the Camera', Tate Modern, London, 28 May–3 October 2010, http://www.tate.org.uk/whats-on/tate-modern/exhibition/exposed.

Performances

Cale, John and Liam Young. 'Drone Orchestra', 2014.

Crandall, Jordan. 'Materialities of the Robotic', 2015.

Kov, Nina. 'Copter', performed by Nina Kov and Jack Bishop.

Sternberg, Donna and EZTV. 'Fly-BY', 2014

Movies

Dirty Wars (dir. Jeremy Scahill, 2013).

Drone (dir, Tonje Hessel Schel, 2014).

Drones (dir. Rick Rosenthal, 2013).

Eagle Eye (dir. D.J. Caruso, 2008).

Eye in the Sky (dir. Gavin Hood, 2015).

Eye/Machine I (dir. Harun Farocki, 2001).

Eye/Machine II (dir. Harun Farocki, 2002).

Eye/Machine III (dir. Harun Farocki, 2003).

Gravity (dir. Alfonso Cuarón, 2013).

Powers of Ten (dir. Charles Eames, 1977).

Rise of Drones (dir. Peter Yost, 2013).

Skyline (dir. Collin Strause, 2010).

Syriana (dir. Stephen Gaghan, 2005).

The Great Dictator (dir. Charlie Chaplin, 1940).

The Rise of Drones: Privacy, Power and Storytelling (2015).

Unmanned: America's Drone Wars (dir. Robert Greenwald, 2013).

LIST OF ILLUSTRATIONS

Figure 1: *Astronaut in Space*. Royalty free, Creative Commons Zero, CCO, Pxsfuel.

Figure 2: Still from Charlie Chaplin, *The Great Dictator*, 1940. Work in the public domain.

Figure 3: Flat Earth internet meme

Figure 4: Flat Earth internet meme

Figure 5: Flat Earth internet meme

Figure 6: Flat Earth internet meme

Figure 7: Cover of *Flatland* by William Abbott Abbott, 1884.

Figure 8: Flat Earth map drawn by Orlando Ferguson in 1893. Work in the public domain.

Figure 9: Azimuthal equidistant projection. CC-BY-SA-3.0-license.

Figure 10: Donnus Nicholas Germanus, cartographer Johannes Schnitzer or Johannes de Armssheim, engraver Ptolemy Jacobus Angelus, *The World*. Work in the public domain.

Figure 11: Martin Behaim, *Globe*. Nouveau Larousse illustré. Work in the public domain.

Figure 12: James Wallace Black, *View of Boston*, 1860. Work in the public domain.

Figure 13: Gaspard-Félix Tournachon Nadar, *Aerial view of Paris*, 1868. Work in the public domain.

Figure 14: Edward Steichen, *Aerial view of ruins of Vaux, France*, 1918. Work in the public domain.

Figure 15: Cockpit view. CCO-license.

Figure 16: Eugene Cernan, Ronald Evans and Harrison Schmitt, *Blue Marble*, 1972. NASA, work in the public domain.

Figure 17: Capt. Albert Stevens, *Record from South Dakota*, 1935. Work in the public domain.

Figure 18: Capt. William Anders, *Earthrise*, 1968. NASA, work in public domain.

Figure 19: One of globalization images. CCO-license.

Figure 20: Monk of Colmar, *Peutinger's map*, 1265. Work in the public domain.

Figure 21: GPS information in photography. Screenshot.

Figure 22: Hyperimage with place tags. Screenshot.

Figure 23: Turgot map of Paris. Work in the public domain.

Figure 24: Geodaten Bayern, *Orthophoto of Augsburg*, 2012. Work in the public domain.

Figure 25: Mount Kilimanjaro Summit photomap. Work in the public domain.

Figure 26: Clement Valla, *Postcard from Google Earth - 40°50'41.94"N, 73°54'42.33"W*. Courtesy of the artist.

Figure 27: *We have never been to Moon*, street poster and Internet meme.